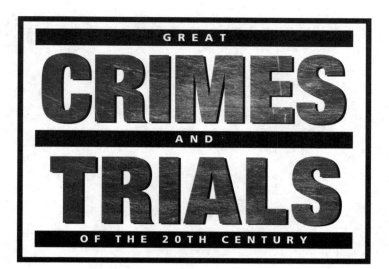

GREAT

CRIMES

AND

TRIALS

OF THE 20TH CENTURY

GREAT CRIMES AND TRIALS OF THE 20TH CENTURY

PETER ARNOLD

HAMLYN

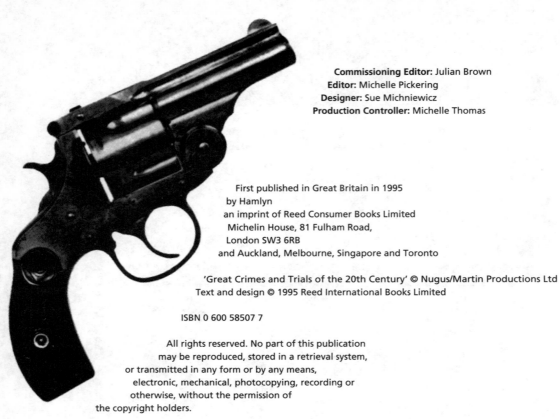

Commissioning Editor: Julian Brown
Editor: Michelle Pickering
Designer: Sue Michniewicz
Production Controller: Michelle Thomas

First published in Great Britain in 1995
by Hamlyn
an imprint of Reed Consumer Books Limited
Michelin House, 81 Fulham Road,
London SW3 6RB
and Auckland, Melbourne, Singapore and Toronto

PHOTOGRAPHIC ACKNOWLEDGEMENTS

All pictures taken from the NMP series *Great Crimes & Trials of the 20th Century* are copyright
Nugus/Martin Productions 1994, except the following:

Barnaby's Picture Library: 7 (Elizabeth Goodwin). Robert Harding Picture Library: 5 top. Hulton Deutsch
Collection: 26, 27, 39, 47, 85, 87, 88, 96, 97 top, 147, 153, 155, 187 (Mirror Syndication International), 193
(MSI), 205 top (MSI), 206 (MSI), 208 (MSI), 211 (MSI). Steve Nevill: 32. Popperfoto: 2/3, 5 centre top, 11, 16,
18, 24, 81, 84, 146, 178 (UPI), 183 (UPI), 192/193, 215, 216, 217, 218, 219. Range/Bettman: 15, 31, 46 (UPI),
56, 61, 64 (UPI), 65 (UPI), 66 (UPI), 67 (UPI), 68 (UPI), 69, 72 (UPI), 90 (UPI), 105, 106, 114 (UPI), 116 (UPI), 121,
134, 138, 139, 142, 164 (UPI), 170 (UPI), 173 (UPI), 182 (UPI), 196 (UPI), 220. Reed International Books Ltd:
5 bottom (Paul Williams). Topham Picture Source: 4, 5 centre bottom (Press Association), 9 (Associated
Press), 29, 33, 45, 52 (AP), 60 (AP), 71, 93 (AP), 97 bottom (AP), 107, 118 (AP), 127 (AP), 128 (PA), 134 top
(AP), 144 (AP); 156; 158; 163 (AP), 175 (AP)

Nugus/Martin Productions gratefully acknowledge the co-operation of the following:

ABC Capital Cities Inc, Independent Television News Ltd, The National Film Archive Washington,
NBC News Inc, Sherman Grinberg Film Libraries Inc, Reuters Television Ltd, Topham Picture Library,
Metropolitan Police London, New York City Municipal Archives, New York City Public Libraries,
Dallas Historical Society, Syndication International, Library of Congress Washington DC.

Printed by Mackays of Chatham in Great Britain

Contents

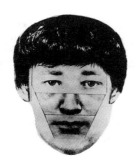

Introduction

The progress made in the twentieth century in all aspects of life has, it would appear, also been made in all aspects of death. Murders and atrocities have increased in scale, frequency, ingenuity and savagery. Evil has always had its attractions for the law-abiding, who realise perhaps how easily crossed might be the line between criminality and respectability. That the Devil has all the good tunes was first noticed by the English preacher Rowland Hill in the eighteenth century, and is confirmed by the millions who 200 years later sit in their armchairs to read about the latest crimes, or, in the United States, to watch the lawyers tease out the gory details in televised courtrooms.

The twenty-six crimes described in this second series of stories from the television series *Great Crimes and Trials of the Twentieth Century* have a wider range than those in the first volume. Indeed, because some of the stories are war crimes and others of political assassinations, it is safe to say that not only have they caused millions of deaths but have affected the lives of most of those now living.

The two stories of Second World War atrocities concern the Nuremberg trials and the massacre at Katyn Forest. The leaders under whose auspices these crimes were committed avoided the punishment of the law, Hitler by suicide and Stalin by retaining his tyrannical power until he died.

Political assassinations also cast a wide influence. That which made most impact on the world at large was the shooting of President Kennedy. After investigations by a Commission, a Select Committee, numerous writers and filmmakers, the whole truth is still not known, and never will be. But the story is fascinating, and is retold here, alongside those of other victims of political assassinations: Gandhi and Martin Luther King. Religion and race, those two great dividers, were responsible for these, and so far as race is concerned, there could hardly have been a more bigoted organisation over the years than the Ku Klux Klan, whose crimes are related here by concentrating on the 1964 case of the murder of three workers for racial equality.

Another organisation whose tentacles are everywhere and whose power does not diminish is the Mafia. The street shooting of the boss of bosses, Big Paul Castellano, and his bodyguard Thomas Bilotti on 46th Street in 1985 is the starting point for the story of 100 years of brutal struggles for power within this crime syndicate. The Mafia also features in one of the stories involving a mystery. Corrupt trade union power and a feud with the Kennedys are other elements in the disappearance of Jimmy Hoffa, still a fascinatingly unsolved crime.

Whatever the lure of organised crime, however, more psychological satisfaction comes from the study of the lone criminal. The type of criminal who has attracted the most attention in the late twentieth century is the serial killer. Several have their grisly deeds recounted in this book.

Who could possibly fathom the mind of Richard Ramirez, who thought himself the child of Satan? The story of his 13 murders and his counsel's concern that he would never see Disneyland again is as strange and powerful as any fiction.

Wayne Williams was another odd personality – an intelligent young black man who was convicted of murdering two black men in Atlanta. Police claimed his conviction cleared 23 murder cases, mostly young black boys. Richard Speck and Charles Whitman were multiple killers who each embarked on a single spree. Speck gained entry to a nurses' home and tied up nine young nurses, eventually killing them one by one . . . all except one, who managed to hide under a bed. Whitman, a studious 'all-American' boy, one day installed himself on top of a university lookout tower with an arsenal of weapons and shot passers-by.

A British serial killer who took young men home with him and then killed them because he didn't want them to leave him, captured the headlines in 1983. Dennis Nilsen's preoccupation with death and his treatment of his victims' bodies as if they were dolls with whom he could watch television were pathetic aspects of his personality which transpired at his trial and afterwards.

The classic case of a man and woman driving stolen cars round the countryside and leaving a trail of corpses behind them is, of course, that of Bonnie and Clyde, a story retold here with new insights. Charles Starkweather casually killed his girlfriend's family and then fled with her, these two also becoming on-the-road murderers, killing seven others as police searched for them.

Female murderers are not always merely partners of male killers, of course. One of the trials to cause immense interest in the 1980s was that of Jean Harris, accused of the murder of Dr Herman Tarnower. He was the inventor of the world-famous Scarsdale Diet, which many women followed, and Harris was his mistress. The jealousy which led her to commit the crime and her independence of thought which led to possible errors in the defence she offered, and thus a longer than necessary imprisonment, make her story tragic and sympathetic.

One could have sympathy, too, with Ethel Rosenberg and her husband Julius, gentle souls who were executed by the state for doing little that they would consider disloyal to their country. It is difficult to know whether or not to feel sympathy for Patty Hearst, at first a kidnap victim, then a bank robber and urban guerrilla. Was she a criminal under duress?

Certainly Caryl Chessman deserves sympathy, not for being the Red Light Bandit, but for his treatment at the hands of the law, which sentenced him to

death for kidnapping and carried out the sentence despite his 12-year campaign for freedom and the fact that the law under which he was executed had in the meantime been scrapped.

James Hanratty, executed for the A6 murder, is another who many think suffered a miscarriage of justice. Readers can judge for themselves the many disturbing elements in this case, not least the existence of an earlier suspect who has insisted more than once that he is the killer.

There was plenty of sympathy for the popular Dan White, who was convicted of the dual murder of the mayor of San Francisco and a homosexual city councillor. White received a light sentence after a bizarre defence, but his conscience was less easily satisfied than the San Francisco court, and he committed suicide on his release.

Jeremy Bamber, who not only killed the five members of his adopted family but plotted carefully to place the blame on his sister, one of his victims, and Harry Roberts, the killer of policemen, scarcely deserve sympathy, unless one thinks that nobody should be locked up for 30 years.

Not all of the crimes and trials in this book relate to murder. The Boston Brink's robbery, brilliantly executed, will provoke admiration in many readers and possibly some amusement. The hoax by which the spurious autobiography of the recluse Howard Hughes was sold to an international publishers also has its elements of farce. The 1946 escape attempt from the famous island prison of Alcatraz, like all those before and since, was unsuccessful, and did not lead to a trial, but the story of this fortress is inseparable from a 'golden' period of US crime.

The twenty-six crimes and trials discussed in this book, plus the pictures, many of which have been taken as stills from the television series and have never been seen in a publication before, give readers an intriguing insight into the criminal mind.

BONNIE AND CLYDE WERE FOLK HEROES WHO INSPIRED A FEATURE FILM AND A WELL-KNOWN SONG. WITH THE DEPRESSION TIGHTENING ITS GRIP THROUGHOUT THE US, THEY WERE SEEN AS ROMANTIC FIGURES AS THEY EVADED THE LAW ACROSS HALF-A-DOZEN STATES, ROBBING AND KILLING. BUT THEIR LIVES WERE FAR FROM ROMANTIC. THEY WERE MEAN, PETTY CROOKS WHO WERE DESPISED BY THE REAL BANK ROBBERS LIKE JOHN DILLINGER JUST AS MUCH AS THEY WERE DESPISED BY THE LAW ENFORCERS. THEIR ENDS WERE AS MESSY AND VIOLENT AS THEIR LIVES, AND THEIR SMASHED BODIES BECAME A PEEPSHOW.

Bonnie and Clyde

In 1934, Europe was suffering great political unrest with the assassination of King Alexander of Yugoslavia by a Croatian nationalist while on a state visit to France, and with the looming shadow of the forthcoming world war. Adolf Hitler was strengthening his hold on power in Germany and meeting his fellow dictator and ally Benito Mussolini in Venice. The British had more tranquil matters to occupy them, with Queen Mary launching her namesake, the largest ocean liner in the world.

The USA was preoccupied with gangsters and crime. Jubilant crowds in Chicago greeted the capture in a shoot-out of Public Enemy Number One, John Dillinger, the bank robber. He soon escaped.

There was no escape, however, for the occupants of a Ford motor car speeding up a country road in Louisiana on the morning of 23 May. Waiting for it in the bushes were six men with guns at the ready. The man and the girl inside the car had a price on their heads. As the car drew level with the ambush, the men in the bushes stepped out and blasted it with a barrage of more than 100 bullets. The riddled car skidded to a halt.

Inside the car the ambushers found two bleeding bodies, all that was left of America's most wanted outlaws, Bonnie Parker and Clyde Barrow. They had been chased by the law across half-a-dozen states after a long rampage of robbery and violence, during which they had never hesitated to kill anyone who crossed their path. Now they themselves had perished by the gun.

The news burst across the world's newspapers and airwaves. In two short years Bonnie Parker and Clyde Barrow had become almost legendary figures, feared and hated by many, grudgingly admired and even hero-worshipped by others. They were to become folk heroes, a latter-day Robin Hood and Maid Marion.

But not to their victims, nor to the lawmen who tracked and shot them down. To them they were now just trophies, to be put on show for the world to see. Naked and unwashed, they were put on slabs and filmed: Bonnie Parker, aged 23; Clyde Barrow, just one year older, who had been in trouble with the law all his young life. Utterly remorseless, the couple had encouraged each other to take what they wanted, and to live the way they liked.

FROM HUMBLE BEGINNINGS TO CRIME

Clyde Barrow was born on 24 March 1909, the sixth of eight neglected children, in Telico, Texas, a small town near Dallas. His hero was the outlaw Jesse James, and he rarely went to school. His parents were too busy scraping a living on their farm to look after their children. At nine he was consigned to an institution for delinquents as 'an incorrigible truant, thief and runaway'.

Telico was in the dustbowl, a vast area of the southwestern states devastated by drought and over-cropping during the 1930s. Two-thirds of the population migrated, among them Clyde's father, who sold the farm for what he could get and started a garage.

Clyde wanted to provide for his mother. But his only skills were outside the law and in 1929 he and his brother Ivan, known as Buck, were shot at by police while driving a stolen car. Buck was arrested and got five years in jail for a long list of offences. Clyde managed to get away.

A few weeks later, at a girlfriend's house, he met Bonnie Parker. Soon she took him home to meet her mother. Bonnie was 19, slim and tiny, funny and clever. She delighted him.

Bonnie and Clyde's Ford V-8 car, pierced by over 100 bullets, being escorted back to the police pound in Arcadia through the crowd of sightseers which quickly flocked to the scene of the killings

Bonnie had been born in Rowena, Texas, a year after Clyde. Her father died when she was four, and she and her mother went to live with her grandmother in Cement City, a rough section of Dallas.

Bonnie and her sister Billie escaped into marriage as soon as they could, both of them to petty crooks. Bonnie married Roy Thornton, who for a while was in prison with Billie's husband Bud. Within a year of Bonnie's wedding, Roy had left her and she got herself a job in a Dallas café.

The morning after Clyde moved in with her the police came looking for him. He got two years in jail for car theft, with twelve more years suspended. His brother Buck was already inside and both began scheming to break out. Buck managed it in March 1930, when he got over the wall of Huntsville Penitentiary. While on the run, Buck married a Dallas girl named Blanche who didn't know who he was. When she found out that he was an escaped prisoner, she persuaded him to give himself up. Brother Clyde's girl, Bonnie, on the other hand, preferred her man on the outside. She taped a slim-handled Colt to her body and slipped it to Clyde through the bars. That night he used it to escape from Waco Jail but, only a week later, he was recaptured in Middletown, Ohio, after bungling a burglary.

Now he was faced with his full 14 years to serve, but he managed to engineer his release by asking a fellow inmate to chop off two of his toes.

A WORLD OF GANGSTERS

In prison, Clyde had been educated by hardened criminals and now emerged into a world of widespread lawlessness. For crime and gangsterism had been encouraged by Prohibition. The cities were ruled by the Mob, and the run-down rural areas were the hunting grounds of such outlaws as John Dillinger.

The Depression that had followed the Wall Street Crash had America in its grip. Three-and-a-half million families were forced on relief, and jobs for untrained men just out of jail didn't exist. Many people regarded those who turned to robbing banks as heroes, attacking the symbols of riches in the midst of degrading poverty.

Clyde Barrow promised his mother that he would try to go straight, but he found it simply impossible. The loyal and lively Bonnie joined him in a crime spree across Texas. At a robbery in Kaufman they were separated. She was caught and jailed for three months. But Clyde and his friends kept robbing. In April of 1932, he and former fellow prisoner Raymond Hamilton killed jeweller John Bucher, grabbing rings worth $2,500 from his safe.

From Bucher's town of Hillsboro, Clyde and Hamilton roamed the Texas backwoods holding up gas stations, waiting until Bonnie could join them. When she did, they continued as before. Between robberies they larked about, posing for snapshots. These added to their notoriety, giving the press the chance to portray Bonnie and Clyde as ruthless lovers who roamed the countryside of Texas, Louisiana, Oklahoma, Arkansas and Missouri, robbing and killing while remaining a romantic couple.

The truth was more complicated. During his time in jail, Clyde had learnt to be bisexual, and he and Bonnie shared their fellow gang member Ray Hamilton, who enjoyed sex any way he could get it. Throughout 1932, the gang cut a swathe through the South. Anyone who stood in their way was either

A demure picture of Bonnie Parker which Police Chief Percy Boyd, held hostage by the gang for 24 hours, said was a good representation of the real woman

killed or kidnapped. They shot four people dead in that year alone. They stole cars and guns whenever they needed them.

Before Christmas, however, Ray Hamilton was arrested on a trip home. They wanted a replacement and, while robbing a gas station, kidnapped 16-year-old William Daniel Jones and persuaded him to join them. W.D., as he was known, soon discovered what he was in for. He was stealing a Ford V-8 with Clyde when the owner jumped on the running board. Clyde casually shot the man in the head and killed him. The next week, their hideout was surrounded and, in escaping, they killed a deputy sheriff.

In March of 1933, Buck Barrow was paroled, thanks to the tearful pleas of his wife, Blanche. Then she and Buck promptly joined up with Bonnie, Clyde and W.D. to form the new Barrow Gang.

First the gang needed some more guns, which Clyde obtained by raiding the federal armoury in Springfield, Missouri. They celebrated by holding up a loan company in Kansas City. While the police searched vainly for them over six states, they were nipping back to Dallas to visit their families.

Next, they robbed a jewellery store in Neosho, Missouri, before renting a house nearby. But a neighbour spotted them carrying guns. They had to leave some of the guns behind when the house was raided. But with them they also left two dead lawmen. That night they drove 400 miles from Neosho to get into Texas. Clyde had caught a bullet in the arm. Bonnie prised it out with a hairpin.

A COUPLE OF PUNKS

For all their fame, the sums they stole were tiny. The most they ever got was $3,500 in May 1933, from the First State Bank in Okabena, Minnesota. John Dillinger commented: 'Couple of punks. They're giving bank robbing a bad name.'

A few days later, Clyde, driving fast as usual, crashed the car on a bend in flames. Bonnie was badly burned. They sought help at a nearby house, but when Clyde was reluctant to call the doctor, the family that had taken them in phoned the police.

Two officers arrived but were ambushed and taken hostage. The Barrows stole their cars – and kidnapped the officers. But once the gang was safely across the state line, the two men were released. Bonnie slowly recovered, but the gang was forced to keep on the move through Kansas, Iowa, Northern Texas and Missouri.

On 19 July they narrowly escaped a police ambush near Platto City, Iowa, in which Buck was shot and wounded in the head. On they went but, less than a week later, they were spotted at a campsite near the town of Dexter. The police surrounded the site but Bonnie was up early. As shots rang out, she, Clyde and W.D. got away by swimming across a river, where they hijacked a car.

Bonnie and Clyde frequently played around for the cameras and sent shots such as this to the press who eagerly printed these portraits of the ruthless lovers

Buck, however, was hit in the back and Blanche stayed behind with him. When the lawmen reached the couple, Blanche was bent over him. They pulled her away, and arrested them both. Buck hung on to life for five days afterwards, during which time Blanche, regarded as a dangerous criminal, was not

Blanche being pulled away from the body of her husband, Clyde's brother Buck, after he was fatally wounded in a police ambush. She stayed behind with him while the other gang members escaped across a river

allowed to spend any time with him. He died calling for her, but she was locked in a cell. Later she was sentenced to ten years imprisonment.

W.D. Jones now decided to flee from the gang, but he was arrested in Houston. He claimed he had been forced to take part in the gang's activities but was, nevertheless, sentenced to 15 years in jail.

Over the next four months, Bonnie and Clyde continued their rampage. They killed four more lawmen as they evaded capture. In November, the pair arranged to meet their families near Dallas. The sheriff there heard of the rendezvous and got ready to ambush them. As they drove up, he sportingly gave them the chance to surrender, but they quickly sped off amid gunfire.

Enraged at losing them, Sheriff Schmid gave three of his deputies orders to bring them back, dead or alive. Ed Caster, Ted Hinton, who had known Bonnie when she was a waitress, and Bob Alcorn were told to go after the couple full-time.

But the outlawed pair were defiant. Early one January morning they crept up on a work gang at Eastham Prison Farm and set five convicts free. In the operation, a guard was killed.

Now they had a new team, including their old accomplice and lover, Ray Hamilton. Another convict insisted on staying with them until he was paid money Hamilton owed him. After they robbed a bank he allowed himself to be recaptured.

Another new recruit was Henry Methvin. A lot of sexual tension developed as Ray had introduced his new girlfriend, Mary O'Dare, into the gang and she made a play for Methvin. But the new gang pressed on, holding up gas stations and stores as they went, as well as stealing larger sums from banks, including a haul in the town of Lancaster. The press continued to give the gang sensational coverage. Further tension arose with a bitter row over the division of the spoils. Clyde accused Ray of secretly pocketing some of the proceeds. So Hamilton and his girl quit. But now Clyde worried that Hamilton would betray him. He decided to follow and kill Hamilton.

Meanwhile, a new hunter had joined the trail: ex-Texas Ranger Frank Hamer, paid by the governor of Huntsville Prison to get Clyde.

PUBLIC OPINION CHANGES

Then came the incident which finally changed the public's perception of the outlaws and took away their romantic image.

Bonnie and Clyde were keeping a rendezvous with some of their henchmen near Grapevine, Texas. They were waiting to intercept and murder Raymond Hamilton. While they waited they drank whisky, made love to each other and practised their marksmanship by shooting at birds. Presently two state highway patrol officers came by and decided to investigate what was happening. They approached a parked car on their motorcycles, totally unaware of the identify of the owners.

Suddenly Henry Methvin started firing on the officers. Then Bonnie and Clyde joined in. The two patrolmen were left dead on the road by their machines. They had no chance. This atrocious murder sealed the doom of Bonnie and Clyde. The cold-bloodedness of it turned public opinion against the couple, regardless of the fact that it was Henry Methvin who had begun the shooting.

Rewards for the capture of the Barrow Gang were now being offered, and the public, no longer in thrall to the gang, increased its vigilance. In April 1934, Raymond Hamilton was arrested for robbery and given 362 years in jail. After a second trial, for the murder of the guard at the prison farm, he ended up in the electric chair.

Now the lawmen on Bonnie and Clyde's trail joined forces, determined to catch the whole gang. Led by Frank Hamer, who had killed 60 outlaws as a ranger, the group included Hamer's deputy Manny Gault, Ted Hinton and Bob Alcorn from Dallas. Together they were a formidable team.

> ## "COUPLE OF PUNKS. THEY'RE GIVING BANK ROBBING A BAD NAME"
>
> John Dillinger

With Hamilton taken care of, Clyde led his little band northeast into Oklahoma. Never far behind now, their pursuers actually saw them in Duvant on 4 April but hesitated to open fire on the gang of outlaws for fear of killing passers-by.

It was near Commerce in Oklahoma that two policemen flagged down a car with a bullet hole in its windscreen. As they approached the car, Constable Cal Campbell was hit and killed by machine-gun fire. Percy Boyd, Commerce's Chief of Police, received a slight head wound and was taken prisoner. The gang held on to him for 24 hours but liked him enough to let him go. Boyd reported that Clyde was cocky and vain and that Henry Methvin was very much in his shadow. But he really liked Bonnie, and said she was nothing like the pictures which had been shown in the press of her and Clyde playing with guns and of her puffing a cigar. She had

The six lawmen who joined forces to catch the Barrow Gang, led by ex-Texas Ranger Frank Hamer (front right). After a wait of three days and nights, they eventually cornered their prey

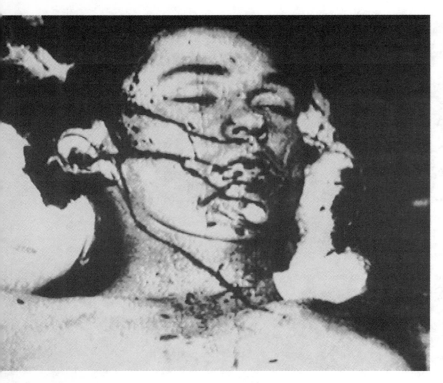

Clyde Barrow, only 24 years old, grew up 'an incorrigible thief, truant and runaway' in Telico, Texas. He lived by the gun and died by it, riddled with 50 bullets

been annoyed by the headline 'Clyde Barrow's cigar-smoking moll' and regretted posing. He reported that in real life she was more like a photograph which showed her looking much more demure. He said that she and Clyde seemed genuinely in love. In the car with them Bonnie had a pet rabbit named Sonny Boy which was intended as a present for her mother.

With this clue, the tracking party headed south, making for Dallas. Here the couple had already met up with Clyde's parents and Bonnie's mother on a country road and had enjoyed browsing through recent snapshots. Bonnie's mother later remembered Bonnie quietly saying: 'When they kill us, don't ever say anything ugly about Clyde.'

Bidding what was to turn out to be their final farewell to their folks, Bonnie and Clyde then headed eastwards. Their pursuers turned the screw with another warrant for their arrest, for the murder of Constable Campbell.

THE PURSUIT ENDS

Desperately tired of the long chase, the rangers hoped that their quarries would make a fatal mistake out of sheer fatigue. When their car was spotted parked

outside of a café in Shreveport, Louisiana, Hinton guessed that the couple intended to rendezvous with Henry Methvin at his father's nearby farm.

So, while every local robbery was ascribed, mostly wrongly, to Bonnie and Clyde, the six rangers staked out the Methvin farm near Shreveport. When Hinton spied them driving down the road from Arcadia, he knew he was right. Rather than risk an abortive chase he and his fellow rangers settled down to wait for their prey. Their cars now carried a massive armoury of automatic weapons, but little to make their ambush a comfortable one.

For three days and nights the group of lawmen endured a miserable, wet and mosquito-bitten wait by the road. But Bonnie and Clyde were wary.

While hiding in the undergrowth on 23 May the officers had a break. At 4am they stopped Henry Methvin's father as he drove up the road. They hand-cuffed him to a tree and left his truck by the side of the road as a decoy.

Then, just after 9.15, a tan Ford V-8 was seen approaching. To the lawmen it looked like the car they were waiting for. Then Ted Hinton recognised Clyde, who was driving. 'That's him for sure, get ready now,' he said.

As Clyde saw the Methvin truck parked by the side of the road he started to slow down, and as he did so the ambushers opened fire. Riddled with bullets, the car stopped.

When the lawmen finally approached the car, they found Bonnie leaning against Clyde. A pistol and a shotgun were ready on the floor of the car next to Bonnie, but the ambush had taken her by surprise.

THE PUBLIC SIDESHOW BEGINS

Within hours the ambush site was filled with sight-seers. A procession of more than 50 cars escorted the shattered Ford as it was towed into the police pound in Arcadia to be put on show. A chain-link fence had to be erected because ghoulish souvenir hunters had already tried to rip parts off the car and seize bits of Bonnie and Clyde's clothing and hair before they were removed from it.

On the back seat of the couple's car, the lawmen had found more weapons: three light machine guns, two shotguns, a dozen pistols, and at least a thousand rounds of ammunition. But the pair had had no chance to fire any of these before the six lawmen had loosed 107 rounds into the car in less than two minutes. Their bodies had been riddled with about 50 bullets each.

There was chaos at the Arcadia funeral home where the bodies were taken as a crowd fought to see the famous corpses. There they were filmed to prove that they were really dead. On show again back in Dallas Bonnie was seen by 40,000 people, Clyde by some 30,000. Also on show for the curious crowds were Clyde's coat, with its 40 bullet holes from the ambush, and his gun which, when closely examined, was found to have seven notches, one for each of the men whose lives he had claimed.

While on the run, Bonnie had written poems and sent them to various newspapers. They included this prophetic epitaph:

They don't think they're too tough or desperate,
They know that the law always wins . . .
They've been shot at before, but they do not ignore
That death is the wages of sin.
Some day they'll go down together,
And they'll bury them side by side;
To few it'll be grief – to the law a relief –
But it's death for Bonnie and Clyde.

The men who had hunted down the murderous couple became national heroes. On the other hand, 30 relatives and friends of Bonnie and Clyde stood trial for harbouring them during their period as out-laws. While the men were chained together to pre-vent any attempt at overpowering their guards, the women, despite Bonnie's example, were not regarded as dangerous. W.D. Jones, already serving 15 years, and Henry Methvin, life, each got an extra two years. Among the women, Mary O'Dare, Bonnie's sister Billie, and Buck's wife Blanche, were sentenced to a year and a day in prison.

Both mothers were also on trial, and their lawyer pleaded that mother love took precedence over the law. However, the judge was not impressed by this defence or by Mrs Barrow's infirmity (she attended the trial in a wheelchair) and sentenced them both to 30 days.

Clyde was buried next to his brother Buck at West Dallas Cemetery. An aeroplane dropped a huge floral wreath on the spot. Despite her wish to be buried next to Clyde, Bonnie was taken to be buried at Dallas's Fishtrap Cemetery.

But the emotions of their families, the legends which later grew up around the couple, and the awful inappropriateness of the epitaph on Bonnie's grave:

As the flowers are all made sweeter
By the sunshine and the dew,
So this old world is made brighter
By the lives of folks like you

could not disguise the fact that Bonnie Parker and Clyde Barrow were two of America's most cold-blooded and callous killers.

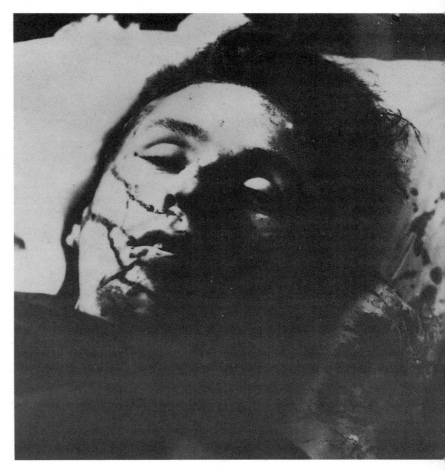

Bonnie Parker, only 23 years old, slim and tiny, funny and clever, but nonetheless ruthless and deadly. She never managed to reach the guns at her feet before being blasted with a barrage of 50 bullets

AN ANNOUNCEMENT THAT THE BODIES OF THOUSANDS OF POLISH OFFICERS WITH BULLET HOLES IN THE BACK OF THEIR NECKS HAD BEEN FOUND BURIED IN A DITCH IN KATYN FOREST IN POLAND CAUSED DISBELIEF AMONG THE ALLIES IN 1943. FOR THE ANNOUNCEMENT WAS MADE BY RADIO BERLIN, WHO ACCUSED THE RUSSIANS OF THE MASSACRE. LATER, WHEN THE RUSSIANS RECAPTURED THE SPOT, THEY POINTED THE FINGER AT THE GERMANS AND IT WAS CONVENIENT AT THE TIME FOR THE ALLIES TO BELIEVE THIS VERSION. BUT LATER, THE REALISATION OF THE RUTHLESSNESS OF STALIN FOLLOWED BY THE COLLAPSE OF THE SOVIET UNION HAVE HELPED TO UNRAVEL THE TRUE SECRETS OF THIS TERRIBLE SLAUGHTER.

Stalin

The Massacre at Katyn Forest

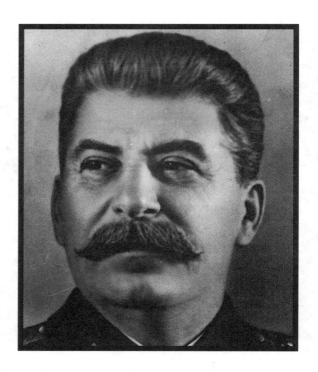

The tide was turning in the Second World War. The German Sixth Army surrendered at Stalingrad after losing a hundred thousand men. Rommel's troops were chased out of Libya and the entire Mediterranean shore was freed of Axis forces. Germany was pounded by bombs. Britain was flooding Russia with military aid. The two countries were allies and partners.

So there was both embarrassment and disbelief when, on 13 April 1943, Radio Berlin announced that the Germans had found the bodies of at least 3,000 Polish officers massacred by the Bolsheviks. Dr Goebbels' propaganda ministry rushed a newsreel camera to the spot – a place called the Hill of Goats, in Katyn Forest – and showed the grisly exhumations of corpses in Polish uniforms. Diaries and documents in the pockets ceased in April 1940. At that time the officers had been in the hands of the Russians.

To confirm their claim that the Russians were responsible, the Germans brought a delegation of professors of forensic medicine from nine neutral countries. They agreed that the state of decay indicated that the victims were shot in 1940. They also confirmed that the bodies had bullet holes in the nape of the neck, a method of execution regularly used by the Soviet secret service. More bodies were found, bringing the total up to more than 4,000.

RUSSIAN DENIALS

Stalin immediately denied the charge. Radio Moscow said that the Poles had fallen into the hands of the invading Germans, who were trying to cover up their own crimes. The German-appointed group published their report in May 1943. By September the advancing Russian tanks had retaken the nearby key city of Smolensk. A few days later, the Russians arrived in the Katyn region.

With the German occupying army scattered and captured, the Russians were now in a position to refute what they called the 'lies and calumnies' about the mass executions of the Polish officers. They appointed their own commission of Soviet experts, who arrived on 26 October to carry out their investigations. The bodies were again exhumed.

'Not the work of our men in 1940; the perpetrators were the Germans in 1941.' That was the conclusion of the Soviet investigators, based on the state of the bodies and documentary evidence they said they found in the pockets of the Polish officers' uniforms. This was a relief to the Allies, who didn't want to fall out with Stalin.

The postwar Nuremberg trial of the Nazi leaders was the obvious place to punish them for the massacre at Katyn Forest. So it duly went on the charge sheet. But the tribunal found the case unproven, and it was not mentioned in the judgement. The evidence at Nuremberg that did condemn the Nazis certainly showed them to be capable of such a crime: six million Jews systematically slaughtered and five million other so-called enemies of the state eliminated in concentration camps.

In 1946 few people believed that Josef Stalin, while a ruthless leader, was capable of callously murdering the 15,000 officers the Poles said were missing. But it is now known that, ever since the Russian Revolution, he had been as brutal as Hitler.

THE RISE OF STALIN

Stalin was never as close to Lenin as he later had himself portrayed. Leon Trotsky, Stalin's greatest enemy inside the Kremlin, called him 'the Party's most eminent mediocrity'.

But he was talented, and in 1922 he was made General Secretary of the Communist Party. When Lenin died two years later, he left a will warning against Stalin's power and suggesting finding somebody 'more loyal, more polite and more attentive' to replace him.

Stalin stayed because the Bolshevik leadership feared that, without him, Trotsky would establish his own dictatorship. The split between the two widened and, in 1927, Stalin had Trotsky exiled to Siberia and

Josef Stalin was a ruthless leader who masterminded plots to kill and remove anyone who stood in his way. Nikita Krushchev called him a brutal, despotic murderer with an all-consuming vanity

then banished from the country. Fourteen years later, Stalin ordered an assassin to find Trotsky in Mexico and murder him with an ice-pick.

Meanwhile, Stalin had succeeded in making himself all-powerful. In 1929, he sent in the army to take over all successful individual farms. Two million peasants were eliminated, and their land confiscated and collectivised. At least five million people died of starvation during the upheavals.

Stalin's ruthless five-year plans pulled industrial Russia into the twentieth century. He forced workers to increase their output and created the legend that Alexis Stakhanov had dug 100 tons of coal in six hours. Workers in all factories who emulated him were honoured as 'Stakhanovites'.

The air force, navy and army were regarded by Stalin as threats to his power, and he set about eliminating potential challenges to his total authority. A reliable estimate is that a fifth of the officers of the Red Army were liquidated. He purged every section of the Communist Party, putting thousands of its officials on trial. They were charged with sabotage – which meant, in effect, questioning any policy which Stalin advocated. Within ten years all the surviving top leaders of the 1920s were in the dock. The accused were tortured and intimidated until they believed it was their duty to confess.

> ## "THE PARTY'S MOST EMINENT MEDIOCRITY"
>
> Leon Trotsky's opinion of Stalin

Those not executed were banished to a gulag. Gulags provided vast reservoirs of free labour and were designed to kill off inmates after extracting as much work as they were capable of. It has been estimated that ten million men and women died cutting the Baltic Sea Canal, building the railways in Siberia and the Far North, and other schemes which needed slave labour.

Stalin sought adoration. Birthday presents were obligatory. Every town had to put up his statue. He basked in such designations as 'Father of the People' and 'Greatest Genius in History'.

Exhumed bodies on the Hill of Goats in Katyn Forest, Poland. The Germans pointed the finger at the Russians, but it was convenient at the time for the Allies to accept the Soviet denial and counter-claim that it was in fact the Germans who were guilty of the atrocity

STALIN ENTERS THE WAR

Actually a cynical opportunist, Stalin was prepared to make a deal with his enemy, Nazi Germany, for a temporary advantage. On 23 August 1939, Joachim von Ribbentrop went to Moscow to offer Stalin half of Poland in return for allowing Hitler to invade it. So, on 1 September, German tanks were able to lead a million-and-a-quarter members of the Wehrmacht into Poland on the first of its blitzkriegs. Then, on 17 September, Russian troops crossed Poland's eastern frontier, breaking existing treaties. That blow in the back sealed the country's fate, and its government fled to Romania the next day. The Red Army swiftly moved in to link up with the Germans, and annexed 76,000 square miles of territory with twelve-and-a-half million people.

While the troops of the German and Russian armies greeted each other as fellow conquerors, both sides knew that it was only a matter of time before Hitler's long-threatened plan to invade Russia would be put into action.

Poland soon surrendered, on 22 September. The poorly equipped and bitter Polish soldiers handed over their arms, and the Russians took 250,000 prisoners. Among those who managed to get out of the country was a former Prime Minister of Poland, General Wladyslaw Sikorski. First in Paris and then in London he took on the double job of head of the government in exile and Commander-in-Chief of the Free Polish forces. Under him, the remnants of the army became the nucleus of a distinguished fighting force.

Back home the two occupying powers were busy decimating Poland. On 3 October 1940, the Germans established the Warsaw Ghetto, forcing 150,000 Jews who had previously lived outside the Jewish district to move in, joining its 250,000 existing inhabitants. So now a third of Warsaw's population was walled up in a fortieth of its space.

THE RUSSIAN MILITARY CAMPS

In the Russian half of Poland, captured soldiers were marched into a hundred prison camps. At first officers and men were kept together, but gradually 14,736

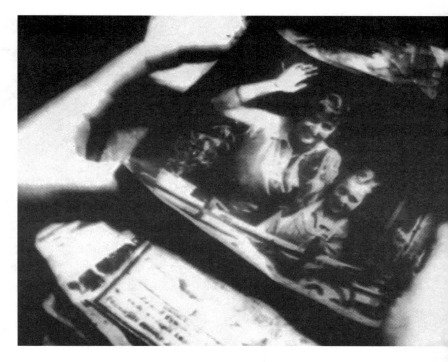

officers and others regarded as potential leaders were put into three separate camps. There they were subjected to a barrage of communist propaganda, and individually questioned by a team from the NKVD, who reported back to Moscow which, if any of them, could be re-educated.

The Kosielsk camp was in the grounds of a former monastery near Smolensk, and 4,254 prisoners were kept there. Letters written to them after March 1940 were returned to sender. The reason given was that the camps were being cleared, and by mid-May only 400 of the prisoners remained, in a special camp. What had happened to the rest, nobody knew – or was saying.

A year later, German tanks turned eastwards, after having conquered most of Western Europe. The time had come for Hitler's long-promised invasion of Russia, and the first weeks were all he had hoped for. By September of 1941 his troops were encircling Leningrad and were ready to head towards Moscow. Smolensk was burning and the former Polish camps were captured.

Close behind the front-line troops came the SS units, killing anyone hostile to the invaders. It was they who would have shot the Polish officers at

Some of the photos and documents found in the pockets of the murdered Polish officers at Katyn Forest. Diaries found with the bodies dated the massacre to April 1940 when the officers had been in the hands of the Russians

A still from Goebbels' newsreel of the exhumation of bodies in Polish uniforms at Katyn Forest in May 1943. This film was used as propaganda against the Allies

Katyn if, as the Russians claimed, the prisoners had been left in the area.

One result of the invasion was that all remaining Polish prisoners in Russian hands were released and formed into a Polish army to fight alongside Soviet forces. On 3 December 1941, General Sikorski flew from London to inspect this new army and to raise with Stalin the question of where the missing officers were. They could now be immeasurably useful in the Polish armies of both West and East.

While Sikorski had heard disturbing rumours about their fate, he had had no firm news of them and was hopeful that they had been sent to work camps in the Soviet Far North, and could now be reunited with their men.

Stalin assured General Sikorski that all captured Poles had been released. He speculated that the missing officers may have escaped to Manchuria. General Anders, head of the Polish army in Russia, claimed that that was impossible, and Stalin promised to look into the matter.

THE DISCOVERY OF THE BODIES

The Poles heard nothing more until the German announcement in April 1943, which confirmed their worst fears. They reluctantly accepted the German version of events as the truth. This version claimed that Katyn Forest, through which the River Dniepr flows, had long been known locally as a place of execution for the NKVD. A dacha had been built there in 1929 by the Soviet secret police and all outsiders barred from its grounds.

In 1942, Poles in the German compulsory labour corps had come across a body in Polish uniform and reburied it with a birch cross over the grave. A local peasant told the German commandant that in 1940 he had seen prisoners being transported to dig deep trenches on the Hill of Goats. Now, as soon as the snow had cleared sufficiently, the Germans started digging by the birch cross.

The horrific secret was out. A total of 4,143 bodies were exhumed. They had all been shot in the neck and most had their hands tied behind their backs.

Among the thousands of men, there was one woman, identified as Janina Lewandowski of the Polish air force. She had been among the prisoners in Kozielsk.

Stalin denied responsibility, but he vetoed an International Red Cross investigation. He then severed all relations with the Polish government for requesting one and set up a puppet Polish government in Moscow.

RUSSIANS CAPTURE KATYN

Stalin's counter-attack, following the routing of the German army at Stalingrad in January 1943, pushed the Germans back 200 miles in the first three months. Throughout that year the Red Army was to maintain its offensive, forcing Germany to continue its retreat all along the Front.

The Red Army retook a shattered Smolensk on 15 September. The Forest of Katyn lay just 250 miles

> "NOT THE WORK OF
> OUR MEN IN 1940;
> THE PERPETRATORS WERE
> THE GERMANS IN 1941"
>
> The conclusion of the
> Soviet investigators in
> October 1943

away. Once they were firmly re-established there, the Russians determined to fix the blame for the massacre of the Polish officers on the Nazis.

The Russians imported their own forensic experts with instructions to prove that the bodies had been in the ground only since the Germans were there, thus exonerating the Russians. The commission duly went through the grisly motions and came up with their preordained findings. While this charade was going on, Russia's leaders knew exactly what had happened. Documents have come to light since the fall of the communist regime which show that it was Beria, head of the NKVD at the time of the massacre, who recommended that these 'enemies of the Soviet regime be shot'. General Tokaryev was present at the first executions, and, in 1991, he gave an account of them.

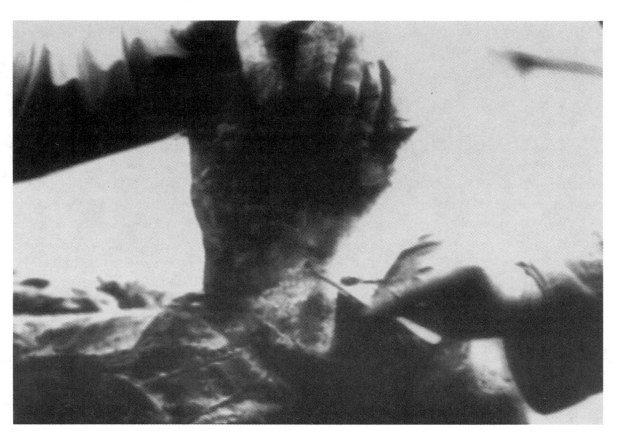

The Germans invited a delegation of forensic doctors from nine neutral countries to examine the corpses at Katyn Forest. They confirmed that the bodies had bullet holes in the nape of the neck, a regular method of execution used by the Soviet secret service

Harold Truman (centre) shaking hands with Winston Churchill (left) and Josef Stalin (right) at Potsdam, Germany, in July 1945. As the Nazi concentration camps came to light, no one questioned the Soviet version of the massacre at Katyn Forest and Nazi leaders were charged with the crime at the Nuremberg trials. Interestingly, the judges remained silent on the matter

They had shot the Poles, one by one, in a sound-proof prison cell at the rate of 250 a night. The main killer was an officer named Blokhin, who wore a brown leather apron and long brown leather gloves reaching above the elbows. Each man was asked his surname, first name and date of birth. Then he was taken to the soundproofed room and shot in the back of the head. The bodies were loaded into covered lorries and taken to the burial ditch. When it was all over the NKVD organised a big banquet to celebrate.

Now the bodies were shown to Western journalists, who, it was assumed, could hardly ask any awkward questions since the local peasants had all been silenced and dead men tell no tales.

However, one of the visitors was the daughter of the American Ambassador, Averill Harriman. She pertinently asked why if, as the Russians claimed, the Polish officers had been shot by the Germans in the summer, the bodies had been clothed in greatcoats and winter underwear. All her guide could answer was that the climate varied greatly in that area and it

must have been a cold summer. The bullet holes were passed off as proof of Nazi involvement, no mention being made of the NKVD's favourite method. The man who had signed the authorisation for the killings on 3 March 1940 knew he was safe.

PUPPET GOVERNMENT INSTALLED

With the D-Day landings imminent, it was politically inexpedient to listen to the suspicions of the London Poles. As the Western Allies fought their way across Europe, towards the victorious Russians in Berlin, nobody was going to care about who was responsible for the deaths of a few thousand men at the start of a war that eventually killed fifty million people.

In the euphoria of the link-up with the Russians, Stalin was allowed to install his puppet government in Poland. They weren't going to ask any awkward questions about Katyn. Stalin's influence over Eastern Europe was confirmed at Potsdam in July 1945. He dismissed all accusations from Winston Churchill and Harry Truman about Eastern Europe as 'fairytales'.

The opening up of the Nazi death camps at the end of the war revealed the extent of their policies of extermination, and few people doubted that Adolf Hitler's mass murdering extended as far as the Forest of Katyn. The Russian prosecutors were allowed to include the Polish massacre among the crimes levelled at the Nazi leaders who were in the dock at Nuremberg, and the eventual silence of the judges about Katyn was hardly noticed.

Then, with West Berlin isolated and the crashing down of the Iron Curtain, a sense of reality about the state of Europe finally dawned. The Russians began the blockade of West Berlin and the Allies responded with an airlift of supplies. The Cold War had begun and with it came a cooler analysis of the past.

PARANOID STALIN

Stalin, who was always on the lookout for treachery to match his own, became completely paranoid. He began planning to liquidate all witnesses who could testify against him to posterity, however senior. When Mao Tse-tung triumphed in China in 1949, Stalin invited him to Moscow, rightly suspicious that this great new ally would turn out to challenge his authority over the now widespread world of communism.

In 1952, at the celebrations of the October Revolution, Stalin appeared gloomy and worried. He had just had nine doctors arrested and accused of murdering his trusted aide Zhdanov, and he blamed a Jewish conspiracy. His colleagues saw this as the curtain raiser to a new series of show trials.

So there was more relief than sorrow in the Kremlin when, on 5 March 1953, at the age of 73, Josef Stalin suddenly died from a clot on the brain. A million people waited in line to see the body.

> "THERE HAVE BEEN DIFFICULT MOMENTS, BLANK SPOTS IN OUR HISTORY. AROUND THEM HAS BEEN BUILT MORE EMOTION THAN KNOWLEDGE. THERE IS ONLY ONE WAY TO THE TRUTH. INVESTIGATE THE FACTS. HISTORY CAN'T BE CHANGED, BUT CONCLUSIONS CAN"

Mikhail Gorbachev's oblique reference to the massacre at Katyn Forest in 1988

GRADUAL ADMISSIONS

Three years later, Nikita Khrushchev made his 'Secret Speech', in which he called Stalin a brutal, despotic murderer with an all-consuming vanity. He talked about Stalin's paranoia and how he had masterminded plots to kill not only his critics but friends he thought might pose a threat to him. For example, of the 1,966 delegates to the 17th Party Congress, 1,108 had been executed. He did not mention Katyn, but later Russian leaders have, and a memorial now stands on the Hill of Goats.

When Mikhail Gorbachev visited Polish leader Jaruzelski in Warsaw in 1988 he spoke publicly about the Katyn Forest massacre for the first time, but obliquely. He stated that: 'There have been difficult moments, blank spots in our history. Around them has been built more emotion than knowledge. There is only one way to the truth. Investigate the facts. History can't be changed, but conclusions can.'

What Gorbachev knew but did not say, either on the occasion of his visit to Warsaw in 1988 or later when Jaruzelski went to Moscow, was that, in addition to the 14,736 soldiers who had been murdered, a further 10,685 Polish civilians had been shot and buried at the same time.

This was revealed in 1992 after the fall of communism in Russia when various papers were cleared out of a top-secret safe.

The victims' only memorial is a cross on the Hill of Goats. But they will be remembered as long as history is studied. On the order authorising the death of the 25,000 is a pencilled signature: J. Stalin. The murders at Katyn and other still unknown sites are no longer a mystery. The murderer has been found guilty by posterity.

HOW CAN ONE MAN DIRECT ACTIONS WHICH LEAD TO THE

TERRIBLE TORTURE AND MURDER OF 11 MILLION PEOPLE?

OR WAGE WARS WHICH CLAIM THE DEATH OF 50 MILLION?

THE CRIMES OF ADOLF HITLER AND HIS NAZI PARTY,

WHOSE AIMS WERE WORLD DOMINATION AND THE TOTAL

ELIMINATION OF THE JEWS – THE FINAL SOLUTION, AS IT

WAS CALLED – WERE BEYOND IMAGINATION. IN THE END,

HITLER'S PLANS DID NOT COME TO FRUITION – THE REST

OF THE WORLD PROVED JUST TOO STRONG. HE AND SOME

OF HIS SUPPORTERS MANAGED TO ESCAPE RETRIBUTION

THROUGH SUICIDE. THE HORRORS OF HIS ACTIONS WERE

OUTLINED IN THE TRIALS OF THOSE WHO REMAINED AND

WERE BROUGHT TO JUDGEMENT AT NUREMBERG.

Hitler

The Nuremberg Trials

I n 1945 the Second World War was reaching its climax. The Russians entered Berlin, and the Americans were advancing to meet them. At the River Elbe, near Leipzig, the two armies met. As the Allies celebrated, the German army surrendered in its thousands. On 7 May, Acting Führer Admiral Doenitz signed an unconditional surrender. Hitler had boasted his Reich would last a thousand years. It survived for just twelve.

With Germany in ruins, the Allies concentrated first on organising a temporary government and then bringing to book the men who had caused the misery of war and its attendant horrors.

New camps sprang up to house the refugees of the final days, and the guilty men attempted to hide among the prisoners of war. But their former prisoners were on the lookout for the people who had treated human beings as units to be numbered, exploited and slaughtered.

As Belsen and the other 23 Nazi concentration camps yielded up their horrific secrets, the wheels of retribution began to turn. The Allies agreed that the men and women who ordered these crimes and those who carried out their orders would be punished.

Tens of thousands of camp victims, barely left alive, were ever-present reminders of the pledge to try the accused before an international tribunal.

The city chosen for the trial of the major war criminals was once the scene of the Nazi Party's greatest showpieces of choreographed militarism: Nuremberg. Here Adolf Hitler had addressed the faithful in rallies designed to mesmerise his followers and to impress the rest of the world. This was the Mecca of the Nazi religion, where the faithful flocked to glorify the man they worshipped almost as a God, to hear him extol them as the master race, and to listen to him promulgate his latest decrees. Now his creation was to be exposed by the dry process of law, far removed from the hysteria of the rallies, but just as effective.

THE ACCUSED

On 30 April, Hitler shot himself under his shattered Chancellery in Berlin. He had married his longtime mistress, Eva Braun, then given her poison to take. By his orders, their bodies were burned by the SS, Hitler's security service. Among the henchmen to follow his example were Heinrich Himmler, head of the SS, who swallowed a cyanide capsule, and propaganda chief Josef Goebbels who, after poisoning his six children, gave his wife poison and shot himself.

So the most senior Nazis on trial were: Hermann Goering, Commander of the German air force, the Luftwaffe, and founder of the Gestapo, the Nazi secret police; Rudolf Hess who, until his flight to England in 1942, was Deputy Führer for Party matters; and Joachim von Ribbentrop, Hitler's Foreign Minister.

Their trial with 18 other top Nazi leaders lasted from 20 November 1945 to 30 September 1946. The accused faced four main indictments, and the trial was opened by Britain's Chief Justice, Lord Lawrence.

The trail which led to Nuremberg had begun when Winston Churchill met US President Franklin

> ## "MEN LIKE THESE MUST NEVER MARCH AGAIN. THE WORLD MUST NEVER FORGET"
>
> US newsreel commentary at the Nuremberg trials

Roosevelt at Arcadia Bay in August 1941 to start defining a set of war aims. Joined by Stalin at Yalta in 1945, they agreed that although the German Kaiser had escaped retribution for the First World War, this time would be different. Later that year, the London Charter prepared the way for the trial of the leading Nazis.

The opening address for the prosecution was made by Justice Robert Jackson of the United States: 'The wrongs which we seek to condemn and punish have been so calculated, so malignant and so devastating that civilisation cannot tolerate their being ignored, because it cannot survive their being repeated.'

This commentary on an American newsreel gives a good impression of Allied attitudes at the time: 'Out of the decisions of the international military tribunal has come a new concept of law, to fix the guilt for international crimes and conspiracies. Four of the world's great powers have agreed that a war of aggression is a crime. A warning to future Hitlers: to erase the crimes against peace, a start has been made. Men like these must never march again. War crimes: guilt has been fixed on those who turned Europe into a wilderness of ruin, homelessness and hunger. Crimes against humanity: guilt has been fixed upon the man who brought death to uncounted millions, to the man behind concentration camp horrors. The world must never forget.'

THE RISE OF ADOLF HITLER

Although Adolf Hitler had not been able to face the humiliation of a trial, he was present in spirit at every moment of it. He was the man who had given the orders. Every indictment was an indictment of him.

From the moment in 1924 when, with the war hero General von Ludendorff, he attempted to seize power in the Munich putsch, Hitler intended to dominate first Germany and then Europe and Russia. Given a light sentence for high treason, he used his industrialists, led by Krupp. In return, he destroyed the Communist Party and doubled the size of the army, ignoring the Versailles Treaty limit of 100,000 men. Industry was turned over to armaments with the slogan: 'Guns before butter'.

Goering's mighty new air force formed part of a war economy. The armed forces expressed their satisfaction. However, in July 1934 Heinrich Himmler's security service, the blackshirted SS, was made independent of the stormtroopers and soon became even more powerful than the army.

In August, Hitler abolished the Presidency and combined it with his own office of Chancellor. He also made himself Commander-in-Chief of the armed forces, which now swore the oath of allegiance to him and not to the state. He could relax, secure in the knowledge that in a plebiscite 90 per cent of the German people were said to have voted to approve his dictatorship. It was now that the planning for aggressive expansion could begin.

HITLER'S WAR EFFORT

At Nuremberg, the niceties of justice were observed. The trial turned the spotlight from one group to another. Those accused on the first indictment, the crimes of war, included the diplomat Joachim von Ribbentrop, Hitler's Foreign Minister; Field Marshal Wilhelm Keitel, Chief Commander of the armed forces – his defence was 'I am just a soldier'; Alfred Jodl, Hitler's military adviser and Operational Chief of Staff; Admiral Erich Raeder, Commander-in-Chief of the German navy, who was instrumental in persuading Hitler to invade Norway; Admiral Karl Doenitz, Commander of the U-boat service whose orders were not to pick up any survivors; Hjalmar Schacht, Minister of Economics, President of the Reichsbank, and Hitler's early financier; Walther Funk, Reich Minister of Economics, who planned the economic and financial side of the war; Alfred Rosenberg, Minister for Occupied Eastern Territories, author of the Nazi race theory; and Albert Speer, Minister for Armaments and War Production who knowingly used slave labour.

Adolf Hitler, flanked by Deputy Führer Rudolf Hess (left) and chief of Nazi youth organisations Baldur von Schirach (right), at a rally of the Hitler Youth Movement in Nuremberg in 1938

colleague, Rudolf Hess, to help him use the time of his imprisonment to write his blueprint for the future. His autobiography, *Mein Kampf* (My Struggle), spelt out his theory that the Aryan race was superior, and revealed his plans for the Jews and other racial groups, and the conquest of Europe.

Within six years, at the 1932 elections, his Party won a majority of votes and 230 seats in Weimar Germany's Parliament, the Reichstag. By the following year he had made an ally of Chancellor Franz von Papen, who ushered him into power. On 30 January 1933, Hitler became Chancellor of Germany.

Now Hitler got vast funds from the bankers, headed by Hjalmar Schacht, and support from the

Prosecutor Robert Jackson said they were 'living symbols of racial hatred, terrorism and violence, and the arrogance and cruelty of power'.

HITLER MARCHES

In 1935, Hitler occupied the Saar. He preached peace, while preparing war. The following year, his troops marched into the Rhineland. 'I have no territorial claims,' he lied. In 1938 he moved into Austria, using von Papen to soften it up, Seyss-Inquart to take over the Chancellorship, Goering to command the troops and von Ribbentrop to deceive the world. Next came the turn of Czechoslovakia: first the Sudentenland on the border, then Prague itself.

Ready or not, Britain and France drew the line at his next victim: Poland. A deal with the Soviet Union allowed Hitler to move into Poland on 1 September 1939. Now he had the war he wanted. 'I shall give a propagandist reason,' he confided. 'The victor is not asked if he told the truth.'

The Polish eagle lasted a mere six weeks under the German blitzkrieg, surrendering on 22 September. Now the Nazi Party turned the assembly lines of their armament industry up to full speed. They initially attempted to negotiate peace with the West, but, when that failed, they prepared for attack.

THE AIM: WORLD DOMINATION

The setting out of the case at Nuremberg under this first indictment took several weeks as a range of witnesses were called to testify about the underlying aim of the Nazis to achieve world domination.

Nuremberg was the scene of many of the Nazi Party's greatest showpieces of choreographed militarism, attended by thousands of banner-waving Nazis eager to listen to the speeches of their leaders. Eight years later in the same town many of those leaders were making their speeches in court

The United Kingdom's Chief Prosecutor, Sir Hartley Shawcross, then outlined every illegal step that Germany had made to take over the territories of other countries, in defiance of all international treaties and covenants.

Among his targets were: Franz von Papen, who was instrumental in helping Hitler to power in 1933, and later became Ambassador to Austria and Turkey; Constantin von Neurath, Minister of Foreign Affairs, known as the Butcher of Czechoslovakia; Fritz Sauckel, chief organiser of the importing of nine million slave labourers; Wilhelm Frick, Hitler's first Minister of the Interior; and Hans Frank, Governor General of Poland, which he called 'a booty land'.

NORWAY, BELGIUM, FRANCE, THEN EAST

In April 1940, the Nazis made their move into Norway. Rosenberg softened it up; Doenitz, Jodl and Keitel were instrumental in the planning.

The following month, paratroops ignored the neutrality of Belgium and the Netherlands. Tanks and infantry joined in a blitzkrieg that was a repetition of the successful campaign against Poland.

Simultaneously came the push through France, with the much trumpeted Maginot Line outflanked by 750,000 troops that the Nazis had been training for years for this moment of fulfilment for *Mein Kampf*. Paris fell on 14 June, France surrendered on the 22nd. Hitler's forces reached the English Channel but he was prevented by the RAF in the Battle of Britain from invading England. Instead he turned his attention to the East.

In April 1941, German armour struck in the Balkans, shattering Yugoslavia, then pushing on into Greece with little opposition.

Now Hitler was ready to complete his master plan. On 22 June he broke the Nazi-Soviet Pact, and within a week his forces were halfway to Moscow. They found a burnt-out landscape, with the Soviet people obeying Stalin's ordered policy of a scorched earth retreat.

Following the troops came the extermination squads: Jews were often shot on the spot by Himmler's men. Seven million foreign workers were soon imported as slaves and their homes looted under orders from Hitler.

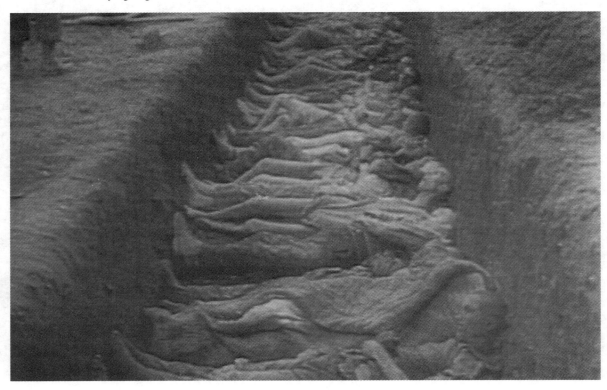

Crimes against humanity: 11 million innocent people were murdered in the Nazi concentration camps created by Hitler as the Final Solution to the 'Jewish problem'

THE MEN RESPONSIBLE

Among the men who conveyed Hitler's orders and supervised the stripping of Russia was Hermann Goering. He and his fellow defendants listened impassively as the prosecution case developed.

Then it was the turn of the French Prosecutor, François de Menthon. He dealt with crimes of war and against mankind, saying that the Nazi doctrine raised inhumanity to the level of a principle, and gave a series of examples including: the systematic murder of Russian prisoners of war; the methodical killing of hostages; the destruction of the Czech village of Lidice and the execution of all its men and boys, with the deportation of all its women and children. There was forced labour and economic looting, including the use of millions of slaves brought from all the occupied territories. There was also the building of

the Warsaw Ghetto, into which thousands of Jews were herded, and its ultimate destruction.

These were all premeditated acts of degradation. They were not, said de Menthon, the result of warlike anger or an avenging resentment but conscious applications of a pre-existing, calculated doctrine.

Then came the turn of the Soviet Prosecutor, General Roman Rudenko, representative of the country which had suffered most from Nazi brutality. The Russians had been among the most determined that a full and public trial of the Nazi leaders must be held.

He demanded the death sentence for all the accused. He listed their crimes including those of: Julius Streicher, editor of the Jew-baiting *Der Sturmer*, who called himself Jew Hater Number One; Ernst Kaltenbrunner, head of the security police, who was responsible for the gas chambers and the camps;

Defendants, sitting in the dock at the Nuremberg trials, listening as sentences are meted out on 10 October 1946. The trials lasted almost a year and all but three were found guilty

Artur Seyss-Inquart, Minister of Security, infamous as the Butcher of the Netherlands; Hans Fritzsche, Political Supervisor of Broadcasting, expert in twisting the truth; and Baldur von Schirach, chief of Nazi youth organisations who wanted to see 'the glint of the wild beast in their eyes'.

This section of the prosecution detailed the crimes against the Jews. These began from the moment the Nazi Party reached power. Anyone, Jew or Gentile, who uttered a word of protest was thrown into one of the concentration camps, carefully hidden from the rest of the world.

KRISTALLNACHT

On 9 November 1938 came Kristallnacht (the 'Night of Glass', so-called because so much glass was broken), when 7,000 Jewish shops were smashed and looted, synagogues burnt to the ground, and hundreds of Jews were killed. Goering commented: 'They should have killed more Jews and broken less glass.'

With the war came the ghettos, where Jews were herded. Each day, lorryloads of them were rounded up. They were told they were being taken to the country. But Himmler, as commissar for the strengthening of the German race, had other plans: he deported, then exterminated, millions of them.

Reinhard Heydrich was his chief executioner. In January 1942, Heydrich chaired a conference at Wannsee, near Berlin. There was planned the Final Solution of the Jewish problem: total elimination. Preparations were made to purge Europe's 14 million Jews and other so-called undesirables. Gas chambers were selected as the most economic method.

The chosen were sent in cattle trucks without food or water. Thousands died on the way. At the entrance to the camps, music greeted them, to lull them and to cover the screams of those who had guessed the truth. Those who looked unfit to work – the old, the infirm, mothers and children – were marched to the chambers straight away. After death,

> **"THEY SHOULD HAVE KILLED MORE JEWS AND BROKEN LESS GLASS"**
>
> Hermann Goering's judgement of Kristallnacht

their bodies were burnt in the cremation ovens. Just the children killed totalled over one-and-a-half million. To save time, many of the smaller children were thrown into the ovens alive. At Nuremberg, Soviet Deputy Prosecutor Smirnov produced some soap made out of the dead bodies, and tanned human skin for gloves and briefcases.

THE DEFENCE

Now it was the turn of the defence. Each prisoner had the lawyer of his choice, and he could speak himself for as long as he wished. They mostly testified that they were only carrying out orders. Asked if there was anyone who said 'No', Goering had laughed and replied: 'Not above ground!'

During his testimony, Goering claimed that the ends of Germany's resurgence justified any means, and he claimed that while some of his actions were ruthless, they were all necessary.

The reaction of the prisoners to the films shown in court was at first delight in seeing themselves, and then gloom at the record of their atrocities. At the proof of what was found at the liberation of the camps, Hess appeared to be the most emotionally affected; von Ribbentrop, sitting next to him, steadied him with a comforting hand.

After final pleas came the reckoning. The SS security service, the Gestapo and the Leadership Corps of the Nazi Party were all declared criminal organisations; the Cabinet, the General Staff and the High Command of the armed forces were acquitted. Then the individual verdicts were read out.

THE RECKONING

Herman Goering was found guilty on all counts, but he cheated his sentence of death by swallowing a smuggled poison capsule just hours before execution. Thus died Hitler's most able and ruthless lieutenant who had created the Luftwaffe, the Gestapo and the concentration camps, and mobilised Germany.

Those who did not escape hanging were Julius Streicher, Jew baiter-in-chief, whose last words were: 'Heil Hitler!'; Fritz Sauckel, slave master, who declaimed: 'God make Germany great again!'; Field Marshal Wilhelm Keitel, Hitler's weak and willing tool who delivered the armed forces to the Nazis, who cried: 'Deutschland Uber Alles!'; Wilhelm Frick, who helped the Nazi Party seize power and ran the police to keep it there; Alfred Jodl, who led the Wehrmacht into betraying its code of honour; Hans Frank, cursed by the memory of the three million Polish Jews he sent to their deaths; Artur Seyss-Inquart, who gave Austria to the Nazis and then pillaged the Netherlands; Ernst Kaltenbrunner, who took over supervision of the Final Solution when Heydrich was murdered; Alfred Rosenberg, who provided justifications for the policy of race hatred; and Joachim von Ribbentrop, who fooled so many for so long.

Life imprisonment was ordered for Walter Funk, but he was released in 1957. Life meant life for Rudolf Hess, who died in Spandau Prison at the age of 93, after serving 40 years there. There was a life sentence too for Erich Raeder. Released in 1955, he died in 1960. Albert Speer and Baldur von Schirach received 20-year sentences; Constantin von Neurath 15 years; and Karl Doenitz ten years.

Three were acquitted: Hans Fritzsche, a propagandist but not a participant; Dr Hjalmar Schacht, a supporter but not a participant; and Franz von Papen.

Nazism had been brought to justice, but there was no official judgement on Adolf Hitler. However, there can be little doubt what it would have been had he lived to stand trial: guilty of the slaughter of 50 million people who died in the war he started, and particularly of the 11 million murdered in the camps his ideology created.

Top Nazi leaders during a lull in proceedings at the Nuremberg trials in January 1946. Herman Goering (left) was sentenced to death but committed suicide; Karl Doenitz (centre) who signed Germany's surrender was given ten years; Rudolf Hess (right) was sentenced to life and died after 40 years imprisonment

THE GANGSTERS OF 1930s AMERICA WERE MADE INTO
MYTHICAL FIGURES BY THE CINEMA. EQUALLY MYTHICAL
WAS THE MILITARY PRISON ADOPTED TO KEEP THEM IN
CAPTIVITY: THE ISLAND STRONGHOLD OF ALCATRAZ. OVER
THE 30 YEARS OF ITS USE MANY OF THE MOST HARDENED
KILLERS AND ROBBERS TRIED TO ESCAPE FROM ALCATRAZ,
BUT IT IS PROBABLE THAT NONE SUCCEEDED. THE MOST
FAMOUS AND BLOODIEST ATTEMPT OCCURRED IN 1946,
WHEN PRISONERS OVERCAME GUARDS AND SECURED ARMS,
ONLY TO FIND THEY HAD THE US MARINES TO BEAT.

The Escapes from Alcatraz

n 1946, in the aftermath of the Second World
War, Nazi war criminals were brought to judgement at Nuremberg, while holocaust survivors
demanded their own state from the British in
Palestine. In India Mahatma Gandhi was also
demanding independence from the British. The
liner *Queen Elizabeth* resumed trips to New York,
and Winston Churchill warned that an 'Iron Curtain'
had descended across Europe.

In San Francisco, on 2 May, people lined the
shores as gunfire was heard across the bay. It came
from the notorious island prison of Alcatraz. The
warden had sent a telegram to all media. It read:
'Serious trouble. Convict has machine gun in cell
house. Have issued riot call and placed armed guards
at strategic locations.'

The report made sensational headlines. The
warden went on to advise that: 'Many of our officers
are imprisoned in the cell house.'

As the day went on, local radio station KGOP
added to the hysteria, reporting that: 'Rampaging
convicts have stormed and captured the prison arsenal. Prison officers have been slaughtered. Armed
prisoners are over-running the island. Women and

children, families of prison employees are in desperate peril. The warden has sent out a call for help to all military and police agencies. A desperate emergency confronts everyone in the San Francisco Bay area.'

As it turned out, this was an exaggeration. But before the emergency was over, 80 marines in full combat order had landed on the island of Alcatraz, bombs and gas were exploded over the prison, two guards and three prisoners had been killed, and fifteen men were injured.

It was the most dangerous attempted escape in the chequered history of the supposedly escape-proof prison, and one which damaged both its buildings and its reputation.

A SECURE FEDERAL PRISON

Alcatraz means Island of the Pelicans, a name given by Spanish explorers in 1775 when the big-beaked birds covered the island. It became a military fort and then a jail for Confederate prisoners during the Civil War. The island and its garrison were heavily armed. The warders brought their families to live with them. Later, the island housed the most troublesome Indian chiefs and Spanish troops captured in the Philippines. During the First World War, deserters and German spies were shut up there. But during the 1920s its buildings fell gradually into ruins.

Then, in 1933, it was decided that a secure federal prison was needed. Attorney General Homer S. Cummings announced a new role for Alcatraz. It was needed as part of a new drive against gangsterism: 'Let the underworld take heed of these convictions, as proof of the grim facts that a criminal career leads inevitably to prison.' The need for an escape-proof prison was shown by newspaper headline after headline. The escape of such infamous criminals as John Dillinger, the notorious bank robber, were making a mockery of existing jails.

The early 1930s were a lawless time in America. Cities were ruled by gangster bosses, with private armies, ruthless and ready to kill. In rural areas many out-of-work farm boys turned to crime. Some robbed banks. Many law-abiding citizens had been so hurt

by the Depression that they secretly cheered on the bandits tormenting the businessmen who had foreclosed on them.

The newspapers and radio bulletins were full of crime. Hardly a day went by without some violent killing. While those who crossed them died, the most notorious gang leaders seemed to have a charmed life, openly running the major cities without retribution from the lawmen, who were all too often prepared to look the other way in return for bribes and favours. And when the forces of law and order did close in, the crooks were often able to shoot their way out. Even when they were jailed, too many of them escaped with the ease of Houdinis.

THE LEGACY OF PROHIBITION

The structure of the underworld was the result of supplying liquor during the 14 years of Prohibition,

The exercise yard of Alcatraz, surrounded by barbed wire and watchtowers manned by armed guards. It was estimated that it cost twice as much to maintain a convict here than at any other federal prison

from early 1920 to late 1933. However, despite the ban on alcohol, America drank at least a hundred million gallons of bootleg booze every year. A lot of it came in by sea. The gang wars between rival suppliers were vicious and bloody. In Chicago alone, at least a thousand men died.

While the US coastguards stopped thousands of boats bringing in bootleg liquor, many hundreds of thousands of journeys were made by ships and boats bringing supplies from Canada, the Caribbean and elsewhere. When the Prohibition laws were finally repealed, bootlegging did not cease. Avoiding alcohol taxes was, and still is, a lucrative way of making money. The authorities did what they could to stop the trade by destroying the barrels and bottles which they found. But, as Prohibition ended, the men at the top had already begun moving into an even more lucrative area of smuggling – drugs. Heroin alone made them an annual profit of $2½ billion.

The authorities took advantage of the conflicts between rival gangs. If they couldn't hijack their competitors' supplies, gangsters would frequently betray their whereabouts to the authorities.

The public's attitude was ambivalent. They liked booze, and they rather admired the outlaws. So when John Dillinger was shot in a police ambush when

Unlike at many other prisons, no inmate at Alcatraz was allowed any special privileges or luxuries. The regime was strict and prisoners were not even allowed to speak to each other inside the cell house

coming out of the movies, the crowds that came to stare were sorry to see the end of such a colourful character, criminal or not.

Similarly, they were not nearly as upset as the authorities would have liked by the success of Al Capone – his riches, his women and his apparent omnipotence. All this adulation of bootleggers and criminals deeply upset J. Edgar Hoover, then head of the FBI. In 1933, he declared war on men he called 'Public Enemies'.

THE NEW ROLE OF ALCATRAZ

As part of this 'war', Hoover wanted the publicity coup of setting up a really tough prison for the country's worst criminals. When the former military prison on Alcatraz was suggested he put all his support behind turning it into the world's harshest prison. The defences of the island were modernised to prepare for the arrival of America's most dangerous criminals. On 14 August 1934, the first 53 hard cases were sent from Atlanta Penitentiary in what was called the Atlanta Boys Convoy. They were herded on to a special train and chained to their seats. Its windows had steel bars and close-mesh wire. The carriages were rolled on to a special boat to take them across the bay.

Among its infamous passengers was Al Capone. Prison had so far meant little hardship for Capone. He had been able to use his power to buy all sorts of luxury and privilege. But the journey to Alcatraz was a journey to another world. For there were to be no special favours for anyone. On Alcatraz the crime boss became anonymous prisoner number 85.

He was given the same sort of spartan cell as everyone else. He asked for special visiting rights but was turned down. He was put to work cleaning up the bath house and became known as 'the wop with the mop'. He was disliked by the other prisoners and in June 1935 bank robber Jim Lucas crept up behind him and stabbed him with scissors. He spent a week in the hospital. Capone became an excellent cobbler, but he was released after five years on Alcatraz to die at home from syphilis.

The importance which Hoover and the FBI attached to building up Alcatraz's reputation as the last home of America's worst criminals was shown by the excitement and publicity generated by Machine Gun Kelly's transfer to the island.

In reality, Kelly never fired any kind of gun in anger in his life, and was known to be, as one reporter put it, 'a good-natured slob, a bootlegger who spilled more than he delivered'. Arrested for a bungled kidnapping, Kelly's misfortune was to be saddled with his flamboyant nickname, which made him a natural guest of the Rock. Unco-operatively, he behaved so well there that he was sent back to a mainland prison where he died of a heart attack.

Other notorious prisoners on Alcatraz included Alvin 'Creepy' Karpis. He became the longest-serving prisoner on the Rock, serving almost 30 years there. He had been part of the Barker Gang, and was joined by the deadliest of Ma Barker's bank-robbing sons, Arthur, better known as Doc, who enjoyed killing, with or without provocation.

Robert Stroud, misnamed the 'Birdman of Alcatraz', had three convictions for murder. In Leavenworth, he had written books on bird diseases. Altogether, he spent 56 years behind bars, nearly all in solitary confinement. But on Alcatraz he wasn't allowed by Warden James Johnston to keep birds, or to continue his studies.

EVERYTHING TOUGH BUT THE FOOD

Johnston, the first warden of Alcatraz from 1934 to 1948, initiated a merciless regime. Prisoners were not allowed to speak to each other in the cell house or mess hall. A single whisper would bring a guard's gas stick down on a prisoner. He could then be taken to the dungeon 'holes', to eat just four slices of bread a day and sleep on the concrete floor.

The cells themselves were only about 6ft by 9ft and prisoners spent 14 hours a day locked in them. Knives were banned from the mess hall in case convicts stole and sharpened them.

The food, however, was surprisingly good, but every scrap had to be eaten. 'Saltwater' Johnston, as

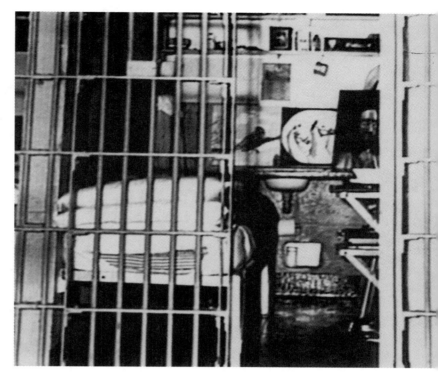

the convicts called the warden, banned newspapers and radios. In the library, only uplifting books were allowed. Other punishments which the guards could use included hosing with icy water and loss of the coveted 'good time', by which a third of a sentence could be lopped off for good behaviour.

Prisoners were put to work doing laundry for nearby navy and army bases. There was also a shoe repair shop, and furniture, clothing and brush factories. Prisoners could only mix in the exercise yard for less than an hour a day. They could have only one visitor for two hours per month, and they were kept separated by shatterproof glass. Conversation was by telephone and was heavily censored.

The towers around the prison were permanently manned by guards with two guns: a carbine for close shots, and a high-powered rifle in case a convict did manage to launch himself on some crude craft into the surrounding water.

THE PUSH-UP PRISON CURRENCY

There was one warder for every three inmates, costing the taxpayer twice as much to keep a convict on Alcatraz as at any other federal prison. But, strangely

Each inmate's cell at Alcatraz was only about 6ft by 9ft and prisoners had to spend on average around 14 hours a day locked in them

enough, among the supplies ferried regularly to the Rock were three packs of cigarettes a week for every inmate. This was because Warden Johnston decided to prevent tobacco, the usual prison currency, from becoming the money substitute there. Instead, the men gambled with push-ups, the standard keep-fit exercise. In other words, prisoners paid off their debts to each other by doing an agreed number of push-ups.

ESCAPE ATTEMPTS

The harsh regime encouraged many prisoners to take on the almost impossible odds and attempt to escape. The first man to try was Joe Bowers, who climbed a wire fence on 27 April 1936. But he was picked off by a sharpshooting guard. His head shattered, he tumbled down into the sea.

The next attempt came one foggy night in December 1937. Theodore 'Sunny Boy' Cole and Ralph Roe had the job of disposing of excess rubber from the mat factory. They threw it all in the same spot under the cliffs, so that they could jump safely on to it and then use the rubber to buoy a raft made

of petrol cans to get across the dangerous currents which swept round the island.

Police on the mainland were issued with photographs of the pair, but nobody ever saw either Ralph Roe or Ted Cole again. They were written off as drowning in the turbulent, freezing, current-twisted waters of the bay. But every prisoner on the Rock hoped that they had managed to escape, and Alvin Karpis sent the warden a mocking Christmas card every year signed 'Ted and Ralph'. The next attempt was in May 1938, by kidnapper Tom Limerick and Jim Lucas, the man who had stabbed Al Capone. They murdered a guard with a hammer, but found themselves locked out on the roof of the prison. Limerick, shot in the eye, fell to his death. Lucas received an extra sentence of life.

'Doc' Barker was the next one to try. In January 1939, he and four others managed to saw their way out of their cells. Barker ran to the water's edge, but there he was shot dead.

In April 1943, Floyd Hamilton, brother of Raymond Hamilton, Bonnie and Clyde's associate,

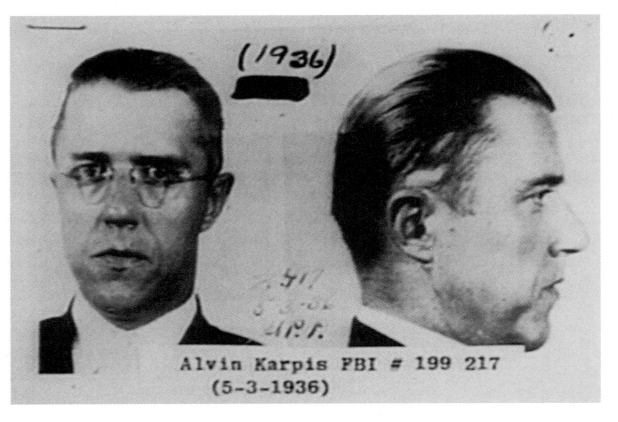

Alvin 'Creepy' Karpis, a member of the Barker Gang, was the longest-serving prisoner on Alcatraz, spending 30 years there. He taunted the warden of the prison by sending a Christmas card every year signed with the names of two inmates who had tried to escape and were never found

Alvin Karpis PBI # 199 217
(5-3-1936)

The Battle of the Rock: for 41 hours prison guards and marines maintained constant fire on the cell block held by revolting prisoners. Many fires broke out and smoke can be seen rising in the prison grounds in this news picture taken during the siege

led three other prisoners and managed to overpower a guard. But none got far from the shore.

BATTLE OF THE ROCK

Then, in 1946, came the celebrated Battle of the Rock. The commentary on one newsreel contained this description: 'As Alcatraz guards are overcome by such vicious criminals as Bernard Paul Coy, with a lengthy prison record, Joseph Paul Cretcher, facing a life term as a cold-blooded killer, and Marvin Franklin Hubbard, kidnapper. Coy and his crew of desperados fought furiously with guards and marines. Caught in their attempted escape by the heroism of a guard who refused to surrender the main key, the barricaded convicts carried out a pitched battle which raged for two days and nights. Grenades found their mark, and fires flared in the prison grounds. With the three ring leaders dead in their fox hole, Federal Prison Director Bennett and Warden Johnston count the cost. In addition to the dead convicts, two prison guards lost their lives. Fifteen wounded men completed the casualty list, Assistant Warden Edward Miller

being one. Three other convicts may pay the death penalty for their part in the grim Battle of the Rock.'

THE REAL STORY

An official inquiry was set up to establish what had really happened. The Battle of Alcatraz began at 1.45pm on 2 May when a prisoner who had been working in the kitchen block was returning to the main cell block. Only one guard, William Miller, was on the floor of the cell block, and as he went to let in Marvin Hubbard, a notorious gunman, he was slugged from behind by Bernard Coy, who was being moved from his cell.

Miller was beaten up and placed in a cell, while the two prisoners then released several accomplices, including Clarence Carnes, who had a record of murder, kidnapping, assault and escapes, and Joseph Cretzer, who was notorious as a ruthless and cold-blooded killer.

Coy then climbed up the bars to the gun gallery which dominated the cell block. There was only one guard on duty there and Coy was able to overpower him. He took the guard's revolver and Springfield rifle and used these to force the unarmed officer who was on duty in cell block D to let him in. Once inside, he released twelve men who had been in solitary confinement.

The prisoners' plan had been to get across the recreation yard, go down the steps to the landing area, and then seize the prison launch and speed across the bay to waiting cars. But Miller had hidden the vital key which would have let them into the yard, and they jammed the lock when attempting to open it with other keys they had found.

Meanwhile, reserve officers had been alerted when Miller failed to answer a routine call. They left the administration block but were intercepted by armed prisoners, and nine were locked in cell 403.

The alarm was now raised with the prisoners isolated in the cell block and the guards imprisoned in a cell. Joseph Cretzer and another freed prisoner, Sam Shockley, started beating up the captured guards, and then Cretzer shot at them. He thought he had killed them all, but seven of them survived, and one was able to scribble the names of the ring leaders on the wall of the cell.

Coy was furious when he thought that Cretzer had destroyed their trump card – hostages. A triangular shoot-out followed as Coy and Hubbard on one hand and Cretzer on the other stalked each other, and military reinforcements surrounded the cell block as night fell.

By the next morning, crowds filled every vantage point. All available prison officers were on duty backed up with 80 marines, and the remaining prisoners were taken from their cells and put in the recreation yard. There they were guarded by the marines, while officers now began their assault on the cell block. Constant fire was maintained on it.

> **"RAMPAGING CONVICTS HAVE CAPTURED THE PRISON ARSENAL. PRISON OFFICERS HAVE BEEN SLAUGHTERED. A DESPERATE EMERGENCY CONFRONTS EVERYONE IN THE SAN FRANCISCO BAY AREA"**
>
> KGOP radio transmission on 2 May 1946

Officers dug holes in the roof through which grenades were dropped. Others broke windows to throw in smoke bombs. A pall of smoke rose over the prison as the marines fired bazookas and mortars. At last, 41 hours after the revolt began, the cell block was finally stormed and the surviving guards released.

Cretzer, Coy and Hubbard were found dead. The three remaining killers were brought to trial. Thompson and Shockley were executed and 19-year-old Carnes got an additional life sentence.

A SUCCESSFUL ESCAPE?

Perhaps the only escape attempt to succeed came in June 1962. Three bank robbers gouged out their cell ventilators to make holes large enough to climb through. The authorities said they used spoons stolen from the mess hall as tools.

Frank Morris and the brothers John and Clarence Anglin had prepared thoroughly. Morris was the mastermind, and obtained plaster of Paris, a makeup kit and hair from the barber shop to make dummies which they placed in their beds to fool the guards making their night-time rounds. Painted cardboard hid a hole through which they had all squeezed.

It wasn't until morning that their ruse was discovered. By then, they had clambered up drainpipes and slipped through a skylight on to the roof. From there, they climbed down an unguarded wall and ran to the sea. To get across the bay they had planned to inflate rubber raincoats as rafts.

All searches failed, and the authorities are said to have hushed up finding some of the prisoners' effects on Angel Island, their planned staging post in their flight across the bay.

The last and physically most impressive escape came on 16 December 1962. Bank robbers John Paul

Scott and Darl Lee Parker slipped through the bars of a kitchen window which they had weakened with string and scouring powder. Parker only got as far as a small group of rocks about a hundred yards away, but Scott reached the shore before collapsing with exhaustion and being recaptured.

ALCATRAZ CLOSED

It was ironic that this near success came only months before officials made an historic announcement: Alcatraz was to be closed. Journalists arrived to hear Warden Owen Blackwell announce that its crumbling structure had been weakened by the explosions it had endured during the siege. It would have needed at least $5 million to repair. So, on 15 May 1963, the last 27 prisoners left the island to the feathered successors of the original pelicans and the gaze of tourists.

The island became an essential part of every VIP's tour of San Francisco. Nikita Krushchev arrived a few months after it closed. He was followed by Charles de Gaulle. Ordinary tourists could catch a boat to the island from pier 43. In 1969 eight hundred native Americans illegally occupied the island for 18 months. The group, which said it was protesting against white oppression, claimed that a treaty in 1868 allowed Indians to take possession of all unoccupied federal land. They were finally evicted by an armed government force without serious bloodshed.

TOURIST TRAP

Today, the dreaded prison island of Alcatraz is just one more stop on the San Francisco tourist beat.

One of the most popular sights is the dummy head which sent an unsuspecting guard into hysterics because he thought Frank Morris had been decapitated. The hole which Morris hollowed out and squeezed through has been left as it was. Cell 42, used by Robert Stroud, the so-called Birdman of Alcatraz, is another show piece. Filmgoers think of Robert Stroud as he was portrayed by Burt Lancaster, but in reality Stroud was never able to keep any birds on the island.

Liquor is now readily available on Alcatraz, if you put on a party, and one wonders what the ghosts of the men who lived on bread and water would make of some of the festivities which take place today. For it is hard to look across San Francisco Bay without suppressing a small shiver for the lost souls who lived and died within the grim walls of the island of Alcatraz.

Often referred to as Devil's Island, Alcatraz was closed in 1963 due to its structure having been weakened during the siege of 1946. It is now open to tourists and can even be hired for parties where alcohol, ironically, is readily available

Mahatma Gandhi was the epitome of non-violence. He made fasting a political weapon. Gandhi was so loved by India's teeming millions that a threat to fast to death could halt riots and civil wars. He made the independence of India his aim and used every possible opportunity to draw attention to the injustices faced by the Indian peoples living under foreign domination. Despite being regularly imprisoned by the British rulers, his frail body in the end proved far stronger than the massed forces and self-interests of the Raj. But in the struggle between Hindu and Moslem he finally went too far in granting justice to the other side.

On 15 August 1947, 400 million people in the new states of India and Pakistan became independent. But while the new Governor General, Earl Mountbatten, and the new Prime Minister, Pandit Nehru, saluted the cheering crowds, the man who had done more than anyone else to make this come about was missing. Mahatma Gandhi was attempting to calm the rioting that had broken out between the 70 million Moslems of Pakistan and the 300 million Hindus of India.

Five months later, on his way to prayer, he was shot by a Hindu fanatic, enraged by his tolerance towards Moslems.

The funeral of the man called the Mahatma, which means 'Great Soul', or Bapu, meaning 'Father', took place two days later in New Delhi. On the banks of the Jumna River his body was placed on a pyre and his son set fire to it. It burned for 14 hours. A bullet was found in the ashes, and the train which carried them to Bombay, where they were immersed in the sea, had only third-class carriages. Bapu had insisted on always travelling in the lowest class for the previous 50 years.

Gandhi
The Assassination

At Delhi's Red Fort, Nathuram Godse and Narayan Apte went on trial. Godse, who fired three shots, claimed that he had no hatred of Gandhi, but 'Ghandiji' had betrayed his religion and culture by supporting Moslems at the expense of Hindus.

THE MAKING OF GANDHI

The India in which Mohandras Karamchand Gandhi was born into the merchant class in 1869 was as divided into castes as the soil is layered. In the top stratum were the Maharajahs and the princes, who, despite their wealth and power, still had to bow to the might of the white Raj. And at the pinnacle of that pyramid sat Queen Victoria, the monarch on whose empire the sun never set.

On state occasions in London, the Indian cavalry was a reminder of the exotic sub-continent across the world, helping to protect their ultimate ruler but at the same time acknowledging their fealty to the throne and dependence on Mother England.

However, an occasional shadow passed over that comfortably established state of affairs. At a levee in 1912 celebrating the consecration of Delhi as the new capital of India, a bomb was thrown at the Governor General, Lord Harding. It wounded him and killed an aide. It seemed that there were extremists who did not want to be part of the British empire and who did not join in giving it three cheers.

When the 19-year-old Gandhi came to London to study law in 1888, he was keen to become as English as possible. He had a suit made in Bond Street and took lessons in ballroom dancing. However, he soon fell among radicals, attracted to them because they shared his rejection of eating flesh. He became a member of the council of the Vegetarian Society and met politicians.

When he had finished his studies, he went to South Africa where he had been offered a legal post among the Indians there. He stayed for 21 years, working for their equality. In the war against the Boers he supported the British. He felt that Indians who claimed citizenship of a country were duty bound to defend it. So he raised an ambulance corps and was decorated for it.

Gandhi arriving in England for a Round Table Conference in London in 1931 as leader of the Indian Congress Party. Whilst the conference did not herald any great progress, Gandhi staunchly maintained his own agenda: complete independence for a united India

Then he forced General Smuts to give Indians many rights they had previously been denied. When Gandhi eventually returned to India in 1915, Smuts wrote: 'The saint has left our shores, I hope forever.'

Gandhi found the British Raj in India as repressive as the South Africans, and he became convinced that it was imperative for India to win its independence. Nevertheless, when the Germans invaded Belgium bringing Britain into the First World War, Gandhi sided with his country's masters and rallied Indians to assist the British war effort, although it meant accepting the status quo for the time being. He even recruited soldiers for the British Indian army. But at the same time, he announced his total opposition to British rule of India.

Gandhi had married his wife, Kasturbai, when they were both just 13 years old, as was the custom. Now, with her support, he began the fasts which were to make him world famous.

GANDHI AND THE VICEROY

On 2 April 1921 Lord Reading arrived in India as Viceroy. He had absolute power over the police and the army; Gandhi had become equally undisputed ruler of the Congress Party which demanded independence. While Reading was determined to keep the pleasures and the privileges of the Raj intact, he proposed a meeting between them. Some of the Mahatma's followers objected. Gandhi's answer was: 'We may attack measures and systems, but we must not attack men. Imperfect ourselves, we must be tender towards others.'

The two men had 13 hours of conversations in which Gandhi baffled Reading by his insistence that non-violence and love would succeed in winning India its independence. The Mahatma said that his major task was to purify India: Britain's expulsion would be a by-product.

> "WE MAY ATTACK MEASURES AND SYSTEMS, BUT WE MUST NOT ATTACK MEN. IMPERFECT OURSELVES, WE MUST BE TENDER TOWARDS OTHERS"
>
> Gandhi

Reading regarded an outbreak of trouble on the northwest frontier as Gandhi's work. Two platoons of a native regiment of the Indian army had refused to go to Peshawar to shoot at their unarmed brethren, and the spectre of another mutiny, a repetition of the violent and bloody uprising of 1857, haunted Reading. He considered arresting the Mahatma. A visit by the Prince of Wales in November 1921 made up his mind, as Gandhi used the opportunity to draw attention to his campaign against one of the economic injustices of the Raj: the import of foreign cloth. While crowds were cheering the Prince in Bombay, Gandhi set off a bonfire of imported cloth and clothes. The police opened fire, and there were dead and wounded on both sides.

THE FIRST ARREST

On 10 March 1922 Gandhi was arrested for sedition. He pleaded guilty to the charge and said he would submit cheerfully to the highest penalty. He was sentenced to six years but, after his wife led a vigil when he had appendicitis, he was released in less than two.

Gandhi was arrested again in 1930 when he deliberately broke the salt laws. These made it a crime to possess salt not bought from the government. Gandhi called it a nefarious monopoly, salt being as essential as water to man and beast. He led hundreds of followers on a 200-mile march to the sea. It took them 24 days. On 6 April, he picked up some salt left by the waves: it was later sold to the highest bidder for 1,600 rupees. Within days, hundreds of thousands of Indians were making their own salt.

This resulted in more than 60,000 people being imprisoned, and there were fatal riots. Over 2,000 of Gandhi's followers, protesting at a salt works, allowed themselves to be clubbed down without protest in a show of non-violence. When his followers continued defying the authorities by making their own salt, Gandhi was arrested again, on 5 May. Nine months later, when he was needed at a Round Table Conference in London, he was released. He arrived in England, triumphant.

Questioned about his meagre dress, he replied: 'You wear plus-fours, I wear minus-fours.' When he had tea with the King and Queen, he wore his usual loincloth. Afterwards he said: 'The King had enough on for both of us.'

He chose to stay in an East End settlement house because, he said, he preferred living among his own kind: 'It has been a matter of the greatest pleasure to me to be in the midst of the poor people of the East End of London. Whatever the result of the mission that brought me to London, I know that I shall carry with me the pleasantest memories of my stay in the midst of the poor people of East London.'

But the conference itself was a deep disappointment to him, as it merely intensified the divisions between the various Indian minorities. He confirmed that: 'It is complete independence that we want.'

He went home via France and Italy, where he continued to spread his message of non-violence. He refused hospitality from Mussolini and spent only ten minutes with him. However, he was tactful about the young fascisti who paraded for him with their guns: 'It has given me very great pleasure to see all these young children so hail and hearty.'

Back in India he found that the Viceroy, Lord Willingdon, had unleashed the sternest repression in the history of the struggle for independence. Arrested again, he began another fast, this time for basic rights for the Untouchables, members of the lowest Hindu caste, whom he called 'the children of God'. Five days into his fast unto death, the laws against the Untouchables were modified.

Although he was still held in prison, he slowly regained his health. But he had powerful enemies, at home and abroad. Winston Churchill said he was revolted by 'the spectacle of this seditious fakir striding half naked up the steps of the Viceroy's palace, to negotiate on equal terms with the representative of the King Emperor'.

PANDIT NEHRU

In 1934, released from prison but upset by what he regarded as opportunism by his followers, Gandhi retired from public life. He lived in an ashram, emphasising spiritual rewards and reducing material wants to a minimum. He even weaved his own loincloth. He said that India must be rebuilt from below.

To Pandit Nehru, who had been his lieutenant for 16 years, fell the task of turning his master's idealism into practical politics. Western-educated, with grace and charm, he could be obstinate and bitter. It was his destiny to bring independence despite Gandhi's opposition to his methods.

A new Viceroy, Lord Linlithgow, arrived in 1936. Behind the pomp of the old British Raj, Nehru was working for a new order to be established. The first goal was self-governing Dominion status.

Then came the Second World War, which suddenly speeded up the process. While Gandhi threw his weight for Britain and against Hitler, the fall of

Pandit Nehru addressing a crowd at Simla where the British Viceroy had called a conference to discuss independence in 1945. Nehru's task was to turn Gandhi's idealism into practical politics and he eventually agreed to a separate India and Pakistan

France encouraged those who saw India's future in a British defeat. But as the Battle of Britain raged, Gandhi told them: 'We do not seek independence out of Britain's ruin.'

Now Britain promised Dominion status, but not until after the war. With Pearl Harbor everything changed again. Suddenly the war was on India's own doorstep. While the Congress Party came out strongly against the Axis, one of Gandhi's former lieutenants, Subhas Chandra Bose, fled the country and, when Singapore fell, raised an Indian national army from captured Indian troops, to fight for Japan. The sight of Asians triumphant over Westerners also encouraged demands for independence.

DEATH FROM FAMINE

Twelve million people migrated between the newly independent India and Pakistan as Hindu, Moslem and Sikh fled for the safety of their respective nations. In less than a year, half-a-million people died as violence erupted amongst the various religious factions

India now became a base for hostilities as well as a vital supply link. Southeast Asia Command was established in Delhi, and it did not have enough trains to keep its forces in Burma fully supplied. So during 1942 famine came to Bengal. The province had depended on Burma for its rice, and the army lacked rolling stock for replacement food. As many as three million people and countless animals may have starved to death.

With pressure for independence increasing, Sir Stafford Cripps was sent to India with new proposals.

He offered a constituent assembly and the ultimate right to leave the Commonwealth.

But Gandhi wanted immediate Dominion status and Cripps had to leave empty-handed. He blamed Gandhi for the failure of his mission. Cripps knew that most Congress Party leaders wanted to accept the offer, if only to pre-empt the fast-rising Moslem League: 'We want to see India a free self-governing nation, free from the Japanese, free from all domination, side by side with us as a great power exercising her influence in the formation of that peace in which we hope will lay the foundations of happiness, the world's civilisation. That was the object of our scheme, that is still our object.'

UNREST AND CIVIL DISOBEDIENCE

Despite unrest in many cities, which led to the army being deployed, the only real enemy on Indian soil were the Hurs of Sind, north of Hyderabad. These bandits were praised by German and Japanese propaganda for their sabotage activities, and the Indian army used them to practise dropping paratroops on a hostile force in the jungle.

Gandhi was imprisoned again on 9 August 1942. With the failure of the Cripps mission, he had adopted a new, uncompromising slogan addressed to the British: Quit India!

His followers were due to start a mass civil disobedience campaign when the police in Bombay swooped and arrested him and 50 other Congress leaders. The whole working committee was interned in Poona. Widespread protests resulted in £1 million worth of damage. At least a thousand protesters and police were killed in the violence and 250 railway stations were destroyed, among damage to government property. Martial law again brought troops on to the streets.

In the midst of all this internal fighting, a new Viceroy arrived in India in October 1943. He was Field Marshal Lord Wavell, who had distinguished himself in the North African campaign but had done less well in southeast Asia. Now demonstrably a civilian, his task was to save India from itself.

The preliminary hearing of nine men connected with the assassination of Gandhi was held at Red Fort in Delhi. Sitting in the front row of the dock are Nathuram Godse (left) who was convicted as the actual killer and Narayan Apte (centre) who was also sentenced to death as the leader of the plot

He began by sending troops to feed the starving millions in Bengal. He went to Calcutta himself and announced that food control was his first concern. The famine was now compounded by a widespread drought. Wavell imposed rationing in all the big cities. He put his troops to distributing food and ensuring that it was fairly shared. Never had the British army been so popular in India.

NEGOTIATIONS WITH LABOUR GOVERNMENT

The end of the war in Europe brought a new urgency to the question of India's future. When Japan surrendered three months later, the pressure for change was overwhelming. Between the two celebrations the Labour Party had defeated Gandhi's old enemy, Winston Churchill, and was much more sympathetic to allowing the sub-continent its freedom.

Wavell called a conference at Simla and released the Congress leaders from jail to attend it. Gandhi came. He was by now an almost mythical figure, worshipped as a demi-God, to his own embarrassment. He was now within sight of his lifelong quest for an independent India.

His successor, the mercurial Pandit Nehru, handled the day-to-day negotiations. But now there was a new player at the table: Muhammad Ali Jinnah, tall, impeccable – and Moslem. Jinnah was determined that the Moslems would have their own country, Pakistan, and opposed Hindu demands for a single India at the subsequent London Conference. Nehru himself was wavering, but Gandhi was unyielding.

Jinnah believed that time was on his side and did not yet insist on partition. He told the British Prime Minister, Clement Attlee, that he would be reasonable as long as the Hindu Congress Party was, as well. All this political manoeuvring was anathema to Wavell, a soldier and poet, and Attlee decided it was time to replace him. His choice as replacement was a stroke of genius: Admiral Lord Louis Mountbatten, uncle to the present Queen, and a lover of India.

One of Mountbatten's first acts on arrival in India was to take his wife to call on Gandhi. But despite mutual goodwill, he failed in an attempt to get agreement to any plan for partition. There had already been bloodshed and the Mahatma foresaw much more blood flowing if partition were adopted.

Nathuram Godse (left) and Narayan Apte shortly before being hanged for the murder of Gandhi. They died shouting: 'May united India be immortal. We salute the Holy Motherland'

VIOLENCE IN BENGAL

The alternative was equally dangerous. In July 1946, the All-India Moslem League had withdrawn its agreement to a federated state and reverted to a demand for a completely separate country of its own. Jinnah had threatened: 'If you want war, we accept it.'

On 16 August Jinnah called for a day of direct action. There were only a few British troops still in Bengal. More than 3,000 people were killed by rioters in Calcutta, and the local Moslem League government was unable or unwilling to control them until British reinforcements arrived.

Bengal was cut off from the rest of the country. Lack of food added to the crisis in the hospitals which were overwhelmed by more than 10,000 casualties, mostly Hindus. Gandhi called on the Governor, Sir Frederick Burrows, during a visit to Calcutta to try to find a way to stem the violence, and one of his most effective fasts was temporarily successful. But the Hindus in Bihar turned on the Moslem minority there in retaliation.

As Nehru gradually came to reject Gandhi's views on separation and agreed to two independent nations, there were other outbreaks of horrific violence in East Bengal and the United Provinces.

THE PARTITION OF INDIA

With independence, the country was split and split again, with Pakistan in two parts. Mountbatten himself became Governor General of the part called India, with Nehru as Prime Minister, and Jinnah became Governor General of the Pakistan sections.

There were problems. At first the Maharajahs threatened to refuse to join an independent Indian state, and religious tensions were also extreme. On Independence Day, Gandhi was in Calcutta, where riots were expected to break out between the Hindus and Moslems, but so powerful was his personality that traditional enemies embraced, shouting: 'Long live Gandhi. Long live Hindu-Moslem unity.'

However, it did not live longer than overnight. Soon the whole sub-continent was in flames. Hindus and Sikhs fled from Pakistan and from what had been Bengal, while Moslems trekked in the opposite directions. Twelve million people took part in the greatest migration in history.

Soldiers did what was possible to intercept marauding bands but before the year was out, half-a-million people had died. Bullock-cart convoys were frequently waylaid; villages were razed to the ground; refugee camps were breeding grounds of disease and death; and floods added a potent natural hazard.

The few who could get a motorised lift were the lucky ones. Refugee trains were frequently held up and most of their passengers slaughtered. The roads were choked with the millions of refugees who passed each other in hostility.

Some of the worst events were in Delhi, and Gandhi decided to go and fast there. Whenever he fasted, he was able to force a halt in the holocaust, but he was in despair at his lack of long-term influence. On his 78th birthday he asked for condolences not congratulations.

His fast succeeded in gaining the rightful compensation for the Moslems that had been promised them on partition, but withheld by the new Indian government. This led directly to his death, as it infuriated a group of fanatical Hindus, who regarded his demand as treachery.

'I WISH ALL EVIL-DOERS WELL'

The fanatics plotted to kill him. In January 1948 they found him in Delhi recovering from a fast. There was a temporary peace in the troubled city, as no other activists on either side wanted the responsibility of causing his death. As the Mahatma walked to prayer on 30 January, he was shot. The murderer and his accomplice were hanged, contrary to Gandhi's teachings. Of an earlier would-be assassin he had said: 'You should pity him. I wish all evil-doers well.'

One of Gandhi's nieces placing flower petals on his brow as he lay in state at Birla House in New Delhi shortly before the four-mile funeral procession to the banks of the Jumna River where his body was cremated. His ashes were divided and scattered in some fifty rivers across India and Pakistan

HALLOWEEN MASKS BECAME A NATIONAL JOKE IN THE

US EARLY IN 1950. BRINK'S ARMORED CAR COMPANY,

WHICH DEALT IN THE SORTING AND DELIVERY OF COMPANY

PAYROLLS, HAD BOASTED OF AN IMPENETRABLE VAULT. YET

IN JUST 20 MINUTES A GANG, WEARING THE MASKS, HAD

CALMLY WALKED IN AND OUT OF THE BUILDING WITH

NEARLY $3 MILLION. OVER A PERIOD OF SIX YEARS THE FBI

SPENT TEN TIMES THAT TRYING TO CATCH THE THIEVES,

BUT IT WAS A DISAGREEMENT OVER A FEW THOUSAND

DOLLARS WHICH FINALLY LED TO THE CASE BEING SOLVED.

The Boston Brink's Robbery

n 1950 US forces were with the United Nations in the Korean War. Meanwhile, the Soviet Union and China were giving the impression of a massive communist alliance. Spy scares were to the fore as Whitaker Chambers accused Alger Hiss of espionage and British scientist Klaus Fuchs admitted to having passed atom bomb secrets to the Russians over a period of six years.

Less global matters concerned seven men who let themselves into the premises of Brink's Armored Car Company at North Terminal Garage on Prince Street, Boston, at 7pm on 16 January 1950. Once inside, they put on grotesque Halloween masks to disguise themselves. They all wore identical navy jackets and chauffeur's caps, gloves and crêpe shoes.

Looking like evil versions of the Seven Dwarfs, they made their way to the vault where the money was. They knew their way. They forced the cashier to open up and then lie on the floor, with his assistants and guards. Their hands and legs were bound.

The robbers used sacks lying around to collect all the cash they could lay their hands on. Soon, they were loading over $2¾ million in cash and securities into a truck their confederate had driven into position.

A VERY PENETRABLE VAULT

Brink's was a company which collected cash from banks, and then counted out and delivered payrolls. Each evening, the next day's deliveries would all be sorted and counted. Overnight they would be locked in what Brink's boasted was an impenetrable vault.

In fact, as the robbers had found out, the vault's inner defences could be cracked and the outer ones were almost non-existent. The gang got away with more money than anyone in America had ever stolen in an armed robbery before. J. Edgar Hoover bizarrely claimed that the robbery proved there was a link between communism and organised crime. The FBI's investigation was to take six years and eventually cost $29 million – ten times greater than the record haul.

Every inch of the vaults was tested for fingerprints, but the heist had been planned meticulously. The disciplined gang had sacrificed an even greater haul of cash because it would have taken longer to move than the time they had allowed themselves.

Brink's officials announced at a press conference that they would pay a reward of $100,000 for information. But despite this massive prize there was silence from the underworld. The FBI staged and photographed its own reconstruction, while Brink's, and Halloween masks, became a national joke.

LITTLE EVIDENCE

The only pieces of evidence left by the gang were the tapes and ropes with which they had tied the men up, and one peaked cap with no markings.

The press was full of lurid reports, but all that journalists and the police had to work with were the recollections of the embarrassed Brink's employees: 'And then I heard them going in the vault, I heard bags being tipped over and ripping open pay envelopes, and they started to drag the bags by me.'

The police were convinced that the gang was not based in Boston. They grilled every local crook, but thought that none of them were clever enough.

Brink's boasted of an impenetrable vault, yet a gang of masked men managed to walk away with the biggest haul in US history at that time. The vault had proved ridiculously easy to penetrate

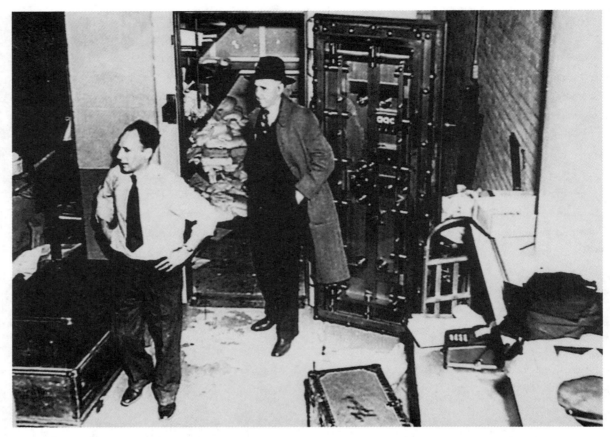

The vault room at Brink's where the robbery took place. Thomas B. Lloyd (left) was the cashier in charge at the time of the holdup and the cap left behind by Specs O'Keefe can be seen in the front right corner of the picture

Their theory took a knock when the getaway truck turned up in a local scrapyard, cut up into hundreds of pieces. When it was reassembled it turned out to be a stolen Ford truck. One of the revolvers taken from a Brink's guard was also found in a heap of garbage.

Among the local crooks now re-interviewed by the police was Joseph 'Specs' O'Keefe. He had been arrested over 70 times in his 47 years. The police kept him under close watch. He had claimed he was with a girlfriend at the key time of 7pm, but under police pressure the girl became less sure of dates and times.

Tiring of the police presence, Specs suggested to his friend Stanley Gusciora, known as Gus, that they should get out of town until things cooled off. They headed west. On the way they robbed a gun store where they helped themselves to various weapons.

Carelessly, they left these visible on the back seat of their car, and very soon both the police and the FBI had them under close observation. Their behaviour had convinced the authorities that they were part of the gang that had held up Brink's, and

the FBI wanted them left free in the hope that they would betray other members. But as they travelled on an overzealous cop arrested them.

While Specs was in jail, the FBI got a lead on another promising suspect. A van of the US Trucking Company, which used a garage next to Brink's, was robbed. Just as at Brink's, somebody had a key and took $750,000. Informers whispered the name of Joe McGinnis, a nightclub owner, as the mastermind of this robbery and possibly also Brink's. The FBI set out to get him and put pressure on Specs O'Keefe. They offered to have his three-year sentence quashed and allow him to share in the reward, if he sang about Joe McGinnis and Brink's. Specs turned the offer down, not wishing to become a target for revenge.

THIEVES FALL OUT

While in prison, Specs believed that one of his cronies, 'Jazz' Maffie, was keeping his share of the loot safe. But when he was released in February 1954 he discovered he had been cheated out of $67,000 of it.

Back in Boston, he threatened to spill the beans, and was stalked around the city by a hitman. After two near-fatal attacks, he gave up on his erstwhile friends and made a deal. He told the FBI how it was done and who to look for. Through a spokesman the FBI went public: 'I appeal to the decent men and women of the United States to assist the FBI and all other law enforcement agencies in the capture of James Faherty and Thomas Richardson.'

Known as the Gold Dust Twins of South Boston, Faherty and Richardson had staged their first stick-up together 15 years before and they had been inseparable ever since. The FBI announcement continued: 'A reward of $100,000 is still open for any information which leads to their arrest and their conviction.'

The others Specs named were either traced and arrested or had died in the six years that had now elapsed since the robbery. The two leaders were Tony Pino, a short, fat, affable rogue from Italy, and the ex-prizefighter Joe McGinnis, the brains of the operation.

The foot soldiers were Jazz Maffie, never yet convicted in ten arrests; Vinny Costa, Tony Pino's brother-in-law, a skilled getaway driver; Henry Baker, an expert in locks and keys; and Vinny Geagan, who provided the muscle for the operation.

Two who were now dead were Gus Gusciora, Spec's great pal, and Barney Banfield, an expert on burglar alarms. The last two were James Faherty and Sandy Richardson, who always worked together.

THE TRIAL

On 6 August 1956 at Suffolk Courthouse, the men behind the Halloween masks were arraigned on 108 counts – from armed robbery to putting persons in fear with intent to rob. One of their attorneys was upset at the bail demanded: 'Well, I don't see how anyone can make a bail of $120,000 with surety. I think that it is an exorbitant bail, and I think that the United States attorney office has adopted a most peculiar position on this whole matter.'

A police detective examining a safe at Brink's containing an even greater amount of money than that stolen. The highly disciplined gang had sacrificed this as it would have taken too long to move

51

The men involved in the Brink's robbery, masterminded by Joe McGinnis and Tony Pino, together with a diagram showing the layout of the Brink's building and the route the robbers took

Joseph S. Banfield

Stanley Gusciora

Vincent Costa

Henry Baker

Michael Geagan

Joseph F. McGinnis

Anthony Pino

Adolph Maffie

Thomas F. Richardson

James I. Faherty

PRINCE ST.

DOTTED LINE INDICATES ROUTE BANDITS USED IN MAKING ROBBERY

HOLD UP TOOK PLACE IN THIS ROOM, EMPLOYEES TIED HAND AND FOOT AROUND ROOM

VAULT

LOOKOUT

HALLWAY

USED THIS ENTRANCE AND STAIRS TO 2ND FLOOR

COUNTING ROOM FILLED WITH DESKS FOR DAY EMPLOYEES

BANDITS LINED UP OUTSIDE GRILL HERE, MADE EMPLOYEE OPEN DOOR

One crucial question was: would they get a fair trial when journalists had already started to print Specs O'Keefe's accusations?

To find legal precedents Judge Felix Forte went back as far as the trial of British Redcoats after the Boston Massacre of 1770. He ruled that the trial could go on. But the problem of finding an unbiased jury was dramatised by the fact that 798 prospective jury members were rejected over 23 days before even one was accepted. At long last the trial began, amid massive security and fears for O'Keefe's safety.

The journalists who swamped the trial concentrated on just one question: would Specs O'Keefe really risk his life by testifying against his former comrades in crime?

On 14 September Specs came through. He began telling the whole story of the Brink's robbery, from the moment that Anthony Pino had told him of his ambitious plan to rob the juiciest target in all New England: 'a vault full of cash'.

Tony had observed the Brink's operations on his own for more than a year. Then he had recruited Specs and Gusciora, and they had followed Brink's armoured cars around the city. More professionals were enlisted, and Tony Pino's living room was the scene of regular planning meetings.

Casing the joint they found a surprisingly easy way of getting in from the North Terminal Garage next door. One night, they explored the whole empty building. Only the vault had an alarm, which was set when the cashiers left, after sorting out the money for the next day's deliveries. Over the following weeks they returned many times, at first forcing the locks.

Then they had the great idea of unscrewing the locks from the doors. They took them to a locksmith who made keys in a few hours. The locks were back in place before morning. They did this for all the doors between the street and the vault. Their most daring achievement was to remove the lock on the street door and temporarily replace it with a dummy.

HOW IT WAS DONE

Having logged all activities meticulously they decided to pull the job early in the evening before any alarms were set. The night they chose was 16 January 1950. The weather was ideal, cold and drizzly, and the streets were deserted.

Seven of the gang were dropped off in Hull Street near the North Terminal Garage. Vinny Costa took up his position on a roof opposite Brink's and gave a signal with a torch just before seven o'clock. Then the seven men went down some steps and through a playground alongside the building until they got to Prince Street. They reached the corner at precisely 7pm.

After a second signal, Specs O'Keefe led Gus Gusciora, Jazz Maffie, Vinny Geagan, Sandy Richardson, Henry Baker and Jimmy Faherty, in that order, into Brink's through the door in Prince Street. Once inside, they disguised themselves with their rubber masks. Their route now lay up some stairs, across a hallway, through the counting room and into the safety room outside the cage where the payrolls were wrapped.

The gang moved in strict order: Specs first with the keys, Gusciora with rope and tape, Maffie, Geagan, Richardson and Baker with empty bags, and Faherty as the rear guard. They were able to slip into the cage leading from the safety room, where a sentry should have been but wasn't, and peered round the door to the grille room where the cashiers were counting the money. The raiders then pulled out pistols and O'Keefe stepped into the grille room.

At first, cashier Joseph Allen thought they were just kids with masks – until he saw the guns. The staff were made to lie on the floor, where Gusciora tied their hands with the rope he had brought. Then he sealed their mouths with sticky tape. Now the gang could walk into the Aladdin's Cave of the vault.

> "I HEARD THEM GOING IN THE VAULT, I HEARD BAGS BEING TIPPED OVER AND RIPPING OPEN PAY ENVELOPES, AND THEY STARTED TO DRAG THE BAGS BY ME"
>
> Brink's employee

The gang did not need the bags which they had brought with them as there were several strewn about the room. Into these they stuffed all the notes they could lay their hands on.

The captives strained to hear a voice to identify, but what little speech there was, was in whispers.

The raiders carried the filled bags back along the route they had come. They discovered three guns which they tossed in with the cash. Outside the truck was circling the block waiting for a signal to draw up.

THE MAINTENANCE MAN

In the garage adjoining the Brink's vault room, a maintenance man named William Manter finished checking the company trucks and got ready to eat his sandwiches. There was a bullet-proof window between the garage and the vault rooms, but he didn't look through it. He did what he always did at dinner time: to tell the vault crew, he pushed the wall buzzer.

From their nights of reconnaissance Specs O'Keefe and Vinny Geagan knew how to get round the garage. They went to check on the man who could possibly wreck their whole enterprise. Thanks to the crêpe-soled shoes they had all been told to wear, they couldn't be heard by William Manter. They decided that he was no threat and let him get on with his a sandwiches.

Working to a strict schedule, the gang realised it was time to start leaving. But they were frustrated by a large strongbox on wheels they couldn't get into and that was too heavy to carry. Inside it, if they had but known, was the payroll of the General Electric Company – adding up to $800,000.

But with more than half-a-ton of treasure in bags, hampers, baskets and trays, they had more than they could handle and they were forced to abandon some of the booty on the stairs and in the corridors.

As he gave his evidence Specs revealed that he had had difficulty keeping his cap on, and at some point during the loading he lost it. Unaware of this, the gang continued to race up and down the corridors with their precious loads.

The haul was so great that all seven men had joined in moving the sacks. When they realised that no one was making sure that the guards did not escape, Specs O'Keefe volunteered to go back.

THE TALE OF THE CAP

It was then that they noticed his cap was missing. He raced back and, having made sure the cashiers were still securely fastened, started to search every inch of the now empty vault but there was no sign of his cap.

Outside, the van got the signal to pull up by the door which the raiders had entered. Hearing it arrive, six of the seven gargoyles prepared to start the loading, but Specs was still searching for his lost hat.

Vinny Geagan went back upstairs to fetch Specs and told him he would have to leave without the cap. Together the two men raced back through the offices to where their companions were still loading the truck. On the way they tried to pick up some bags which had been abandoned.

The police later found O'Keefe's cap on a shelf, where it must have been picked up and placed by some tidy-minded robber, who then forgot his automatic action. It was not the only clue the gang overlooked: in his hurry, Gusciora left some ends of spare rope and tape on the floor which were later traced by the FBI to Sears Mail Order.

The driver of the truck, Barney Banfield, and the caper's originator, Tony Pino, who had been waiting with him, joined in the loading of the van.

The lookout man, Vinny Costa, had come down from the roof and was now in his car at the end of the street ready to drive out and block any vehicle that came along. The eleventh conspirator, Joe McGinnis, was to join the gang at their hide-out and dispose of the evidence.

THE HAUL

As they drove away, it was not yet twenty past seven. In less than twenty minutes, they had pulled off the biggest cash robbery in American history. In

Picture from the FBI reconstruction of the Brink's robbery showing the types of masks and caps worn by the robbers. Both Brink's and Halloween masks became a national joke all over the US

total, they had managed to steal $1,218,211.29 in cash and $1,557,183.83 in bearer bonds.

Dropping off some members of the gang so that alibis could be established, they ended up in Roxbury, 15 minutes drive away, at the home of Jazz Maffie's parents, who couldn't speak English. It was at this house, the police later found out, that the used cash was split up into shares of about $100,000 each.

The rest was supposed to be destroyed.

THE VERDICT

For three long weeks, Joseph 'Specs' O'Keefe was on the witness stand, telling all he knew about the robbery. It was 5 October before the defence attorneys got their chance to address the court. But this stage of the trial did not take long. None of the other defendants testified. There was nothing they could say except to dig their own graves deeper.

Their lawyers did their best to discredit the testimony of a 'Judas', whom they characterised as self-serving and untrustworthy. But it was a hollow defence, and nothing was said to persuade the jury that they had not heard an accurate account of the famous robbery.

Late that same afternoon, the jury retired, and by 12.15am, they had reached a unanimous verdict. The next morning they returned to court and delivered it: guilty on all counts.

The judge made the gang wait three days before he sentenced them. They were taken back to jail while he conferred as to whether the amount of cash should affect the number of years they should go to jail. In Boston at that time the usual term for armed robbery was around the five-year mark. While the gang had brandished guns, no bullets had been fired and nobody had been hurt.

But the publicity for this hold-up had been so enormous that they had to be made examples of: Judge Forte sentenced each one of the gang, except the helpful O'Keefe, to life imprisonment at the Massachusetts State Prison. Specs got a modest four years and was freed by June 1960. The rest of the gang were taken away under heavy guard.

Judge Forte's harsh sentences were appealed to the State Supreme Court, which upheld them, and the United States Supreme Court later refused to review the convictions.

Specs O'Keefe got $5,000 from the FBI, changed his name, and for a time was a chauffeur to the unsuspecting film star, Cary Grant.

Tony Pino served the longest sentence, 14 years, and put out an unfulfilled contract on Specs O'Keefe for ratting on the gang. Joe McGinnis turned to religion. Jazz Maffie became a car salesman. Vinny Costa went back to jail for helping to counterfeit $1 million in $20 bills. Henry Baker died in the prison hospital. Vinny Geagan lost most of his money in a dance hall that failed and resumed work as a longshoreman. Jimmy Faherty became a hopeless alcoholic.

The FBI still considers its investigation and breaking of the Brink's case among its foremost achievements. In its official account of the robbery it calls it 'the perfect crime'. But not so perfect that the gang didn't get caught.

Specs O'Keefe who confessed six years after the robbery when arguments over the stolen money broke out between gang members. He received a four-year sentence and a $5,000 reward from the FBI whilst the rest of the gang were given life sentences

JULIUS AND ETHEL ROSENBERG WERE TWO GENTLE PEOPLE WHO HAD LED HARD LIVES. THEY JOINED THE COMMUNIST PARTY IN THEIR EFFORTS TO IMPROVE THE SITUATION OF WORKING PEOPLE. CHANCE GAVE THEM THE OPPORTUNITY TO HELP THE SOVIET WAR EFFORT AT A TIME WHEN THE UNITED STATES AND THE SOVIET UNION PROCLAIMED THEY WERE ON THE SAME SIDE. BUT AS WORLD AFFAIRS CHANGED, THEY FOUND THEMSELVES CHARGED WITH ESPIONAGE. THEY WOULD NOT CONFESS, AND THE STATE COULD HARDLY HAVE BEEN MORE VINDICTIVE IN REVENGE.

Julius and Ethel Rosenberg

Atom Spies?

Queen Elizabeth II was crowned on 2 June 1953. In the same year the United States acquired a first Republican President for 20 years, Dwight D. Eisenhower. Josef Stalin died, and Winston Churchill met with renegade Yugoslavian communist Marshal Tito. Meanwhile, an armistice was signed to end three years of war in Korea.

But the Cold War between East and West continued, and on Death Row in Sing Sing Prison a husband and wife awaited execution. Julius and Ethel Rosenberg had been convicted of conspiring to pass America's most vital military and scientific secrets to the Soviet Union. A confession could still save them from the electric chair, but if they refused to admit their guilt, they would be the first Americans ever executed for spying in peacetime.

The secrets they were convicted of betraying were the workings of the atomic bomb, enabling the Soviet Union to build one of its own.

The press of the world arrived to record the moment when Julius and Ethel Rosenberg would pay for a crime that the judge at their trial called worse than murder. There had been violent protests around the world from those upset at the prospect of killing the mother of two children on evidence provided by her own brother and his wife. Despite the promise of a reprieve if she confessed, Ethel Rosenberg continued to deny any involvement.

Three million letters were received by the White House. Among them were pleas from Albert Einstein, the Pope and the President of France. But Eisenhower, who had twice turned down their lawyer's plea for clemency, remained unmoved.

ROSENBERG ARRIVES IN AMERICA

Julius Rosenberg, electrical engineer and card-carrying member of the Communist Party, was the youngest of five children of an immigrant garment worker. His father, Harry, arrived in steerage from Czarist Russia in 1902. He was part of the great wave of Jewish refugees from the pogroms. To them, the United States of America was the long-promised land of liberty and equality.

Once through immigration on Ellis Island, the family went to live on the top floor of a five-storey tenement on Broome Street in the Lower East Side of New York. The roof leaked. In winter, icicles hung from the ceiling and windows, and Julius as an infant was often cold and hungry.

His father was an active trade unionist and took part in an unsuccessful strike against sweatshop conditions in the garment industry. He was sacked and blacklisted. Julius vowed to grow up to avenge him, and was a diligent and studious child.

The slums were a fertile breeding ground for revolutionary politics, and by 1933 Julius had abandoned his studies as a rabbi. The following year, he entered City College and became a member of the Communist Party, reading Marx, Lenin and Stalin, and explained the Depression as the inevitable result of a capitalist economy and exploitation of the labour of the masses.

Nearby, but as yet unknown to him, lived Ethel Greenglass, three years his senior. Her father ran a small shop for repairing sewing machines in the basement of the coldwater tenement in which they lived on Sheriff Street. Like many slum children, Ethel was sickly. She had rickets, causing curvature of the spine.

After school, she took a stenography course and started looking for a job. In 1932, at the height of the Depression, this was a heartbreaking task. Her life was changed radically when she was knocked over when a fire hose was turned on a thousand rioting applicants for a job as a clerk in a factory. Unhurt but angry, she vowed to fight to change the system. When she did get a job, at the New York National Shipping Company, she led a strike of 150 women that led to a shutdown. Her employers surrendered but then fired her a week later.

JULIUS AND ETHEL

On New Year's Eve, 1936, Ethel sang at a union fundraising party. Julius was there. They fell in love. He introduced her to Stalinism. The Soviet Union was Utopia. By shutting their eyes to the purges, the gulags and the forced labour, they thought they were seeing the future and that it worked.

When the Spanish Civil War broke out in 1936 Julius wanted to volunteer for the International Brigade to help the Republicans, and felt like a coward when he allowed himself to be talked out of it.

2,000 protesters held a round-the-clock vigil outside the White House in January and February 1953, but failed to impress President Eisenhower. He steadfastly refused to commute the Rosenbergs' sentence

In February 1939, Julius graduated from college. Three months later he and Ethel were married – in a synagogue for the sake of their religious relatives.

When the Soviet Union signed a pact with the Nazis, Julius managed to justify it on the grounds of expediency. At first, he opposed US involvement in the world war that resulted. But when Germany attacked Russia he changed his tune. He even got a civilian job with the US Signals Corps, falsely stating that he had never been a member of the Communist Party. Now he agitated for American entry into the war on the Allies' side. Japan provoked this when, on 7 December 1941, its planes attacked Pearl Harbor without warning.

The Rosenbergs rejoiced. Now America, their home country, and Russia, to which they had pledged their hearts, were on the same side. But they were worried that the United States didn't fully trust the Soviet Union and was not helping it enough. To attempt to counter this, while American forces began to fight back, it was later alleged that Julius allowed himself to be recruited as an unofficial information link to the Soviet Union.

THE BEGINNINGS OF ESPIONAGE?

Certainly, in 1943, after the birth of their first child, Michael, the couple stopped open Party activities. It was said that Julius was soon asked by his Russian contact to see what he could find out about a military town being built in New Mexico under conditions of top security. It was to do with using atomic energy in a new top-secret weapon.

Julius Rosenberg's chance was said to have come when Ethel's brother, David Greenglass, was sent to Los Alamos as a sergeant in the army. Julius had already recruited David into the Young Communist League. Now he convinced David that it was his political duty to pass on all he could about the project, codenamed Manhattan.

> "THE EVIDENCE WAS OVERWHELMING OF THEIR GUILT, BUT I THINK THE PUNISHMENT WAS TOTALLY UNWARRANTED"
>
> Veteran lawyer Louis Nizer

David learned that Dr Robert Oppenheimer was leading a team of scientists to release energy in a chain reaction. Greenglass's own job was to machine a lens to deflect the energy. The fuel used was uranium 235, which was split into two equal halves. Sergeant David Greenglass stole a test tube of uranium 235, as did several other enlisted men, to take home as souvenirs. Where his tube of the vital ingredient ended up, nobody knows.

David Greenglass went on leave from Los Alamos in January 1945. While in New York he claimed to have visited his brother-in-law and sketched the lens he was working on. Julius was interested and asked him to get as much information as he could.

Shortly afterwards, David Greenglass claimed that Julius asked him to come and meet a Russian who questioned him closely about the lens. The Russian was never identified, but may have been Andrei Yakolev. Supposedly a Vice Consul, he is known to have been in charge of the Soviet espionage offensive to crack the Manhattan project.

Greenglass was told to return to Los Alamos and await a messenger who would produce the other half of a jello box which Julius tore in two. Greenglass's wife, Ruth, now joined him at the atomic centre.

When Stalin met Roosevelt and Churchill at Yalta, it seemed that permanent co-operation would be possible between the Allies. Julius was so excited by the prospect that he lost his caution and started talking at work like the communist he was. The Signal Corps fired him as a security risk.

THE ATOMIC BOMB

As the war in Europe ended, a courier named Harry Gold turned up in Albuquerque with the jello half-top. He collected details from David Greenglass about the trigger mechanism of the bomb which David had been able to smuggle out.

The result of the Manhattan project was now used to finish off Japan. On 6 August 1945, the first atomic bomb was dropped with devastating effect on Hiroshima. Two days later, a second bomb was detonated over the city of Nagasaki.

The Second World War ended just three weeks later amid general rejoicing. There was a feeling that, as the only possessor of this terrible weapon, the United States had a tremendous advantage, and for the little band of communist spies this provided the challenge of trying to restore the balance of power. At the Potsdam Conference the month before, Stalin had told the Western Allies that Eastern Europe would be communist.

That September, David Greenglass claimed to have sketched the Nagasaki bomb's inner workings for Julius. His sister Ethel was said to have typed out his ten-page description. Within two years of the end of the war, relations between the victors had deteriorated so much that the Russians blockaded Berlin. The Allies responded with an airlift which kept the non-communist part of the city alive.

As an Iron Curtain fell down across Europe, the Yakolev network ceased operations. The Allies now prepared to resist communism, and anti-communist feeling amongst the general population of America increased as the Chinese communists led by Mao Tse-tung took control of that vast country.

RUSSIAN BOMB

Then on 23 September 1949 the Russians detonated their first atomic bomb. This was three years earlier than the West had expected and the members of the dispersed spy ring knew it could only have come about so soon through their efforts.

US scientists continued to strive to produce an even more terrible weapon: the hydrogen bomb. But now the communist world seemed to have successfully eliminated the one advantage which had kept Western democracy reasonably secure against the massive conventional forces of communism.

Among the political shock waves of the exploding of the Russian atom bomb was an intensification of anti-communist hysteria throughout the United

Messenger Harry Gold (left) and Ethel's brother David Greenglass in court. David was not given the death sentence despite the fact that it was he who revealed the details of how the atomic bomb worked, but his testimony helped seal the fate of the Rosenbergs

States, known as McCarthyism after its chief exponent and exploiter, Senator Joseph McCarthy.

This hysteria was fuelled by charges made by Whittaker Chambers, an ex-Soviet agent urged on by Congressman Richard Nixon, that American diplomat Alger Hiss had passed him state department documents. Hiss denied it: 'I am not and never have been a member of the Communist Party.'

But Nixon, then serving on the House Un-American Activities Committee, was determined to prove Hiss guilty. He produced microfilms containing secret documents that he claimed Chambers had hidden in a pumpkin on his farm. Hiss was imprisoned for almost four years for perjury. It was amid this hysteria, on 2 February 1950, that there came the arrest in Britain of a scientist, Klaus Fuchs, who had worked on the Manhattan project.

KLAUS FUCHS

The FBI had tipped off British intelligence that a recently deciphered KGB message dated 1944 pointed to the identity of the traitor. It seemed likely that Klaus Fuchs, a naturalised Briton born in Germany,

had been betraying secrets to the Russians. Faced with all the evidence, he confessed.

Like Rosenberg, Fuchs was a dedicated communist. He had been feeding the Soviet Union with atomic research information from 1942 to 1947, including secrets from Los Alamos. He was sentenced to 14 years in prison and his treachery caused a rift between the wartime Allies.

Fuchs revealed that his American contact with the Russians had been a courier he knew only as Raymond, who came to Los Alamos to see him. He identified him from a photo as Harry Gold. Gold was arrested and began to sing to save his neck. He admitted going to Albuquerque with the jello half-top and giving $500 to a soldier in return for an envelope, but he couldn't remember the soldier's name.

By a process of elimination, the FBI identified David Greenglass, and on 15 June 1950 they arrested him. He too confessed.

ROSENBERGS ARRESTED

Ten days later the US went to war again to protect South Korea. Once again American troops poured across the ocean, and the anti-communist feelings of the American people deepened as they saw their troops dying again. In the midst of this new mood, Julius Rosenberg was arrested on 17 July, and Ethel on 10 August.

Another courier in the Yakolev spy ring, Morton Sobell, fled to Mexico but was brought back. All three stood trial for conspiracy to commit espionage. David Greenglass and Harry Gold pleaded guilty and agreed to give evidence, so were not tried with the others. In return for also giving evidence against the Rosenbergs, Ruth Greenglass was not prosecuted at all.

In March 1951 the trio pleaded not guilty at New York's Federal Courthouse. The most telling evidence against them came from David Greenglass and his wife Ruth. David testified that his sister had typed his analysis of the atom bomb, which Julius had called 'very good'.

Julius denied everything. He didn't know where David was stationed. He had never given him money

Ethel and Julius Rosenberg, separated by a metal grille, en route to Sing Sing Prison after being found guilty of conspiring to commit espionage

Two protesters displaying posters and placards before embarking on the Rosenberg Clemency Train to Washington to demand a review of the couple's case and their death sentence

or seen his sketch of the bomb. Ethel testified that everything her brother and his wife had said was false. She was a loyal citizen. Harry Gold gave evidence that he picked up envelopes from Fuchs and the Greenglasses in New Mexico. He told David that 'Julius sent me' and received what Greenglass called 'the secret of the atom bomb'.

The Rosenbergs' attorney Emmanuel Bloch, inexperienced in criminal cases, presented what was, by general consent, a poor defence. In contrast, prosecutor Irving Saypol impressed the jury with his charge that 'the Rosenbergs have magnified their treachery by lying here'.

On 29 March, after a single night of deliberation, the jury found the Rosenbergs and Sobell guilty of conspiring to commit espionage.

SENTENCE OF DEATH

Judge Irving Kaufman told the Rosenbergs: 'Your conduct in putting the A-bomb into the hands of the Russians has already caused the communist aggression in Korea.' He sentenced them both to death and went on somewhat wildly: 'I believe your conduct has already caused 50,000 casualties in Korea, and who knows but that millions more innocent people may pay the price of your treason.'

Sobell was given 30 years, the same as Harry Gold. David Greenglass got 15 years. Ruth went free. As the Rosenbergs sat on Death Row in Sing Sing Prison, a two-year legal and political battle was waged to get their sentences commuted. Many people felt that it was barbaric to deprive their two children, Michael, aged eight, and Robert, not yet seven, of both their parents. Their visits to their mother and father in Sing Sing, with their defence council, Manny Bloch, received sympathetic coverage. It seemed wrong that Klaus Fuchs should receive only 14 years in jail for an enormous betrayal over many years, while Ethel's worst proven crime was to type out some pages of notes.

While they waited in prison, demonstrations and counter-demonstrations went on all over the world. Not all the demonstrators were friendly to the Rosenbergs. A small band of counter-pickets did what they could to disrupt a round-the-clock vigil of 2,000 protesters who converged on the White House in January and February of 1953 in an attempt to urge the new President Eisenhower, who had been left this political hot potato by President Truman, to exercise executive clemency.

Eisenhower refused, saying: 'The nature of the crime involves deliberate betrayal of the entire nation. A freely selected jury rendered its judgement. I am determined not to set aside their verdict.'

Despite this, the agitation went on, both for and against the Rosenbergs. As the day appointed for the executions drew near, the demonstrations increased in size and fervour.

The Supreme Court had never examined the case itself, only whether it was a suitable one for it to take up. Now with only days to go, two new lawyers on the case found a legal loophole. A recent revision of the law stated that the jury must recommend the death sentence. It had not. They convinced Justice William Douglas to issue a further stay. Once more

the execution was postponed, and on the new day set for the execution, the Supreme Court convened in extraordinary session.

They considered whether Justice Douglas's view was correct and that the death penalty should be declared invalid. Eventually Chief Justice Vinson read the majority opinion: by five votes to four the stay of execution was refused. The government lawyers quit the Supreme Court triumphant, and the Rosenbergs' lawyer Emmanuel Bloch was left to make a final plea to the President.

A spokesman for the White House soon gave the President's response: 'I am convinced that the only conclusion to be drawn on the history of this case is that the Rosenbergs have received the benefit of every safeguard which American justice can provide. There is no question in my mind that their original trial and the long series of appeals constitute the fullest measure of justice and due process of law.'

THE EXECUTIONS

At Sing Sing Prison all the preparations had been made for the execution. It had been brought forward from the usual hour of eleven o'clock to 8pm so as to avoid the Jewish Sabbath.

Despite a last mass protest in New York's Union Square, the Rosenbergs were electrocuted, still protesting their innocence. Julius died swiftly with one shock; it took four before Ethel was pronounced dead

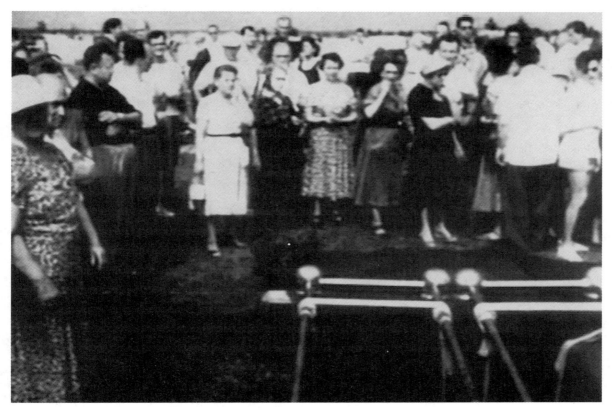

The graveside of Julius and Ethel Rosenberg. Whilst some still dispute whether they were guilty, few believe that they should have been executed

A rabbi arrived to give final words of comfort and prayer. State troopers barricaded all entrances. The offer of a reprieve for a confession still applied, and a telephone line was kept open for any news that the couple had accepted the deal. A prison matron revealed that Ethel refused to believe she was going to die and still protested her innocence.

Because of the change in time there was to be no last meal of their choice. The five permitted witnesses arrived. They were the US marshal and his deputy, and three journalists, one from each of the main wire services. Thirty-five other newspapermen awaited their reports in another room.

In New York's Union Square, the crowds gathered in one last mass protest. For many the question now was not whether the couple were guilty, but whether they deserved to die after a trial conducted in such an hysterical atmosphere. At the prison, Julius and Ethel were saying a last farewell to each other. As the clock overlooking the square moved past the hour of execution, a few people in the crowd fainted and several men and women wept.

Julius was the first to go into the death chamber. Although he had to be helped to the chair, he died swiftly once the switch was pulled. But when Ethel's turn came it took four long shocks before the doctor pronounced her dead.

Controversy about the justice of their execution followed them beyond the grave. However, despite the Rosenbergs' protestations of innocence, for many people any doubt that they were Russian spies was dispelled once and for all by Nikita Krushchev in his memoirs, which appeared in the 1970s. He reported: 'I heard both from Stalin and Molotov that the Rosenbergs had provided very significant help in accelerating the production of our atomic bomb.'

A widely held opinion was that of the veteran lawyer and author Louis Nizer: 'The evidence was overwhelming of their guilt and the jury had the right at least to say so, but I think the punishment was totally unwarranted.'

Today, most people agree that the punishment was excessive, and many still dispute whether the Rosenbergs were guilty at all.

CHARLES STARKWEATHER WAS A 17-YEAR-OLD WHO FANCIED HIMSELF AS A JAMES DEAN REBEL. WITHOUT A CAUSE OF ANY KIND, HE EMBARKED ON A SENSELESS MURDER SPREE, KILLING TEN PEOPLE IN EIGHT DAYS. MORE INTERESTING THAN STARKWEATHER WAS HIS COMPANION, 14-YEAR-OLD CARIL FUGATE, WHOSE MOTHER, SISTER AND STEPFATHER WERE THE FIRST THREE VICTIMS. WAS SHE A WILLING ASSISTANT, OR A HELPLESS CHILD CARRIED ALONG BY FEAR? OR PERHAPS A LITTLE OF BOTH? IT WAS A QUESTION WHICH EXERCISED AMERICANS FOR YEARS.

The Badlands Killer

Charles Starkweather

General Charles de Gaulle was brought back as leader of France, while at the other end of the military hierarchy Elvis Presley was called up for the army. An ex-General, Dwight D. Eisenhower, was in the White House, while American scientists were racing to match the Russians' success with *Sputnik* and get the *Explorer* satellite into space.

The year was 1958, and it opened mysteriously in Belmont Avenue, an unpaved road of low quality housing on the edge of Nebraska's capital city, Lincoln. Nobody had seen the Bartlett family in number 924 for several days. There was a notice on the door reading: 'Stay away. Everybody is sick with the flu.' When relatives called to see the family, 14-year-old Caril told them to go away.

On 25 January, they called the police, who came and talked to Caril. She told the police that everyone inside was ill and they went away, satisfied. But when Caril's grandmother went back two days later and got no answer at all, she decided that somebody had to break in.

When, at last, relatives did just that they found three bodies. They belonged to Marion Bartlett, the

57-year-old night watchman who was Caril's step-father; her mother Velda, who was 20 years younger than him and had divorced Caril's father four years before in order to marry Marion; and, even more horrifying, the body of their two-year-old daughter, Betty Jean, stabbed and beaten to death.

The police were told that Caril's boyfriend Charlie Starkweather had called on the family some days earlier, and he was a known troublemaker.

A 17-year-old who fancied himself as a rebel in the James Dean mould, Charlie was fascinated by guns and crime. His parents had seven other children to cope with, and Charlie had run wild. Among his exploits was racing stolen cars on a local track.

On 21 January, Charlie had set off for Caril's home with a gun, apparently to shoot rabbits with her father. The police put out an all-stations call to find Charlie Starkweather. They searched for Caril's body but there was no sign of it.

Then came a sighting of the missing couple: Caril was with Charlie in his car, and they appeared to be heading south on route 2 towards the nearby village of Bennett.

Had she been kidnapped? Was she an accomplice? Or was she just a kid who was doing as she was told by her boyfriend?

TRAIL OF SLAUGHTER

The runaway pair ended up in Bennett on 27 January. Charlie was heading for the house of a family friend, but his car got stuck in the mud. They walked the rest of the way to August Meyer's house.

When they got there, Charlie shot him and stole $100, another gun and some clothes. By the time the police checked out the farm, the couple were long gone. In the wash-house, covered with a blanket, they found 70-year-old Meyer. He had been shot in the head at close range.

Local citizens formed a posse and joined in the manhunt. But the couple had headed back to Lincoln in a car Charlie had hijacked after asking for a lift. The bodies of the driver and his girlfriend were found riddled with bullets in an abandoned storm cellar with the door jammed tight over them. They were identified as Robert Jensen, a 17-year-old high school student, who lay at the bottom of the storm cellar steps with six

17-year-old Robert Jensen and 16-year-old Carol King. Jensen had been shot repeatedly in the back of the head, although Starkweather claimed it was self-defence. He also claimed that it was Caril who had murdered Carol King in a fit of jealousy

bullet wounds in the back of his head, around his left ear; and 16-year-old Carol King, who lay on top of him, half-naked. She had been shot and stabbed.

While the posse of locals combed the surrounding countryside in search of the couple, Charlie and Caril went back to Lincoln to check whether the bodies of Caril's family had been found yet. When Charlie saw police around the house, he drove straight on, ending up at one of the town's biggest homes on 24th Street.

Inside, he lay in wait for the owner, C. Lauer Ward. When Ward came home, Charlie murdered him. Clara Ward tried to telephone the police, but Charlie saw her and stabbed her in the back with his hunting knife. Then the maid, Lillian Fencl, was tied up and knifed to death.

The discovery of these three bodies caused a panic. Lincoln was quickly sealed off for a house-to-house search. Gun stores sold out five times over. A $1,000 reward was offered. The local sheriff appealed

> ## "I DON'T CARE IF SHE LIVES OR DIES"
>
> Charles Starkweather on his way from Death Row to testify against Caril Fugate

for help in the capture of the rampaging Charles Starkweather and his companion: 'Our search discovered the last three bodies which makes a total of nine that we know of so far. Mary Martin and I have made an appeal for all adjoining counties including Omaha to send all the available help they can to Lincoln. It is our opinion that the car is still in this vicinity. We know he has been for the last three days and we want to cover Lincoln block-to-block.'

But, now driving the Wards' Packard, Charlie and Caril were heading away from Lincoln towards Wyoming and the neighbouring Badlands.

THE PANIC SPREADS

Armed guards were stationed at local schools in Lincoln. But terror soon spread throughout the Great Plain and Rocky Mountain states. No one knew where the teenage killer would strike next. The national guard was called out. Roadblocks were set up and every home was barricaded. Citizens formed vigilante squads and searched every possible hiding place, by day and night.

As they sped across the state line, Charlie heard on the radio that the police were looking for the Packard he was driving. It was Merle Collison's bad luck to take a nap in his Buick on highway 20 as the couple drove along it. When he wouldn't get out of his car, Charlie shot at him through the window.

Then, as Collison opened the door, he was killed by another seven shots. But Charlie had trouble starting the car – the handbrake had jammed. When a deputy sheriff pulled up, he jumped back into the powerful Packard and drove off alone.

He sped through the city of Douglas at up to 120 miles per hour, now with police cars on his tail. Caril was left behind, pleading with the police for help. Finally, bullets smashed his window. Hit on the ear by flying glass, he pulled up.

The police had to fire warning shots into the ground in front of Charlie before he would surrender.

Merle Collison, shot eight times at point-blank range, was the last of the Badlands victims. Starkweather was trying to get Collison's car started when a deputy sheriff spotted him

Sheriff Merle Karnopp (left) and Safety Patrol Chief Investigator Harold Smith (back) escorting Charlie Starkweather from Wyoming, where he was caught, back to Nebraska to stand trial for the murders

But, at last, to the delight of the pursuing press and local residents, Charles Starkweather was in jail, after ten slayings in eight days.

STARKWEATHER'S STORY

Charlie admitted to eight killings, claiming that they were in self-defence. He confessed to murdering Caril's family, saying that they had accused him of getting her pregnant. A quarrel had flared up and her stepfather had attacked Charlie with a hammer. Charlie had shot him, and when Velda came at him with a knife he had first shot her and then hit her with the rifle butt as she went down. The baby was crying, so he threw a kitchen knife at her to shut her up. Then he finished her off with a blow to the head and stabbed her father several times to make sure he was dead.

Starkweather also admitted to a murder which had been baffling the police – the killing of Robert Colvert, a gas station attendant, two months before. Charlie had robbed the station of just over $100 and driven Colvert to an isolated spot where he shot him.

On 29 January, Charlie was charged with murdering Merle Collison in Wyoming, but the Governor was only too pleased to extradite Charlie back to Nebraska and no trial was ever held there. On a cell wall Charlie wrote that Caril had killed two of the women, but the girl denied this, protesting that she was just one of his victims as well. Caril claimed that she was tricked into helping him because Charlie had told her that her mother and stepfather were being held hostage. The proof she offered was that when they were caught, she had run to the deputy sheriff, crying: 'Take me to the police.'

But the state of Nebraska believed that she was Charlie's willing partner in crime, not an innocent captive. It was decided to put both of them on trial for murder in the first degree.

A CULT HERO

The two alleged killers elected to be tried separately, and Charlie's trial for the murder of Robert Jensen began in Lincoln on 5 May 1958.

His claim that he had acted in self-defence was seriously undermined by testimony that all the bullets were found in the boy's back. His defence team called three psychiatrists but none of them felt able to testify that he was legally insane.

Sheriff Earl Heflin (right) caught Starkweather after a high-speed chase through the city of Douglas. Sheriff William Romer (left) and Assistant Police Chief Eugene Masters (centre) also gave evidence at Starkweather's trial

Among some of his generation, Charlie was elevated to the status of cult hero. As he had hoped, they saw him as a James Dean character, a misunderstood teenage rebel. But the jury were not impressed, and on 23 May they found him guilty of murder in the first degree. The sentence: death.

Now the state encouraged Charlie to give evidence against Caril. He claimed she had egged him on to murder her parents. While he cleaned up afterwards she watched TV. He hadn't tied her up and they had stayed in the house for five days.

When their car had stuck in the mud and snow, she had eagerly helped him ransack August Meyer's house. And when they hijacked Robert Jensen's car, it was Caril, Charlie claimed, who had emptied the high school student's wallet.

It was Caril, according to Charlie, who had jealously attacked Carol King, because she thought Charlie had been having sex with her. Finally she knifed and shot the girl, while he was away trying to extricate their car.

At C. Lauer Ward's house, Charlie alleged, she had packed herself a suitcase of stolen clothes. She had then stabbed Clara Ward, sprinkling perfume to hide the smell of blood, and then knifed the maid, Lillian Fencl. Caril denied all this, insisting that all she did was to alert Charlie when Ward drove up. Charlie had then taken Ward to the cellar to shoot him, and it was Charlie who had killed the women: she swore she hadn't touched them.

But Charlie insisted that when he left the maid, she was alive, and that he had stabbed Mrs Ward only once. In the face of this blow, her attorneys decided to use their client's trump card – her youthful charm.

TELEVISION TRAILER

Not yet fifteen years old, Caril Fugate would be the youngest girl in the United States ever to be tried for first-degree murder. Her lawyers decided to arrange an interview on a local television station. It was an extraordinary prelude to an extraordinary trial.

Putting her on television didn't go as well as they had hoped, however. The police had cropped her hair of its ponytail, and dressed her not in jeans but in a tight blouse and long skirt which made her appear ten years older. And nervousness made her seem sharp and hard as the interviewer questioned her.

Interviewer: Why do you think he would even implicate you if you didn't have anything at all to do with it? Why do you think he'd want to implicate you?

Caril: Well, by now I'm sure he hates me for running away, and is starting to make it look like I am just as guilty as he is.

Interviewer: Have you gone with him for quite a while?

Caril: Yes, I went with him a year before and I told him that I didn't want to see him again, but he came back. And up to that Sunday I went with him and then I kept telling him to leave. And that Sunday I told him to leave and I told him I don't ever want to see him again.

Interviewer: What had brought you to this conclusion that you didn't want to go with him any more?

Caril: I think he's crazy.

Interviewer: Do you still think that?

Caril: Yes, I do.

But many viewers wondered whether this had been her feeling during the week of the murders. At the forefront of everyone's mind was also the possibility that Caril could be sent to the electric chair.

Interviewer: Did you ever break down and cry and beg Charlie to let you go, or anything like that?

Caril: Yes, I cried all the way.

Interviewer: He just wouldn't let you out of the car at all?

Caril: No.

Interviewer: Have you thought if you were convicted that you might go to prison or you might even go to the electric chair? Have you thought about that?

Caril: Yes I have, and I don't really believe that I have anything to worry about . . . Lord knows that I'm innocent and I know it and the people who are involved in it know it.

Among the viewers were the mother and father of one of the victims, high school student Robert Jensen. Mrs Jensen gave her opinion of Caril's performance: 'The thing that struck me most about her then and still was her very cold eyes, the unfeeling look that she would have.'

Mrs Jensen's husband got the same impression: 'At that time I thought she was the most defiant person I'd ever seen. I don't think that she would have stopped right then if she could have got away. I think she wasn't bothered. I didn't see any remorse or any such thing like that.'

THE TRIAL OF CARIL

Caril Fugate's trial for being an accomplice to murder and robbery began on 27 October. Years later she recalled her bewilderment: 'During my whole trial I was not totally aware of what was going on.'

A string of witnesses testified that Caril had helped Charles Starkweather in the killings, and the press was hostile. Nor were the jury of five women and seven men strictly neutral. One of them later recalled that the day before the trial he had bet a

friend $1 that Caril would get the electric chair. There was also the view that if she sat in Charlie's lap it would save the double expense.

Charlie Starkweather left Death Row to bear witness against Caril. 'I don't care if she lives or dies,' he shrugged. He testified that she had threatened to blow her mother's brains out, that she'd had plenty of opportunity to get away if she had wanted, that she had held a gun on Carol King, and that she had taken Robert Jensen's billfold.

In rebuttal, her attorney pleaded that she was a frightened child who saw the terrible things that happened to people who defied Charlie Starkweather.

The jury was out for 24 hours while Caril waited with her surviving family, who rallied round and supported her throughout her arrest and trial. The jury's first decision was that she should not be executed.

There was pity for her. But whatever compassion the jury may have felt, they had to follow the facts. As one juror said: 'She was guilty, they didn't ask us why.'

They found her guilty of murder while in the perpetration of a robbery. In Nebraska the jury decides the sentence, too. They chose life imprisonment. Caril cried out: 'No, I'd rather be executed.'

14-year-old Caril Fugate being led from her cell to be fingerprinted and have her mugshot taken. It was at this point that she began fully to grasp the reality of her situation

Judge Harry Spencer asked her: 'Is there any reason why sentence should not be pronounced at this time?' 'Yes,' she replied. 'I'm not guilty.'

The judge pronounced: 'You are sentenced to imprisonment at the state reformatory at York for the period of your natural life and you are ordered to pay the costs of the prosecution.'

Caril was taken away to face the added punishment of 222 days in solitary confinement. As she was still only fifteen years old, she could not, by law, enter the general prison population. So she had to spend the first eight months all alone in the prison.

She later recalled: 'There were days when I would just cry out of loneliness, you know, for another human being. Or I used to sit by my window, because my window looked out to our gate and I used to think they're going to come and they're going to find out, you know, that I didn't . . . and I'd wait and I'd wait and I'd watch out of the window and every time a car would come I'd just kind of hold my breath.

'And I used to just sit and, you know, look out and, you know, cry and everything. And I think when it really dawned on me and I knew I wasn't leaving – that it was going to be permanent – was the day that I was fingerprinted. And then they take what they called prison-term mugshot, and after this I really felt that, you know, this is it: you're not leaving. You're going to stay here. And I think maybe this is when I sort of started to adjust to the idea that I would be here, and that day I cried a lot.'

STARKWEATHER EXECUTED

Charlie, meanwhile, was fighting for his life. He had been encouraged to think that by helping convict Caril Ann he would win himself a reprieve. He was disappointed. In April 1959, he fired his attorney and represented himself at a clemency hearing, claiming

he had found God. That won him a short reprieve, but on 24 June he was executed in the electric chair.

At York, Caril found a harsh regime. No talking was allowed except at meals and recreation. Makeup and radios were banned. Little attempt was made at rehabilitation in the late 1950s. Inmates could have school lessons, but for only 45 minutes three times a week. It took Caril ten years just to finish the 8th grade and complete her high school education.

The reformatory's only teacher was Mrs Iris Saddoris: 'Some way or other I just tried to instil into her a quieter voice, a nicer walk, and things that I felt would help her because I had no idea really that Caril would be with us as long as she was.'

This was a problem which increasingly began to trouble people. However terrible the crime of which she had been convicted, she had been very young and impressionable. The regime at York made little allowance for preparing her for the possibility of release.

Inmates were woken at 5.45am. The food was often inedible. Their clothes were dowdy, ill-fitting, rarely washed and smelt strongly of disinfectant. In daylight hours, prisoners were not allowed on their beds. Even if they felt ill they had to lie on the concrete floor until nightfall. Those who broke the rules were placed in solitary confinement, for weeks at a time, where the diet was confined to tea and bread. Inmates were even forbidden to smile.

PREPARING FOR RELEASE

Eight years passed before Caril first left the prison at York. It was for a judicial review where she was refused a new trial. By 1970 she was the longest-serving inhabitant – staff or prisoner. Conditions were gradually relaxed, but sometimes she still despaired: 'This is it – you are forever and ever and ever doomed to a penitentiary.'

> "I WISH THERE WAS SOME MAGIC WORD I COULD SAY THAT COULD BRING THE PEOPLE BACK. I'M SORRY, I'M DEEPLY SORRY IT HAPPENED"
>
> Caril Fugate shortly before her release in 1976

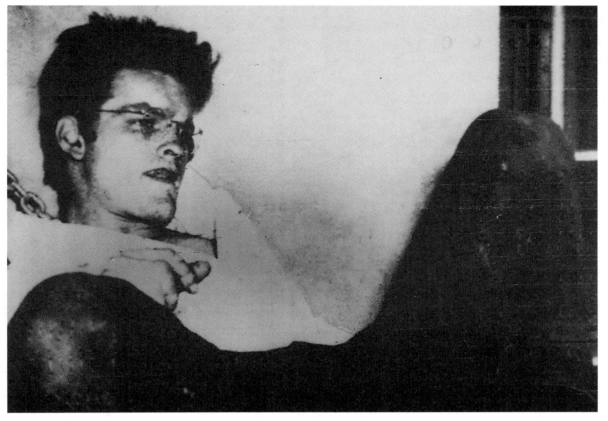

The 'mad dog' killer in his cell after capture. In a letter to his parents, which was used as evidence at his trial, he said he was 'not real sorry' for the killings and that for the first time he and Caril had had 'more fun' than they'd ever had before

But in 1971 the authorities began to prepare her for the possibility of release. A new reform regime at the prison now allowed some prisoners to go into the nearby town. Caril became a regular at the bowling alley, but she was still not allowed on work release because of her life sentence. She was grateful when the town also offered the use of its new indoor pool where she swam every week: 'Maybe I can't just, you know, walk the streets free or something, but they are willing to at least let me come down for a small part of the time and be part of their community.'

Then she was allowed to work in the local church crèche. Some mothers had initial reservations: 'Someone from there! And then I heard the name Caril and I was dumbfounded. Because we lived here at the time that the things happened that she was put in there for. And I remember barring my door at that time and I was scared to death because my older children were young then.'

But the confidence of the authorities seemed justified: Caril had always been a model prisoner.

Prison governor J.J. Exxon sounded optimistic about the possibility of her rehabilitation: 'I feel quite sure that some time in the future, possibly the immediate future, we can put Caril Ann Fugate back into society, where we think that she will have an excellent opportunity to become a valuable working member.'

But there was still a strong lobby in Nebraska which opposed her release, however much she might express remorse at what had happened with statements like this: 'I really wish that there was something I could do. I wish there was a magic word I could say or a magic phrase or something that could bring the people back. I'm sorry, I'm deeply sorry it happened.'

Finally, on 20 June 1976, Caril Ann Fugate was released on parole. She continued to protest her innocence, and even took a lie detector test in 1983 which suggested that she was telling the truth. But the next day a poll showed that a majority of Nebraskans were still convinced that she had accompanied Charlie Starkweather willingly during his appalling rampage.

IN JANUARY 1948 POLICE THOUGHT THEY HAD CAUGHT THE RED LIGHT BANDIT, WHO HAD FORCED TWO WOMEN FROM THEIR CARS INTO HIS OWN FOR SEXUAL ACTS AND ROBBERY. TECHNICALLY, THIS WAS KIDNAPPING, A CAPITAL OFFENCE IN CALIFORNIA. CARYL CHESSMAN CONDUCTED HIS OWN DEFENCE, INEPTLY, AND WAS SENTENCED TO DEATH. ON DEATH ROW, HE READ LAW AND CONDUCTED NUMEROUS APPEALS. HIS EXECUTION WAS PUT OFF AGAIN AND AGAIN. THE LAW UNDER WHICH HE WAS SENTENCED WAS SCRAPPED. THE DEATH ROW STRUGGLE WAS TO LAST TWELVE YEARS, AND WAS DECIDED BY THE FEW SECONDS IT TAKES TO MISDIAL A TELEPHONE NUMBER.

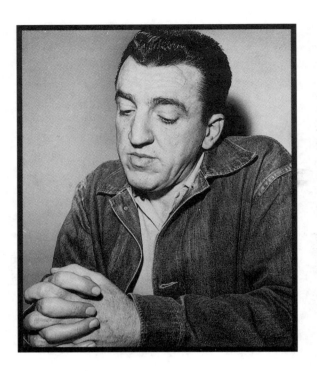

Caryl Chessman

The Red Light Bandit

There was bitter fighting as Katanga tried to break away from the newly independent Belgian Congo, and 56 people were killed by police at Sharpeville when black South Africans protested with civil disobedience against laws which required them to carry identity cards. US Vice President Richard Nixon faced his Democratic challenger for the Presidency, John Kennedy, in a televised debate.

The year was 1960, the last for Caryl Chessman, a man whose 12-year fight for life had captured headlines all over the world.

At 10am on 2 May 1960, United States District Judge Louis Goodman agreed to a stay of execution in the case of Chessman, a convicted kidnapper, who was due to be executed in a few moments time. The judge instructed his secretary to telephone San Quentin Prison to halt the execution. She got the wrong number.

This was the ninth time that a stay of execution had been granted to Chessman since he had been found guilty way back in May 1948. Since then, he had been on Death Row in San Quentin Prison protesting his innocence.

Outside San Quentin on the morning of his execution was a large crowd of demonstrators. Many displayed their disgust at the cat-and-mouse game the legal system had played. Inside the prison, Caryl Chessman, in his stockinged feet, was being escorted from the condemned cell, through guarded doors, and into the little octagonal steel room that was the San Quentin gas chamber. He was strapped into the right-hand of two chairs. The cyanide pellets under it were ready to be released into a pan of acid.

Across San Francisco Bay, Judge Goodman's secretary had checked the number of the prison. As she started dialling again, the door of the execution chamber was closed.

CHESSMAN'S CRIMES

The events that led to that moment began over twelve years before, at 4.30am on Sunday 18 January 1948. A dentist named Thomas Bartle was driving south along the Pacific Coast highway from Malibu, California, with a girl named Ann Plaskowitz. A late-model Ford started to follow them, flashing a red light. Thinking it must be the police, they stopped,

and a man demanded Bartle's driver's licence. When he, in turn, asked to see identification, the man produced a gun. They gave him $15 and he drove off.

Later that day, a second couple were parked on a deserted road when a car with a red spotlight pulled up beside them. The driver stole a small sum of money and drove off.

On the following night another couple were parked overlooking the city. A light-coloured Ford with a red spotlight drew up and a masked man asked for their identification. This time he forced the girl into his car and ordered her to perform sexual acts on him. She kept calm and, when a car approached, she suggested that it might be the police and that he should take off the handkerchief mask. As he did so, she got a good look at his face. He let her go and the couple raced to the police.

At midnight the same night, the robber took exactly $1 off another couple who were parked off Mulholland Drive.

The fourth and last holdup by the man who was to become known as the Red Light Bandit happened in the early morning of 22 January, also high in the

Caryl Chessman, convicted as the Red Light Bandit and sentenced to death under the kidnapping laws of California, spent twelve years on Death Row. In all, he received nine stays of execution, but the last did not arrive on time

Hollywood Hills. This time the Bandit pulled the girl into his car. Her boyfriend escaped and drove to the police, while the masked abductor tried to rape the girl. Unable to complete the act, he again forced his victim to perform fellatio before releasing her.

The next day there was an armed robbery at Redondo Beach, and a suspect car was chased and stopped. One of the men in it ran off. The police arrested him after a chase. His name was Caryl Chessman, and he had a long record of petty crime.

CHESSMAN AND THE POLICE

Caryl Whittier Chessman had been born in 1921 in St Joseph, Michigan. Six months after his birth the family moved to Glendale, California. When he was nine, tragedy struck. His mother was paralysed in a car crash. His father, who twice tried to kill himself, was unable to support his family. Young Caryl began to steal food to feed them.

Chessman had his first brush with the law at the age of 16 when he was sent to a young offenders school for car theft and burglary. He then served two terms at a youth camp for violent juvenile offenders. Over the next eleven years he served time for car theft, robbery, assault with a deadly weapon and assaulting a police officer. He was an unusual prisoner with an IQ of 136. He edited the San Quentin Prison newspaper, taught shorthand and wrote scripts for the prison radio station.

He had been out on parole only a couple of weeks when he was arrested fleeing from the stolen car. The car fitted the description of the Red Light Bandit's vehicle. It had a spotlight mounted by the driver's window and police found a red handkerchief knotted so that it would fit over this lamp and make it into a red light.

What happened next remained the subject of dispute. According to the police Chessman confessed of his own volition to being the Red Light Bandit. But he claimed that he was brutally beaten and agreed to make a false confession only because, in return, the police promised to drop all charges except robbery.

Contrary to the deal he thought he had made, Caryl Chessman was arraigned on 18 charges including kidnapping. In California, following the abduction of Charles Lindbergh's baby son, kidnapping 'with bodily harm with intent to commit robbery' had been made a capital offence, whether or not anyone was killed. So if Caryl Chessman were to be found guilty of forcing the two women from their car to his he would technically be eligible for the death sentence, despite the fact that he had neither murdered nor fully raped anyone.

Many people felt that press reports before and during Chessman's trial inflamed public opinion by greatly exaggerating his victims' ordeals. Between his arrest and the start of his trial on 30 April 1943, Caryl Chessman hired and fired four attorneys. He finally represented himself, incompetently. He allowed so many prosecution errors and excesses to go unchallenged that some observers thought that he was deliberately trying to ensure a mistrial.

Although he was identified by several victims as the Red Light Bandit, the identification procedures were all subject to flaws. Before each line-up, the victims were shown Chessman on his own and had him pointed out to them. Some of the descriptions of the Bandit fitted him; others did not. Nevertheless, the jury found him guilty on 17 counts including three of kidnapping, and recommended the death penalty.

THE APPEALS BEGIN

Now began twelve years of appeals. Like a cat, Caryl Chessman turned out to have nine lives, with eight stays of execution. His first attempt to save his life came in June 1948, shortly after he had been moved to San Quentin. The court reporter at his trial had died having only transcribed a third of his shorthand notes. Chessman appealed for a new trial as there was now no possibility of an accurate transcript.

Another reporter, the brother-in-law of the prosecuting attorney, was employed to complete the job. It turned out he was an alcoholic and, in October, the Court Reporters Association protested that his transcript was unreadable. But in June 1949 the judge

who had tried Chessman certified it as accurate. Chessman was not asked for his approval.

For the next two years, as the US became fascinated by the revelations of major criminals during the Kefauver enquiries, petty crook Chessman fought to prove that the transcript was so inaccurate that a new trial must be called. But in May 1951, the US Supreme Court refused to consider his case.

As the nation mourned the retirement of baseball star Joe DiMaggio, Chessman's appeal was considered by a Californian court. This was rejected and a date for execution of 28 March 1952 was set.

Caryl Chessman's second chance of life came in February 1952, when his execution was postponed for another referral to the US Supreme Court. But Chessman soon heard that this had been refused and then came the devastating news that the execution would be carried out on 27 June. Almost immediately came another reprieve from the gas chamber when Chessman was given fresh leave to appeal his case.

For the rest of 1952, while the American public thrilled to the appearance of a new hero, Hopalong Cassidy, Caryl Chessman continued his bitter and lonely fight to prove that his original trial had been

Caryl Chessman in San Quentin Prison where he educated himself in the law and conducted his own appeals. He turned himself from a bright petty hoodlum into a literate and intelligent thinker

faulty. But in May 1953 the US Court of Appeals turned him down. At the beginning of 1954 a third execution date was set.

It now seemed as though nothing could save Chessman from taking his place in the gas chamber. But, on the day before he was due to die, Chessman's lawyer Berwin Rice convinced California's Judge Thomas Keating to agree to another stay of execution. He rushed to the prison and told Chessman: 'I've got some news for you, Chess, you're going to be around for a little longer, at least.'

CHESSMAN WRITES BESTSELLER

During his three-year ordeal, Caryl Chessman had changed from a bright petty hoodlum into a literate and intelligent thinker. He had turned his cell into a study centre on the law, and had just published the first of three books in which he pleaded his case. This was *Cell 2455, Death Row*. It quickly became an international bestseller and alerted the world to his plight.

Over the next six years, Chessman published two more books in which he argued not only that his original trial had been deeply flawed but that he had done nothing to deserve to be on Death Row.

From his condemned cell, Chessman pointed out that the original identifications of him as the Red Light Bandit had been incorrectly carried out, and that his original confession had been forced out of him. Alongside him in San Quentin were men who had committed far worse crimes but were not now facing the gas chamber.

However, for all his pleading and a great deal of public support, the California Supreme Court again refused to reconsider the case and a new execution date was set for 30 July 1954.

For the first time Chessman seemed totally dispirited. But again there was a last-minute reprieve when a local judge granted a stay so that Chessman could go back to the US Supreme Court. California's Attorney General was infuriated.

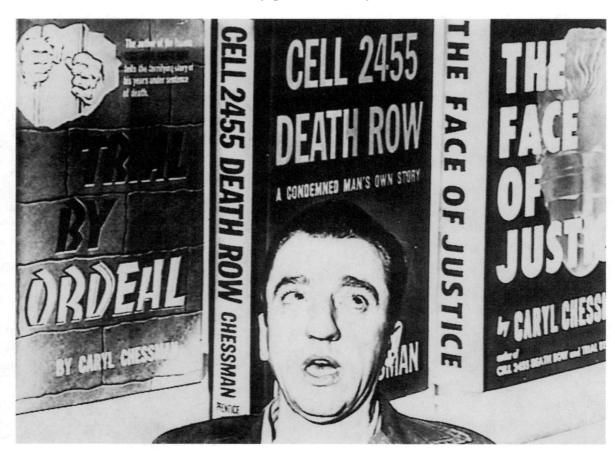

Caryl Chessman wrote three books about his case during his imprisonment, arguing that his trial had been flawed and that the punishment did not fit the crime anyway. These books became international bestsellers and alerted the world to his plight

WORLDWIDE SUPPORT

Caryl Chessman was no longer a lonely figure fighting for his life but a man whose struggle had gained him friends all over the world. He also now had a fiancée, Frances Couturier. Her support, and that of his correspondents, was sorely needed as the see-saw legal battle continued.

Two more years went by, marked by the explosion of the first H-bomb and the deaths in 1955 of Albert Einstein in New York and the nation's latest screen idol, James Dean.

Each appeal to the Supreme Court was referred back down to local courts and then back up again. Both sides were acutely aware of the delicate balance which existed between federal and state rights on such a critical matter and the Supreme Court kept insisting that the decision must be taken at state level. As the months rolled on with earth-shaking events such as the Soviet invasion of Hungary and the Anglo-French invasion of Suez in 1956, the arguments for Chessman's reprieve continued.

NEW HEARING

A year later, in June 1957, while federal troops were busy imposing federal laws on racial integration in Arkansas, the US Supreme Court finally took the dramatic step of ordering the California courts to hold a new hearing on the whole validity of the original court transcripts. For the first time, it was ordered that Caryl Chessman must be present at the hearing. He was taken to the State Supreme Court accompanied by new attorneys whom he was able to employ with the income from his books.

Disputes over the transcripts dragged on for another two years as Chessman and his lawyers went back and forth to court.

By now, a new element had entered the case. California had repealed the 'Little Lindbergh Law' under which Caryl Chessman had been sentenced to death. An increasing number of people felt that the

> ## "ANYONE WHO HAS TO WAIT ELEVEN YEARS FOR THE GAS CHAMBER HAS EXPIATED HIS GUILT"
>
> Italian newspaper

only legal justification for demanding the death penalty had now been removed.

Caryl Chessman had been on Death Row for more than eight years. For many it seemed inhumane that he should still be fighting for his life when the state legislature had decided that the original law under which he had been condemned could no longer be justified. It had also granted parole eligibility to everyone else who had been convicted under it. But the court continued to take the view that it must concentrate solely on the technical legal point of the transcripts and not take any broader issues into account.

On 7 July 1959, Chessman's attorneys Rosalie Asher and George Davis were advised that the California Supreme Court had decided that the transcript was substantially correct – even though 2,000 changes were inserted for the record. A new execution date was set for 24 October 1959.

AN INTERNATIONAL PETITION

After a reprieve of four years, Chessman was again faced with a definite date for execution. But he announced his intention to fight on.

His case was now being followed all over the world. There were protest meetings in many capitals. An international petition was set up and signed by more than two million people. Even in nations which had not abandoned the death penalty at that time, like Britain and France, there was astonishment that a man could have been kept waiting for so many years. In Italy, the newspaper *Osservatore Romano* wrote: 'Anyone who has to wait eleven years for the gas chamber has expiated his guilt.'

Famous names who lent their support included Albert Schweitzer, Eleanor Roosevelt, Queen Fabiola of Belgium, Pope John XXIII, Pablo Casals, Shirley MacLaine and Marlon Brando.

Faced with this pressure, California's Governor Edmund Brown announced that he was considering

Protesters kept an all-night vigil outside San Quentin Prison on the eve of Caryl Chessman's execution on 2 May 1960, disgusted at the cat-and-mouse games that the legal system had been playing. This time the execution took place

the appeals – but local political reaction proved too strong and on 19 October 1959 he refused to grant clemency. Thirty years later in his book *Public Justice, Private Mercy*, Brown wrote: 'Chessman was a nasty, arrogant, unrepentant man, almost certainly guilty of the crimes he was convicted of. But I don't think those crimes deserved the death penalty.'

Governor Brown's experience with Chessman had planted the seeds of doubt about the effectiveness of the death penalty and he said: 'So I moved along, and I watched the people that killed. I concluded it didn't do good, that these people would kill, whether you had capital punishment or not. For the state to do it, it seemed to me that it cheapened the life of everybody.'

The effect on the officials involved also concerned him: 'I never knew whether I did right, and it's a terrible responsibility, even though the jury and the courts all decided he should die.'

Nevertheless, the petitions may have played a part in persuading US Supreme Court Justice Douglas to agree to another appeal. But on 11 January 1960 the court again refused to consider the case. A new execution date was set for 19 February. But in an unexpected new twist with only one day to go, Governor Brown granted a 60-day reprieve. He also announced that he would be recommending the abolition of the death penalty in California.

TELEVISED PRESS CONFERENCE

The battle lines were now drawn in this new attempt to find a solution. Yet again Chessman found himself back in his cell to await events. Even more extraordinarily, it was now announced that Chessman would be allowed to hold a televised press conference.

Smartly dressed, he was asked whether he was now going for broke: 'I believe I have been all along. At one point there was a willingness on my part, when a great many friends prevailed on me, to consider accepting a commutation of sentence. When that was rejected and made a political issue, I have decided since then that I'm going to survive and be vindicated and walk the streets a free man or I'm going to wind up dead.'

A journalist asked: 'What if you were to secure your release tomorrow, what would be the first thing you would do on the outside, do you have any idea?' Chessman replied: 'Probably take a good long look at the sky when there wasn't any bars around.'

A journalist wanted to know if he had ever lost hope: 'Well, I don't know if I actually had hope. It's like the soldier out in the field, the battlefields, I don't know if he has hope or not, he just keeps slogging forward as much as possible, then waits for the results, whether the shell might hit him. Well, in the same way in a legal sense the shell might hit me and that would have been the end of me.'

Chessman was then asked by reporters how many people had been executed in California during the twelve years he had been waiting on Death Row: 'I believe before I left San Quentin it was 75 men and one woman.'

He was asked if these had affected him strongly. 'Well, they did of course in the sense that I saw a man walk by my cell and he never returned and I had occasion to reflect on the fact that it often wasn't murder that was a capital offence, it was ignorance, and the fact that the man was fundless or friendless. You read in the paper where someone perhaps was more fortunate: to get a conviction for second-degree murder on what might be an identical set of facts that would put someone else in the gas chamber. I don't feel that there is anything equitable or fair or sensible or socially valid about capital punishment.'

Even when asked how he now felt, he reacted with dignity: 'I don't feel about it, I've gone beyond the point of feeling. You don't react subjectively after ten years. How can you? You don't have the capacity to feel anymore.'

DEATH BY ERROR

By now Chessman had learnt not to raise his hopes too high. And his caution was justified when the

> **"I DON'T FEEL THAT THERE IS ANYTHING EQUITABLE OR FAIR OR SENSIBLE OR SOCIALLY VALID ABOUT CAPITAL PUNISHMENT"**
>
> Caryl Chessman

State Senate Judiciary Committee confounded his attorney George Davis's hopes when they refused to consider the death penalty abolition bill.

After more than 11 years in the shadow of the gas chamber and a total of eight stays of execution, Chessman still protested his innocence. But more importantly now, he felt that he was fighting to make a contribution to a more humane society. The petty crook who had begun his long struggle defiantly and bitterly was now hoping that his example would lead to the abolition of capital punishment.

That night, protesters gathered outside the prison for a final vigil. By the morning set for Chessman's execution their numbers had been increased by newsmen from all over the world. Chessman's attorneys were making their last pleas to get another stay.

Security at the prison was tight and all other prisoners had been confined to their cells until the execution – due at ten o'clock – was completed. As ten o'clock approached, Chessman's attorneys succeeded in persuading Judge Goodman that there were new arguments that should be considered. As the final minutes ticked away the judge instructed his secretary to get the prison. She dialled its number: GL-4-1460. But she got a wrong number and precious seconds were wasted as she dialled again. Meanwhile, Chessman had been taken from his cell and led the short distance to the gas chamber. He walked unaided into the metal box and was strapped into the right-hand chair.

Even as the judge's secretary got through to the prison Governor, the cyanide pellets had dropped into the acid bowl. All the judge could do was turn to George Davis and say: 'It's too late, the pellets have been dropped.'

Defiant to the last, Caryl Chessman held his breath for one last extra minute before ending his twelve-year ordeal.

RARELY DOES A MAN BOAST OF GETTING AWAY WITH MURDER, PARTICULARLY A MURDER THAT ANOTHER MAN HAS ALREADY PAID FOR WITH HIS LIFE. BUT YEARS AFTER JAMES HANRATTY HAD BEEN HANGED FOR THE SHOOTING OF MICHAEL GREGSTEN IN A PICNICKERS' LAY-BY NEAR THE A6, PETER ALPHON, WHO HAD BEEN THE ORIGINAL SUSPECT IN THE CASE, SEEMED ANXIOUS TO PROVE THAT HE HIMSELF WAS THE KILLER. WHAT WITH TWO CONFLICTING IDENTIKIT PICTURES, A DRAMATIC CHANGE OF ALIBI IN THE MIDDLE OF THE TRIAL AND A KEY WITNESS WHO SUBSEQUENTLY COMMITTED SUICIDE, WHO KNOWS WHAT REALLY HAPPENED? WHAT IS CERTAIN IS THAT FEW NOW BELIEVE JAMES HANRATTY SHOULD HAVE HANGED.

The A6 Murder

John Fitzgerald Kennedy was sworn in as President of the United States in January 1961, just in time for his country to suffer humiliation both with the failure at the Bay of Pigs of an attempted invasion of Cuba and the Soviet Union's success in putting the first man in space. Cold War tensions increased as communists built the famous wall to seal off the Western sector of Berlin.

The Cold War, however, was the last thing on the minds of a young couple enjoying a drink at the Old Station Inn, Taplow, on the evening of 22 August 1961. It was more likely love which filled their thoughts when they left the Buckinghamshire village beside the Thames at about nine o'clock and drove through the village of Dorney to Marsh Lane, where they turned off to a quiet field they knew called Dorney Reach.

Sweeping down to the Thames, the cornfield was a favourite place for lovers to park, and the couple had been there several times before. They were Michael Gregsten, a scientist working at the nearby Road Research Laboratory, and Valerie Storie, a research assistant at the same laboratory. Theirs was a somewhat fraught affair, as Gregsten was married although living apart from his wife.

By half-past nine, it was completely dark, and they didn't see a man come up to their Morris Minor. The first they knew was when he tapped on the driver's window. A gun was thrust in.

'This is a hold-up,' he said, and got in the back seat. He said that his name was Jim and that he was on the run. He sat thinking until, at around 11.30, the gunman made Gregsten drive them towards Slough. He said that he was hungry. The terrifying ride took them through Slough, Hayes and Greenford, with the gunman directing where they should go. His instructions seemed to be pretty random, and near London Airport they had to stop for petrol. Two gallons were put in by an attendant, who didn't notice anything unusual about the occupants. Further on, the gunman allowed Gregsten to get out of the car to buy some cigarettes. With Valerie still a prisoner, Gregsten returned without attempting to escape.

Their back-seat kidnapper seemed to be directing them northwards, and they joined the A5 at St Albans and then the A6. Going through Luton, the still unseen gunman stopped talking about food and said he wanted to 'have a kip'. By then it was half-past one in the morning and they were still heading north. Searching for somewhere to park, the gunman twice made Gregsten turn off, but then told him to drive on again.

Eventually they came to the village of Clophill and drove up to Dead Man's Hill. At the top was a picnickers' lay-by and the gunman ordered Gregsten to stop the car there. Twice, Gregsten nervously overshot it, but the hidden gunman got angry and shouted at him to stop. Then he instructed Gregsten to turn the car round and turn off the lights.

He tied Valerie up and told Gregsten to pass over a bag from the front. Gregsten may have tried to throw it at him. The man fired two shots into the side and back of Gregsten's head, killing him instantly. Gregsten slumped. Valerie screamed: 'You shot him, you bastard.' The kidnapper replied: 'He frightened me. He moved too quick. Be quiet. I'm finking.'

Valerie noticed that he pronounced the word 'thinking' as 'finking', as many Cockneys do. Now he told her to join him in the back of the car, where he assaulted her. She had her one glimpse of his face in the headlights of a passing car. Then the gunman made her help drag out Gregsten's body, and show him how the gears of the car worked. She offered him a pound note and begged him to go. Instead, he fired two volleys of shots at her which knocked her to the ground. She pretended to be dead, and heard him get in the car and drive off.

DESCRIPTION TO STUDENT

At 6.34am a farm worker found Valerie Storie, still alive. He called to a student who was taking a traffic census, who flagged down a car to fetch the police. Before Valerie lost consciousness she described the

A6 murder victim Michael Gregsten who was shot in the head while out for an evening's drive with his girlfriend. He had been forced to drive at gunpoint for over four hours

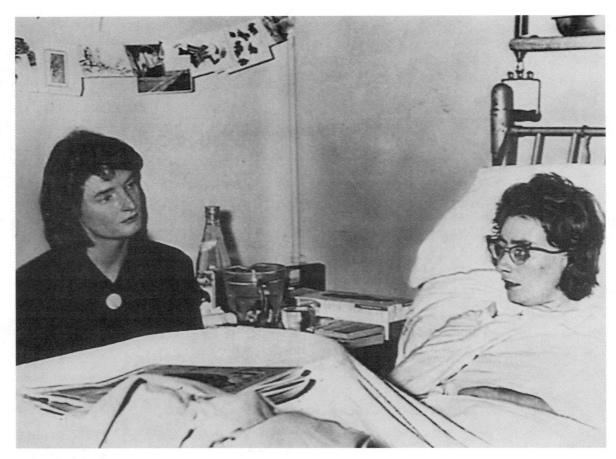

Valerie Storie (right) was raped, forced to drag her boyfriend's dead body from their car and then shot six times, leaving her paralysed from the waist down. Janet Gregsten (left), the murdered man's wife from whom he was separated, visited Valerie during her recovery, stating: 'She is my friend'

gunman. She said he was around 30, about 5ft 6in with a pale face and deep-set brown eyes. The student, John Kerr, said that she was pretty coherent considering the fact that she'd obviously been badly wounded: 'She was able to give a description of the man, she was able to tell me who she was, she was able to say that a gunman had held them up at Slough, or rather that she'd picked him up at Slough and that he'd held them up and shot her.'

A search turned up six cartridge cases. All of them must have been from bullets fired at Valerie, because when the car was found, two more cases were discovered in it, the ones from the bullets that killed Michael Gregsten.

Interviewed later the same day, Superintendent Morgan emphasised the age and eye colour of the man they wanted to find: 'We are anxious to trace a man of the following description: aged about 30 years; 5ft 6in; proportionate build; dark brown hair; palish face; brown eyes, very deep-set; straight

nose; wearing a dark long suit – either dark grey or black, believed to be a dark tie and shirt; and believed to have an East End London accent.'

That description became even more important when a controversy developed over the identity of the murderer.

The car was soon found near Redbridge tube station. Calls to the incident room fixed 7am as the time of its arrival there. It had been noticed being badly and erratically driven, but the description of the man driving differed so greatly from Valerie's memory of him that the police ended up with two conflicting identikit pictures.

The murder gun was discovered the following evening, 24 August. It was under the upstairs back seat of a 36A bus, whose route lay through the north-west London district of Maida Vale, which was soon to figure prominently in the inquiry. The police tried to find the person who had hidden it, but they drew a blank when they talked to passengers and bus crews.

On Sunday, 27 August, the detective who was now in charge of the murder hunt, Superintendent Robert Acott, issued an appeal to the public: 'Do you have a lodger who has not stirred out for the past few days?' His appeal bore fruit when the manager of the Alexandra Court Hotel, in Finsbury Park, phoned to say that a guest named Frederick Durrant had locked himself in. When questioned, this man admitted to police that his real name was Peter Louis Alphon. He was 31, with deep-set brown eyes. When asked about the night of the murder, Alphon claimed that he had met his mother and then slept at a hotel called the Vienna in Maida Vale.

CONFLICTING DESCRIPTIONS

It was at this stage that the police decided to issue the two identikit pictures to the press. But the task of identification was made more difficult by an unexpected development.

Valerie Storie was recovering and now out of danger in St Thomas Hospital, although she would be permanently paralysed from the waist down. On 31 August, she gave the police a new description of her attacker. Now she said that he had staring *icy-blue* eyes. Valerie was visited in hospital by her lover's widow, Janet Gregsten, whose family were said to have tried to break up the affair between Michael and Valerie. Janet explained: 'She is my friend. Mike and she had a lot in common.'

On 11 September, the manager of the Vienna found two cartridge cases in one of his rooms. They came from the A6 murder gun. A man who worked there, real name William Nudds but who had several aliases, made conflicting statements to the police. One of these implicated Peter Alphon and an identity parade was arranged on 24 September. Alphon was among the men lined up for Valerie to look at. But she picked out another man who couldn't have had anything at all to do with the A6 murder. So Peter Alphon was eliminated from Scotland Yard's inquiries, even though the police had already discredited the alibi given by his mother.

Police examining Michael Gregsten's Morris Minor which was found parked near Redbridge tube station. They found two cartridge cases from the bullets which had killed Gregsten

In all, William Nudds gave three contradictory statements to the police. In one of them he named another hotel guest who had stayed in the very room where the cartridge cases were found the night before the murder. This guest called himself James Ryan, but his real name was James Hanratty. Hanratty was already on the run for two burglaries. The police put out his description, and his family, anxious to clear him, went looking for him too.

In Blackpool, on 11 October, he was spotted by two policemen and detained when he came out of a café. He had dyed his hair.

Another identity parade was arranged, and this time Valerie thought to ask the men who were lined up to *speak*. She asked them to say: 'Be quiet will you, I'm thinking.' Then she picked out Hanratty, who was immediately arrested. Detective Superintendent Acott was satisfied that, this time, he had got the real killer. Hanratty had blue eyes.

James Hanratty was born in 1936, the eldest son of a Cockney girl who had married an Irishman. They were devout Roman Catholics and brought up their four sons strictly. His father, also named James, was a dustman and when Hanratty left school, where he was a slow learner, he joined his father's team. But he soon drifted into burglary and stealing cars.

One of his associates was Charlie France, known as Dixie, with whom he fell out after dating Dixie's 16-year-old daughter. France was to give damning evidence against Hanratty at his trial.

HANRATTY'S TRIAL OPENS

The trial began in Bedford, on 22 January 1962, despite objections from the defence that a local jury might be prejudiced. Michael Sherrard QC for the defence concentrated on discrediting the identification of James Hanratty, which the prosecution, led by Graham Swanwick QC, made the centre of their case.

The picnic area at Dead Man's Hill near the village of Clophill off the A6 where the two victims were left for dead by their attacker. A police search turned up six cartridge cases from the bullets fired at Valerie Storie

As well as Valerie Storie's absolute certainty at the identity parade, the prosecution produced another witness, John Skillett. He identified Hanratty as the man at the wheel of the murder car, which had been badly driven near Redbridge tube station. However, Skillett's front-seat passenger, Edward Blackhall, disagreed, and he *was* nearer the driver.

James Trower was another witness of the murder vehicle in Redbridge. He thought the driver was Hanratty. However, the most convincing witness was Valerie Storie, brought to Bedford in an ambulance. She impressed the court with her certainty in identifying Hanratty, although she had seen her rapist's face only for a moment.

The noose tightened around Hanratty's neck when 'Dixie' France testified that Hanratty had told him that a good hiding place was under the back seat of a bus. And also when William Nudds swore that when Hanratty had left the Vienna he had asked the way to the 36A bus stop.

It tightened further when a fellow prisoner, Roy Langdale, swore that Hanratty had confessed to him during exercise in Brixton Prison. His testimony, however, was strongly discredited in the courtroom by Michael Sherrard.

THE ALIBI PROBLEM

The defence evidence at this point seemed to be going well. But they suddenly had to cope with a change in Hanratty's alibi.

Hanratty had always claimed that he was in Liverpool on the night of the murder but he refused to say who he was with because they were fences and afraid of being identified. His only proof of being there was that he had called in at a sweet shop in Scotland Road and asked for directions. An assistant who was serving in the shop at the time, Mrs Olive Dinwoodie, confirmed that a man who looked like Hanratty had asked the way of her, but she wasn't sure which day it was.

James Hanratty, head covered, leaving court after being remanded in custody for the A6 murder. He had been picked out from an identity parade after being asked by the surviving victim to repeat a phrase used by the killer

Then, during the first week of the trial, Hanratty suddenly confided to his counsel that he wasn't in Liverpool on the night of the murder, after all. He had been in Rhyl, in North Wales, 40 miles away. The defence had almost no time to track down proof of the new alibi, but they did manage to find the house where he said he had stayed. They rushed Grace Jones, the landlady of Ingledene, where he claimed to have have spent the night in a bathroom, to Bedford, to give evidence on his behalf. But, without adequate preparation, she went to pieces in the witness box.

> ## "SOMEONE SOMEWHERE IS RESPONSIBLE AND ONE DAY THE TRUTH WILL COME OUT"
>
> James Hanratty

'I AM INNOCENT'

The trial lasted a month – at that time Britain's longest ever for murder. Mr Justice Gorman's summing up took another ten hours and by then, the jury had heard 600,000 words of evidence. It was out for six hours before it asked for a definition of reasonable doubt. Late in the evening it finally returned with the verdict: guilty on all counts. James Hanratty was sentenced to death by hanging. When asked if he had anything to say, he replied: 'I am innocent.'

Plans were immediately made for an appeal. Hanratty's parents, who never wavered in their belief in their son's innocence, devoted themselves to petitioning the Home Secretary of the day, Mr R.A. Butler. Some ninety thousand people signed the petition, reflecting a widespread feeling that convictions based mainly on identity parades were unsafe, and that hanging was horrifically final in a situation where there may be some doubt. But, when the petition was handed in at the Home Office, Mr Butler refused to commute the sentence, and when Hanratty's appeal was turned down the execution was set for 4 April.

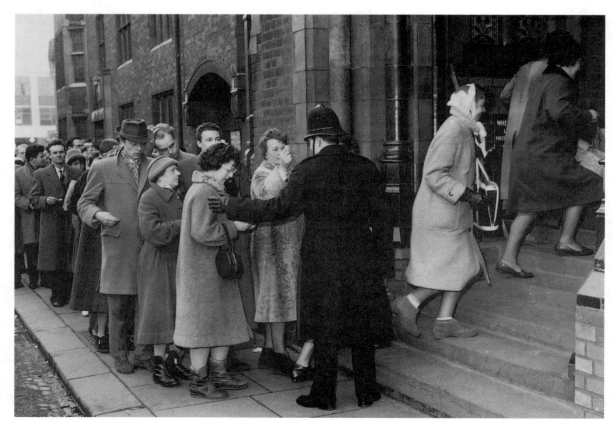

The A6 murder trial attracted huge public interest and, at that time in Britain, was the longest ever for murder. People queued for entry to the court each day of its month's duration

James Hanratty's father (front right) campaigned ceaselessly for his son's posthumous pardon, backed by such public figures as Yoko Ono and John Lennon

In a last letter to his brother Mick, Jim Hanratty wrote: 'I am going to ask you a small favour. That is to clear my name of this crime. Someone somewhere is responsible and one day the truth will come out.'

Crowds gathered on the morning of 4 April 1962 as James Hanratty was taken to be hanged. The two priests who attended him told his parents that he had protested his innocence to the very end.

His execution might have been the end of the story, except for the persistence of a committee that was formed to prove his innocence, and the boastfulness of Peter Alphon.

Over the following years, Hanratty's claim to have stayed in Rhyl on the night of the murder was greatly strengthened. Ivy Vincent remembered a young man she later identified from a photograph as Hanratty, knocking at her door to ask for lodgings. Betty Davies remembered a similar request, and one of the neighbours she mentioned it to was able to pinpoint the date. Christopher Larman recalled a man

with dyed hair asking where he could get bed and breakfast. Larman, too, was sure of the date.

Newspaper seller Charlie Jones remembered Hanratty asking him the way to the fairground, where he hoped to meet an old friend. The friend was Terry Evans. During the previous summer, he had told Hanratty that he knew a fellow who would buy stolen property.

Significantly, Hanratty's reason for going to Rhyl, he had said, was to fence a gold watch he had stolen. If these and other witnesses in Rhyl had testified to all this in court, would the jury have believed he could have got to the cornfield in Buckinghamshire in time to hold up Gregsten and Storie? Hanratty's father was certain they would not.

THE MYSTERIOUS ALPHON

Meanwhile, a French author named Jean Justice was stalking an earlier suspect in the case, the man who had apparently been cleared by the first identity

This is my son. JAMES HANRATTY. murdered by the state for the A.6. murder.

ELEVEN WITNESSES SWEAR HE WAS IN RHYL, 200 MILES AWAY, WHEN THE CRIME WAS COMMITTED.

I DEMAND A PUBLIC INQUIRY AND JUSTICE TO BE DONE

James Hanratty Sr (right) handing leaflets demanding a new inquiry of the A6 murder to passers-by outside the House of Commons in 1969. He died in 1978 without achieving his goal of an official pardon for his son

parade: Peter Alphon. Alphon was a professional gambler, aged 31, with deep-set hazel eyes, thus fitting Valerie Storie's original description. He, too, had a room at the Vienna Hotel. On the night of the murder he didn't come in until after 2am.

In 1967, Peter Alphon confirmed at a press conference in Paris that he was, indeed, the murderer. He repeated his confession later, being asked: 'So you are the man who fired two shots at Michael Gregsten and raped Valerie Storie and then fired at her?' Alphon replied: 'That's what I said at the press conference, and I'm going to stand by it.'

Suspicion had been diverted from him when Valerie didn't pick him out at the identity parade and later chose Hanratty, but he certainly looked strikingly like the first identikit picture.

At the interview, Alphon showed little remorse for the murder: 'All I know is that a gun was put into my hand, was sufficient if the need came, to destroy both of the people and Gregsten had gone with one shot. And as regards this Storie, I'm afraid that she had to go. A vital witness. As it turns out she wasn't, but we weren't to know that, and I'm afraid she went with the others.'

When pressed by reporters, Peter Alphon offered some bizarre explanations for his involvement: 'The Crusade was against indecency, immorality, those two things. That's enough, isn't it? I'd been forced to do it by the actions of these people, to bring it out in the open. The moral reason why I've confessed, and I said it at the press conference, is that I want to drag the name of British justice in the mud where it belongs. I think they neglected to say that at the press conference: where it belongs in the mud. Well, that's maybe a little bit hard for your audience, the general public, to appreciate, but as I've been charged with so many things that I haven't done, I would at last like to see the British police charge me with something that I have done.'

WITNESS COMMITS SUICIDE

In this scenario, 'Dixie' France was given the gun by Alphon, hid it under the bus seat, and planted the cartridges in the Vienna. When Hanratty was hanged, France committed suicide. Alphon also claimed that he had been paid £5,000 by an unknown party to break up the liaison between Mike and Valerie. To prove this, he showed his bank account to the journalist Paul Foot, who wrote a book on the case in 1971 called *Who Killed Hanratty?* It recorded an otherwise unexplained series of payments, totalling £7,569.

Another unexplained discrepancy in the case was Hanratty's acknowledged expertise as a car thief: would he really have had to be shown how to drive a Morris Minor? On the other hand, Peter Alphon was a hopeless driver, which would have accounted for the erratic driving noticed by witnesses when the murder car was being parked near Redbridge tube station. But, despite Alphon's confession and all the new evidence, the pleas for a posthumous pardon made by the A6 Murder Committee, backed by personalities such as Yoko Ono and John Lennon, went unheeded.

> ## "THE CRUSADE WAS AGAINST INDECENCY, IMMORALITY, THOSE TWO THINGS. THAT'S ENOUGH, ISN'T IT?"
>
> Peter Alphon's justfication
> for murder and rape

In 1974, an inquiry was set up by the Home Secretary of the day, Roy Jenkins, under a leading barrister. It sat in secret, and confirmed the jury's verdict.

Although permission was given for the remains of James Hanratty to be reburied in consecrated ground, his father died in 1978 without managing to clear his son's name – at least officially. But there can be few people today who believe that if all the evidence that has accumulated since the trial had been available during it, Hanratty would have been found guilty. With his alibi strengthened and the detailed confession of another suspect, it is extremely unlikely that he would have been prosecuted, let alone convicted and hanged for the A6 murder.

For some years, London's Madame Tussauds included James Hanratty among the murderers in its Chamber of Horrors. Then it put a question mark beside his effigy. Now it has removed him altogether.

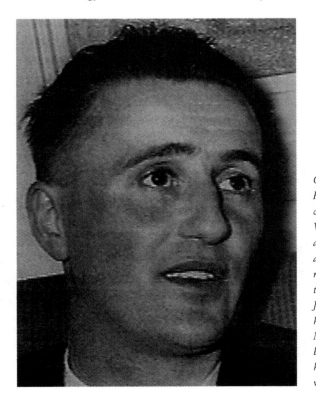

Original suspect Peter Alphon, who closely matched Valerie Storie's first description of her attacker, has repeatedly confessed to the crime for which James Hanratty hanged in 1962. No charge has ever been made against him in connection with the A6 murder

THE ASSASSINATION OF JOHN F. KENNEDY WAS PROBABLY THE BIGGEST NEWS STORY IN THE LIVES OF ALL THOSE THAT HEARD IT, AND OF COURSE IT IS A CLICHÉ THAT THEY ALL REMEMBER WHERE THEY WERE WHEN THEY DID SO. IT WAS INEVITABLE, AFTER THE SUPPOSED ASSASSIN WAS HIMSELF SLAIN, THAT RUMOURS AND INNUENDOS WOULD GROW UP AROUND THE EVENT. EVEN SO, IT IS REMARKABLE THAT AFTER A PRESIDENT'S COMMISSION STUDIED THE AFFAIR FOR MONTHS, A HOUSE SELECT COMMITTEE ON ASSASSINATIONS WAS REQUIRED TO INVESTIGATE AGAIN, COMING TO DIFFERENT CONCLUSIONS. IT SEEMS UNLIKELY NOW THAT THE WHOLE TRUTH WILL EVER BE KNOWN.

John F. Kennedy

The Assassination

By 1963 the Presidency of John F. Kennedy was showing some major achievements. A nuclear test ban treaty had been signed with the Soviet Union. The administration was solidly behind Martin Luther King's campaign for black civil rights. And the youthful President was internationally acclaimed as the West's leader.

On 22 November 1963, the President and his wife Jackie arrived at Love Field, Dallas, during a fundraising trip to Texas. It was a sunny day and the President had asked for the protective bubble top of his limousine to be removed.

At 12.29 the motorcade entered Dealey Plaza. At 12.30 there was a shot. The President's waving hand froze. There was another shot and he reached for his throat.

Jackie scrambled over the back of the car and was pushed back by an agent who jumped on. At least three shots were fired, one shattering the President's head.

As the President's car raced away to a hospital, one of the police motorcyclists dismounted and ran into the Texas Book Depository, believing the shots to have come from there. A spectator told a police-man that he had seen a calm young man firing from the sixth floor of the Depository. An employee, Lee Harvey Oswald, slipped out of the building.

Meanwhile, at Parkland Memorial Hospital, a doctor opened a wound in the front of the President's neck and inserted a tube in an effort to keep him alive. But at 1.03 President Kennedy was dead and a wave of grief spread across Dallas, the United States and the world.

At 2.38 Lyndon B. Johnson was sworn in as President, with Jackie standing beside him in a blood-stained suit. They took off for Washington with Jack Kennedy's body.

A Dallas police patrolman, J.D. Tippit, heard a description of the now hunted Lee Harvey Oswald. At 1.16 Tippit was shot dead in the street while talk-ing to a man who then ran away.

At 1.40 Oswald slipped into a cinema without paying. The police came and arrested him for Tippit's murder and took him to Dallas police headquarters to be interrogated.

A rifle found at the Depository proved to have been bought by Oswald.

Meanwhile, John F. Kennedy's body arrived in Washington. Only now was it taken for a full post-mortem examination to Bethesda Naval Hospital.

Two days later, a van waited to transfer Lee Harvey Oswald to the county jail. But as he was led out, an astonishing scene erupted on the nation's tele-vision screens. A man stepped out from the group of newsmen in the basement of the local jail and fired a single shot from a .38 revolver directly into Oswald's side. The TV commentator shouted: 'He's been shot. He's been shot. Lee Oswald has been shot.'

Oswald's executioner was Jack Ruby, a night-club owner and intimate of both cops and hoodlums. Somehow he had got into the police garage and pushed his way through to the prisoner. He said it was to spare Jackie Kennedy the pain of testifying.

Ruby had also been present at a press conference at police headquarters the night before. At his trial in 1964 he was sentenced to death, but this was later

reversed in 1966. He was preparing for a new trial when he died of cancer in 1967.

Lee Harvey Oswald was rushed to the Parkland Memorial Hospital where he died, just two days and seven minutes after John Kennedy.

THE WARREN COMMISSION
On 19 November, President Lyndon Johnson set up a President's Commission, headed by the Chief Justice of the Supreme Court, Earl Warren, to investigate the crime. The Warren Commission consisted of seven politicians and public servants. It took months to hear 552 witnesses, and concluded that Lee Harvey Oswald, hating his country and acting alone, was responsible for the assassination of the President. There were no conspiracies – in particular, neither the Russians nor the Cubans were involved.

Using FBI men as stand-ins, the Commission reconstructed the Presidential car's progress and decided that Oswald had fired three shots, taking between 4.8 and 5.6 seconds. His rifle needed at least 2.3 seconds to load and fire.

At the Depository the motorcade's route made it slow down. Hidden behind a pile of boxes, Oswald had a perfect target, and fired. He fired again, aiming

John F. Kennedy waving to the cheering crowds in Dallas shortly before the first shots were fired. Jackie Kennedy is sitting next to her husband and in front of them are Texas Governor John Connally, who was also hit by a bullet, and his wife

Depository by the front door, while police discovered the gun, a Mannlicher-Carcano. It had been bought by Oswald for $21.45 under a false name.

One of the bullets it fired was found at the hospital in almost pristine condition. The Commission reckoned that this was the bullet which had hit both Kennedy and Connally and that it had retained its shape despite passing through bone and muscle.

The Commission also concluded that Oswald killed Tippit when the patrolman had got out of his car to confront him. Oswald shot Tippit in the head, chest and stomach, and ran to the cinema, reloading his revolver. He was spotted, the place surrounded, and he was arrested.

At a chaotic midnight press conference, Oswald denied any part in both the Kennedy and Tippit homicides, saying: 'I never killed anybody, no sir!' and complaining that he was just a 'patsy'.

He remained consistent throughout his interrogation, denying that photographs of him were genuine and refusing to take a lie detector test.

LEE HARVEY OSWALD

Born in New Orleans in 1939, Lee Oswald never took school seriously. At 17, he joined the marines and learned sharpshooting. Assigned to Japan, he studied Russian. In 1959, he left the marines, defected to Russia, married and brought his wife back to Texas.

The Commission concluded that he was a militant left-winger there, accepting photographs as proof, including one showing him handing out pro-Castro leaflets. But sceptics later said he was merely attempting to infiltrate the movement.

The conclusions of the Warren Commission were first greeted with relief, but not everyone was convinced. Jim Garrison, the District Attorney of New Orleans, was among the earliest critics of the Commission. He believed that the assassination was a plot by dissident elements in the CIA: 'I believe the Warren Commission was wrong and that it will be shown to be wrong.'

Garrison was swiftly followed by a host of other critics who began to point out major inconsistencies

The rifle allegedly used by Lee Harvey Oswald in the JFK shooting. None of the expert sharpshooters who tried to reenact the shooting were able to load, aim and fire the gun accurately in the allotted time

just to the right of the President's backbone. This second bullet entered Kennedy's back, emerging just below the Adam's apple. It then hit Governor John Connally, who was in the car with the President, entering his right shoulder, passing through his chest, hitting his right wrist and coming to rest in his left thigh. The fact that one bullet hit both men explained the damage done by only three shots. The third shot shattered Kennedy's skull. He fell limp into Jackie's lap. She cried out: 'Oh my God, they killed my husband!' Blood covered the back seat of the car.

The Commission concluded that a hole in the windscreen of the car was probably made by the third bullet. One of the bullets – probably the first, thought the Commission – missed its target and finished up hitting the ground ahead of the car.

The Commission then reckoned that Oswald hid his rifle and raced down five flights of stairs to the lunchroom, where he met the policeman coming up. No shots came from anywhere else, according to the Warren Commission. It believed that Oswald left the in the detailed scenario put forward by the Warren Commission. Soon new theories abounded and calls were being made for fresh investigations.

OBJECTIONS TO THE REPORT

Among the many objections to the Commission's conclusions, one concerned the extraordinary path it claimed was taken by what was mockingly labelled the 'magic bullet'. Could it really have caused seven wounds, *and* turned corners and *yet* remained almost intact? If it didn't the short time-span of the firing meant there *had* to be a *second* gunman, probably firing from in front of the car. To avoid reaching that inconvenient judgement, the Commission ignored the failure of expert sharpshooters to aim and fire a cheap rifle like Oswald's accurately in the allotted time. And his rifle had proved to have defective sights!

Photographic evidence showed that President Kennedy jerked backwards when he was hit. To most people this suggested that he was hit from the front. Believers in a single gunman said that the brace he wore for a back injury forced his head backwards although he was hit from behind. However, if this were so, why were the two motorcycle riders behind him covered in his blood?

No fewer than 51 people said they had heard shots coming from a grassy knoll in front of the car. At least eight people reported seeing puffs of smoke.

At the hospital, there was no immediate confusion over which of Kennedy's wounds were caused by bullets going in and which by bullets coming out. The doctors were sure that the wound in his throat was an entrance wound. If so, the shot came from in front of him. But a rumour was soon going round that the body had been tampered with during the flight or in the ambulance taking it to Bethesda Naval Hospital. The head wound was significantly smaller in Dallas than in Washington. And although the corpse left wrapped in sheets, it was reported to have arrived in a zippered bag.

Another area of controversy was on whose side Lee Oswald had been working when he handed out

A photograph taken immediately after the shooting: the white arrow points to Kennedy's foot protruding over the side of the car and the black arrow to Texas Governor John Connally's wife trying to shield her injured husband. Security officer Clinton Hill climbed onto the car to try to protect its occupants

In all, 51 people gave evidence that they had heard shots fired from the grassy knoll in front of the President's car and eight of them also said they saw puffs of smoke there. In 1979 the Select Committee on Assassinations used acoustical evidence from radio recordings to confirm that the third of the four shots must have come from the knoll

pro-Castro leaflets in New Orleans. The Commission accepted these on their face value, but there is strong evidence that he was actually allied to anti-Castro activists. And the Commission ignored Jack Ruby's underworld ties. But might Ruby not have been acting under orders to prevent the 'patsy' from revealing a conspiracy?

A NEW COMMITTEE

All these questions worried America, and in 1976 over 80 per cent of people polled said they believed that Oswald was not alone. Congress felt obliged to act and set up a Select Committee on Assassinations. This was triggered by two revelations. One was that a letter from Oswald had been destroyed after his death. It was to FBI agent James Hosty, who had been involved with Oswald in New Orleans, but Hosty had failed to mention it to the Warren Commission.

The other catalyst was the discovery that the CIA had masterminded several attempts on the life of Fidel Castro, suggesting a rogue element within this government agency.

The former President, Gerald Ford, a member of the Warren Commission, told the Committee that

knowing of these attempts would have broadened the Commission's original investigation: 'If we had known of the assassination plans or attempts by an agency of the federal government it certainly would have required that the Commission extend its inquiry into those kinds of operations by an agency of the federal government.'

Yes, there had been a fourth shot, the House Select Committee concluded in its report of January 1979. It deduced this from tape recordings taken over microphones of the Dallas police radio networks that had been open at the time of the shooting. Advanced acoustical equipment pinpointed the grassy knoll as the source of the third of four shots.

The Committee determined that at least one other gunman had been firing. Its other major conclusion was that there probably had been a conspiracy, but that neither the CIA nor the FBI were involved.

THE CONSPIRACY THEORIES

So who were the conspirators? If Oswald didn't plan the assassination, who did? A wide choice has been suggested over the years, one of the first being the Soviet Union. After all, Oswald had defected there in

1959 and had married the niece of a colonel some said was in the KGB, bringing her back with him. He had spent time in New Orleans, involved with Cubans. But although he appeared to be an unrepentant left-wing activist, perhaps he was really an anti-communist agent?

In a well-publicised photo Lee Harvey Oswald is apparently clutching a rifle and two Marxist publications, but he claimed in his statement to the Dallas police that it was a fake. There is in fact evidence for this in the conflicting directions of the shadows on his face and on the ground.

It has been suggested that the CIA sent him to Russia. Perhaps he was really one of its moles? Certainly, while he was in New Orleans, Oswald had links with people suspected of working for the CIA. These included Guy Banister, a former FBI agent.

> ## "I BELIEVE THE WARREN COMMISSION WAS WRONG AND THAT IT WILL BE SHOWN TO BE WRONG"
>
> New Orleans DA Jim Garrison

Oswald used Banister's address for the Fair Play for Cuba Committee. Another contact was a pilot, David Ferrie, who had known Oswald when he was a teenager. He flew missions into Cuba for the CIA.

One theory says that certain renegade elements within the Agency used Oswald as their patsy. The CIA did claim that Oswald went to Mexico City to get visas to go to Cuba and the Soviet Union. But when asked for a photo that they had taken of him there, they produced one of somebody who was clearly not Lee Harvey Oswald.

COINCIDENTAL DEATHS

Ferrie died soon after being implicated in the case, supposedly from a ruptured blood vessel, but it was noted that his was only one of more than 20 other mysterious deaths of people connected with the aftermath of the assassination.

Among them were writer Dorothy Kilgkallen, who had claimed to be about to 'blow the assassination wide open'; Tom Howard, Jack Ruby's lawyer, friend and confidante, from a heart attack; reporter Bill Hunter, who interviewed Howard, and who was shot dead in a California police station; Jim Keothe, the only other writer to interview Howard, killed by a karate chop from an intruder; and Hank Killam, who hinted at a link between Ruby and Oswald, and who had his throat cut.

The possibility of a conspiracy becomes more believable when it is appreciated that Jack Kennedy and his brother Robert were not the universally popular heroes that legend has transformed them into. Those in the clan of the President's father, Joe Kennedy, were widely distrusted as opportunists who bought their way to power. Joe Kennedy called in countless favours to win his son's nomination, and spent millions to win the Presidency.

Jack was undoubtedly a skilled and charismatic orator, and a man who seemed to personify a new

This photograph, published at the time of the assassination, shows Lee Harvey Oswald holding a rifle and two Marxist publications. Oswald claimed that it was a fake and the conflicting directions of the shadows on the ground and on his face give his assertion some credibility

minute withdrawal of air support. So both sides could have had a motive – in particular the exiles, since by 1963 Kennedy was showing himself ready to compromise with Castro. He was able to do so because he had proved his toughness a few months before when Cuba once more became a critical flashpoint.

On that particular occasion the Soviet leader Nikita Khrushchev attempted to install nuclear missiles on the island. This time the young President made no mistakes. He refused to back down in his determination to get them removed. He announced a blockade of the island. Then he showed that he would be ready to launch a full-scale attack. Khrushchev backed down and might possibly have sought revenge. But Kennedy was soon back negotiating a test ban treaty with him.

SOUTHERN HOSTILITY

No one was more bitter at Kennedy's betrayal of the Cuban exiles than the team known as Operation Mongoose, which he had set up to co-ordinate anti-Castro activities. One of the most popular theories with conspiracy researchers is that Oswald was a low-level naval intelligence agent, set up as a patsy by Mongoose members.

One group which was particularly hostile to the President was the Southerners of the far right. Not only were the Kennedys showing themselves soft on communism and in favour of civil rights for black citizens, but Kennedy had hurt their pockets by scaling back oil depletion tax credits. He had also fired their local military hero, General Edwin Walker, for handing out right-wing literature to his troops.

There was also the belief that Jack Kennedy was preparing to dump Vice President Lyndon Johnson, one of the South's most powerful politicians, for the 1964 election. The strength of some Southerners' feelings was apparent in a handbill given out just before Kennedy arrived in Dallas.

Another group with a motive to slay Kennedy, and one whose members were experts in murder and could have set up the assassination, was the Mafia. Chicago boss Sam Giancana had swung the 1960

The Kennedy funeral: Jacqueline Kennedy flanked by her husband's brothers Edward (left) and Robert (right) and her two children Caroline and John

spirit for America, but in his efforts to win votes he made promises he could not always keep, and sometimes left supporters disappointed – perhaps bitter enough for revenge. He also made powerful enemies by his actions as President.

Cuban refugees were led to believe that with Jack Kennedy in power they would soon be back on their island, with the communists defeated. Through incompetence or misjudgement, it never happened. The President's sincerity and dedication were not enough. Instead came the humiliation of the Bay of Pigs, when a CIA-sponsored attempt to land a force of exiles on Cuba ended in disaster.

While Castro crowed and swore vengeance, the exiles blamed the 1961 catastrophe on Kennedy's last-election to Kennedy with extra votes cast in his key state of Illinois. He believed he had increased his hold over Kennedy when his girlfriend, Judith Exner, had had an affair with the President.

However, instead of being grateful the Kennedys began to threaten organised crime. Attorney General Bobby Kennedy had vowed to jail their union link, Teamster boss Jimmy Hoffa. Bobby was appalled when his investigations of Hoffa showed how widely the Mafia had corrupted American labour and commercial life. Alongside his campaign to jail Hoffa he began to go after the leading Mafia bosses.

Godfather Carlos Marcello had been temporarily deported by Bobby. He repeatedly threatened to kill both Kennedys. Some say he employed French hitmen in Dallas. Hoffa is known to have sent a message to Marcello saying: 'This has to be done.'

J. Edgar Hoover, the longtime head of the FBI and no friend of Kennedy, did all he could to bolster the belief that Lee Harvey Oswald had acted alone. Questions came to be asked as to whether Hoover was protecting the Bureau. In the six months before Dallas, the FBI had logged some 400 threats to the President's life. Which of these – if any – came to fruition? The Warren Commission's view that it was just one lone madman named Lee Harvey Oswald now seems completely discredited.

The House Assassinations Committee's report, with its acceptance that there had been a conspiracy, seemed to pave the way for a comprehensive investigation. But over the past 15 years there has been no official attempt to answer the questions first asked by Jim Garrison: 'Just keep in mind who profited most from the assassination. Then ask yourself some questions. Who appointed the members of the Warren Commission? And who runs the CIA which has concealed a tremendous amount of evidence? And who runs the FBI?'

On 25 November 1963, John Fitzgerald Kennedy was buried at Arlington National Cemetery. A million mourners lined the streets of Washington and countless millions more joined them through television. It seemed that the finest hopes of a generation were

Funeral procession leaving the Capitol in Washington where the President's body had been lying in state on the Lincoln Catafalque

being buried that day. What cannot be in doubt is that the assassin or assassins had changed history.

Rumour and conspiracy theories have raged since then and all the inconsistencies of the official reports continue to be examined. But what now seems uncertain is whether a final answer to one of the century's greatest mysteries can ever be given.

The shooting of Lee Harvey Oswald by Jack Ruby. He died at Parkland Memorial Hospital where John F. Kennedy had died just two days and seven minutes before

FOR WELL OVER 100 YEARS, THE BIZARRE FIGURES OF

KU KLUX KLAN HAVE STRUCK TERROR INTO BLACK PEOPLE.

THE FULL-LENGTH GOWNS, FACE MASKS AND POINTED

WITCHES' HATS, TOGETHER WITH BURNING CROSSES, WERE

DESIGNED TO FRIGHTEN UNEDUCATED BLACKS. AND THERE

WAS SUBSTANCE IN THE THREATS, AS HUNDREDS OF BLACK

PEOPLE WERE LYNCHED BY THE SINISTER ORGANISATION

THAT AT TIMES COULD BOAST FIVE MILLION MEMBERS. AS

RECENTLY AS 1964, LOCAL POLICE IN NESHOBA COUNTY

ARROGANTLY CONNIVED WITH THE KLAN IN THE MURDER

OF WORKERS OF THE CONGRESS OF RACIAL EQUALITY.

The KKK Killings

There were new world leaders in 1964, both in the Kremlin, where Leonid Brezhnev and Alexander Kosygin seized power in a bloodless coup, and in the United States, where Lyndon Johnson became President, annihilating challenger Barry Goldwater. Britain was also welcoming a new leader, Prime Minister Harold Wilson, and Johnson soon met with him in Washington.

But Johnson was facing real problems at home and abroad. US involvement in Vietnam was increasing with naval forces patrolling off the coast. And at home there was trouble as the country struggled towards racial equality for all its citizens.

A leading role in the opposition to racial equality was played by the Ku Klux Klan, formed 99 years earlier when white Southerners banded together to confront blacks freed from slavery.

In the 1960s there came renewed demands for real equality for blacks. On 3 July 1964 President Johnson signed a Civil Rights Act into law.

Some months before this, three young men had started working in Mississippi to help blacks claim their new rights. Mickey Schwerner, a 24-year-old white man from Pelham, New York, had been working with CORE, the Congress of Racial Equality, for over six months. Andy Goodman was a 20-year-old white student from Queens College, New York, anxious to take part in some positive action. Their companion was black – Jim Chaney, a local boy from Meridian, Mississippi, who found respect for his colour in the civil rights movement.

The boys were repeatedly harassed by local police, finally being arrested on a charge of speeding and taken to Neshoba County Jail in Mississippi. The police records showed that they had been released at about ten o'clock and they drove off in their car. This was discovered the next day, but everyone denied knowing where the boys might be. The FBI was called in, but it wasn't until six weeks later that their bodies were found, buried in an earthen dam nearby. They had been shot. Although the FBI had received a tip-off, they were still up against a wall of silence.

There was a national outcry, with the Reverend Martin Luther King leading demands for speedy justice: 'I think that it is urgent, and it is important, for the federal government, through the FBI, to use all of its resources to discover who killed those men.'

Twenty-one suspected Ku Klux Klansmen were arrested, including the sheriff and deputy sheriff of the county, but at their arraignment they showed justifiable confidence that the charges against them would be dismissed.

This confidence reflected the tradition of white supremacy which had been reborn after the setback of the defeat of the Confederacy in 1865. In the devastated Southern states, former slaves were encouraged to assert their rights. Many sought revenge on former slave owners and their families.

THE BIRTH OF THE KU KLUX KLAN

There was a rapid backlash. At the end of 1865 a group of young ex-Confederate officers met at the town of Pulaski in Tennessee to found a secret society, the Kyklos Klan. They adopted bizarre ghost-like costumes which included full-length gowns and overall face masks designed to frighten uneducated and superstitious blacks, and set out to hunt down any they suspected of harassing and oppressing whites.

Within three years there were Klans in most Southern states with more than half-a-million members. The familiar pointed white hats had appeared and the local emblems and crosses worn on the robes.

Klansmen believed that their movement had begun with high ideals, but the punishments they meted out quickly turned to atrocities. The Klan was outlawed by Congress and by the mid-1870s it had virtually died away. However, white supremacy had been firmly re-established in the former Confederate states, with the blacks being kept both separate and impoverished. The massive waves of immigration which brought millions to the United States at the end of the 19th century kept alive the fears of many poor whites in the cities and Southern states that they would be overwhelmed by non-Anglo Saxons. Newspaper stories and cartoons encouraged and spread the fear of Negro rule.

The spark for the resurrection of the Ku Klux Klan came with the success of *The Birth of a Nation*, the first silent film spectacular made by Southerner

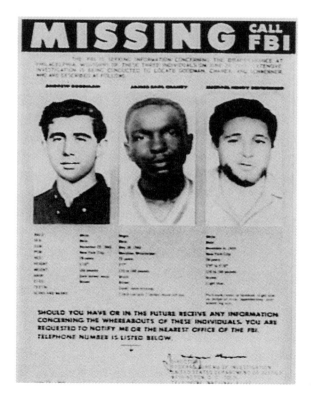

(l to r) Andy Goodman, Jim Chaney and Mickey Schwerner, the three civil rights workers for the Congress of Racial Equality who were murdered as they passed through Neshoba County in Mississippi

By the early 1920s the Ku Klux Klan could boast as many as five million members and 8 August 1925 witnessed the horrifying spectacle of 40,000 KKK members marching through the streets of Washington

D.W. Griffith. This idealistic portrayal of the Klan appeared in 1915, and showed scenes of black violence as former slaves revenged themselves on their owners. Whether deliberately or not, Griffith was reflecting widespread fears in the South of another challenge to white supremacy and the need to band together against this.

By the early 1920s the Klan was able to claim a membership of no fewer than five million people. Its objects of hatred had by now broadened from just blacks to include Roman Catholics, Jews, all foreigners and organised labour. The Klan, with its threatening burning crosses, became an integral part of Southern life, although it was always locally based with several competing organisations. Its members regarded themselves as the militant defenders of white values.

At this period of its existence, the Ku Klux Klan was almost respectable. Local businessmen and civic leaders in the Southern states openly joined its ranks, and being a Ku Klux Klan member didn't stop a young lawyer named Hugo L. Black from later becoming a

Justice of the Supreme Court, despite the fact that Klansmen frequently took the law into their own hands. Each year during the 1920s and 1930s saw several lynchings.

Washington was the scene of an amazing spectacle on 8 August 1925 as 40,000 members of the KKK marched through its streets. Many of them waved American and Confederate flags to demonstrate their patriotism. Only the arrival of heavy rain dissuaded them from carrying burning crosses, but at the head of the procession robed marchers formed a huge white cross.

However, it was to turn out that the Washington march was the peak of the Klan's power. Later that year, the Grand Dragon of its Indiana branch – or 'Realm' – was the centre of a scandal involving the rape and death of a young woman. When his 'Grand Wizard' expelled him from the Klan, he retaliated by revealing the Klan's political links and corruption. During the 1930s membership swiftly fell to around two million, and the Klans sought allies in other organisations on the far right.

A natural companion was found in the Nazi-inspired German-American Bund, which had a similar hate-list of blacks, Jews, Catholics, socialists and trade unionists. On 18 August 1940, the two organisations had a joint meeting, at which the Klan sang Nazi marching songs and the American Nazis burned a forty-foot cross. And when Fritz Kuhn, America's would-be Führer, spoke at a rally of the Bund at Madison Square Garden, Klansmen were able to participate in some of the action they so much enjoyed: beating up dissenters.

THE WAR CEMENTS OPPOSITION

When the United States went to war against fascism in 1941, the extremism of the Klan came to be seen as un-American and unpatriotic. However, when the war ended, the South to which soldiers returned was as poverty-stricken and prejudiced as when they had gone away.

Although nationally the leading Klan had been bankrupted in 1944 for not paying $685,000 in taxes, local replicas soon sprang up to defend the Southern way of life. They were patronisingly friendly to blacks who 'knew their place', but more often they warned that there were dangerous agitators around who wanted to end such Southern traditions as maintaining segregated facilities. The Klansmen prepared to take action against them.

Not all the troublemakers who opposed the ideal of the Klan came from the North. Many blacks and some Southern whites who had served in the armed forces had been affected by all the promises of equality after the war. Now they were demanding equal, not separate rights. There was a movement to boycott the segregated buses. In May 1954, the Supreme Court overturned a hundred-year ruling that blacks and whites could be legally educated at separate schools. But integration didn't happen overnight.

LITTLE ROCK

It was three years later, in April 1957, that nine black children enrolled at the high school in Little Rock, Arkansas. President Dwight Eisenhower had to send a thousand troops to escort the children to school and to maintain order among the objectors.

The crowd was inflamed by speeches from Klan sympathisers talking of dragging the black children out of the high school and lynching them, but the President sent in the troops, saying: 'Mob rule cannot be allowed.' The Klans reacted with terrorism: kidnapping, murder, castration, and bombing black homes, schools and churches.

During the 1950s, dozens of small Klans had sprung up again, many of them bitter rivals. But by 1961 most of them had been consolidated by Robert Shelton of Alabama as the United Klans of America. Politicians such as Governor Barnett of Mississippi echoed its beliefs: 'There is no case in history where the caucasian race has survived social integration. We will not drink from the cup of genocide.'

The Ku Klux Klan was sometimes patronisingly friendly to blacks who 'knew their place', such as this 107-year-old former slave and his wife for whom they arranged a visit from Father Christmas

The pressure for racial integration was maintained when James Meredith became the first black student to register at the University of Mississippi, on 1 October 1962. Federal troops were needed to hold off hostile whites, who included Klansmen imported from as far away as Florida. Two people were killed and 200 arrested.

By June 1963 unrest was coming to such a crescendo that President Kennedy went on television to confirm his determination to enforce civil rights. That same night, in Jackson, Mississippi, Medgar Evers, a field officer working for the NAACP, the National Association for the Advancement of Colored People, was shot and killed. Byron De La Beckworth was tried twice for Evers' murder but both trials ended with a hung jury.

Then, on 28 August 1963, came the largest ever civil rights demonstration, when 200,000 marchers in Washington heard Dr Martin Luther King tell of his dream of an equal and fair non-racial America.

> "THERE IS NO CASE IN HISTORY WHERE THE CAUCASIAN RACE HAS SURVIVED SOCIAL INTEGRATION. WE WILL NOT DRINK FROM THE CUP OF GENOCIDE"
>
> Governor Barnett of Mississippi

But the reality in the South remained violent. Eighteen days after Dr King's speech, the 16th Street Baptist Church in Birmingham, Alabama, was bombed. Four teenage girls were killed. It was twelve years before the state of Alabama finally indicted Robert E. Chambliss and two other renegades from Birmingham's Eastview Klavern for the bombing of the church and the murder of the four girls.

Throughout 1964, the pressure mounted for full integration in the South. Civil rights workers came from all over the US to persuade stores to hire black labour and to enrol voters. They followed the precepts of Martin Luther King. He had learned from the success of Gandhi in India in using passive resistance. Moral pressure was applied without violence, while still causing the maximum possible disturbance.

THE FREEDOM SCHOOLS

Among these volunteer civil rights workers were people like Mickey Schwerner and Andy Goodman, joined by local black activists such as Jim Chaney. They set up freedom schools to teach black people who wanted to pass the literacy test for voting. Mount Zion Church in Longdale was going to house a freedom school until it was burnt down. The three activists went to check out the ruins. It was then that they were arrested for speeding, released, and never seen again. Their burnt-out station wagon was soon found just off the road but there was no sign of the three men.

Faced with the indifference of local lawmen, the FBI sent in its agents and troops to find out what had happened to the three men. Frustrated, they scoured the countryside and dragged the rivers. Forty-three days later, the FBI got an anonymous tip that their bodies were buried in an earthern dam. They excavated 18 feet down, and found them.

On 4 December, the FBI arrested the sheriff of Neshoba County, his deputy and 19 others, and charged them with violation of the murdered men's rights. Since murder is a local crime, not a federal one, conspiracy was the only charge that the FBI could bring. Sheriff Lawrence Rainey was confident that he would escape any punishment, and at first his confidence seemed well-founded. He and all the defendants were freed, even though one of them confessed. The local court ruled that the confession was inadmissible as evidence. The prosecution tried again, and when they finally came to trial in 1967 at Meridian, Mississippi, the truth behind the Mississippi murders emerged.

CONSPIRACY OF KLAN AND THE LAW

The trio had been arrested on a pre-arranged plan to 'get' Mickey Schwerner. They had been held in jail by the deputy sheriff just long enough for the Klansmen to assemble. Then they were allowed to go. They were followed down a highway nearby, their car was stopped and they were all shot.

When the trial finally ended on 20 October 1967 eight of the accused were acquitted, three were released because of a hung jury, and seven were found guilty. Even so, they were immediately freed on a $5,000 bond.

The sheriff and deputy sheriff of Neshoba County, on trial in connection with the murdered civil rights workers, showed justifiable confidence that they would not be found guilty of the charges against them

But pressure on the Klans was now becoming intense, with outspoken speeches by politicians such as Vice President Hubert Humphrey: 'The truth of the matter is when the dignity of one American is denied, all of us have been denied.'

The FBI increased its offensive to infiltrate the ranks of the Klan. Its action brought this muddled response from Sam Bowers, head of the White Knights of Mississippi, who was later to be convicted of the Neshoba killings: 'Now we are met here on the basis of a great struggle. The FBI Anti-Christ system of Nicholas Kassambach has come in here, has been harassing us for a long time. They've now made their move to try to bring a group of white Christians, slaughtered them on the altar of the nigger revolution.'

MORE MURDERS

On 23 March 1965, a carload of Klansmen drew alongside Mrs Viola Liuzzo as she was returning from a civil rights march in Selma, Alabama. They shot her

and her black companion dead. A few days later, the FBI arrested four men but were still only able to charge them with the federal crime of conspiracy to infringe Mrs Liuzzo's civil rights.

That same day President Johnson went on television to denounce the Klans. He ordered the FBI to take every possible step to cripple them.

It later emerged that the FBI had been able to close in on Mrs Liuzzo's killers so swiftly because one of their informers had been in the car with the Klansmen. With his face carefully concealed he later described what had happened: 'We subsequently followed the vehicle down the freeway. Apparently the woman realised she was being followed: she accelerated to a highway speed of over 90–100 miles an hour. The Klan automobile pulled up beside her. Two Klansmen fired shots into the vehicle resulting in the death of both people. To my knowledge the woman was killed instantly and the black man in the front seat was killed instantly.'

The FBI had launched a major campaign to infiltrate the Klan, both to identify members and to stir up rivalry and suspicion among those members and between the various Klaverns. Although immensely successful, it was on occasions criticised for being provocative and causing unnecessary violence.

On 7 June 1965 James Meredith, whose registration at the University of Mississippi had been such a significant landmark two-and-a-half years previously, was part of a civil rights march from Memphis, Tennessee, to Jackson, Mississippi, to encourage blacks to register as voters. As the march neared the Mississippi town of Hernando, there was a sudden shot and Meredith fell, wounded in the back.

Police almost reluctantly arrested a man found carrying a gun by the roadside: 'Did you shoot Melvin? . . . What's your name, buster? . . . Get in the car . . .' were questions and instructions issued with the same urgency as if the offence had concerned parking. James Norvell was driven away and the march later resumed.

SETBACKS TO THE KLAN

Although race riots struck many US cities, the FBI campaign was beginning to succeed in breaking up the Klans. Another major blow to the Klans came from an unexpected quarter in 1967, when the House Committee on Un-American Activities sent Robert Shelton to jail for contempt. The Committee condemned the Ku Klux Klan for both its activities and its misuse of funds.

Another serious setback came in 1972 when one of the Klan's most influential friends, Governor George Wallace of Alabama, was speaking at a campaign rally. A gunman named Arthur Bremer, who had been tracking Wallace, was able to get close enough to shoot at point-blank range. Wallace was hit in the stomach, shoulders, arm and spine, and was never able to walk again.

> "THE TRUTH OF THE MATTER IS WHEN THE DIGNITY OF ONE AMERICAN IS DENIED, ALL OF US HAVE BEEN DENIED"
>
> Vice President Hubert Humphrey

Despite the occasional burning cross, it looked by the early 1970s as if the Klan had no function left. Membership dropped and the average age fell as older members died. It continued to put on the occasional show, but by now even the costumes failed to scare when paraded in the sunlight. Civil rights had ceased to be a massive public issue. Legally at least blacks were now the equal of whites throughout America. The Klan fragmented into rival groups which resorted to tactics of harassment. But despite the threats the Klan could do little to hold back a steady growth in black confidence.

Of the six main Klan groups at that time, the largest was Invisible Empire, Knights of the Ku Klux Klan. This was led by David Duke, a graduate of the Nazi-style White People's Party. His approach was to make the Klan look responsible and reasonable. He later abandoned the Klan, and ran both for Governor of Louisiana and as Presidential candidate.

Duke's arch rival in the Klan power struggle was extremist Bill Wilkinson. He rejected David Duke's 'respectable' approach, used violent rhetoric and surrounded himself with armed bodyguards.

These strongarm tactics meant that for many blacks the threat was still there, as indeed it was for any whites who offended Klan leaders. Then, in 1979, came two incidents which seemed to herald a resurgence of the Klans.

GUN BATTLES

At Decatur in Alabama marchers were protesting against the conviction for rape of a black youth named Tommy Lee Hines, whom they claimed was retarded and had been falsely convicted. Determined to stop them were members of the Alabama Realm of the Invisible Empire, led by the Exalted Cyclops of the Decatur Klavern, David Kelso.

As the marchers reached the shouting Klansmen the KKK, some masked and dressed in the traditional white robes and others wearing motorcycle helmets and carrying clubs, forced a confrontation. Suddenly, there was fighting and then a shot. David Kelso, who was wielding a club, was wounded. A black maintenance man, Curtis Robinson, was arrested and later sentenced to five years, suspended. But he was eventually pardoned on the grounds of self-defence.

The Klan used its guns in November 1979 when two carloads of Klansmen confronted members of the Communist Workers Party at Greensboro, North Carolina. Demonstrators who were holding a 'Death to the Klan' rally set upon the cars. Fighting broke out, and then shooting, which left five demonstrators dead by the side of the road.

The Klansmen were acquitted of murder by an all-white jury, but the city of Greensboro had to pay a victim's widow $395,000 because one of their informers had taken an active part in the operation.

However, despite such incidents the Klan continued its steady decline during the 1980s. In a belated attempt at respectability, it discarded its secret society image. Members were more willing to admit their support publicly, even those like policemen, who should be impartial.

The Klan's troubles multiplied. When it tried to march in the once-fertile ground of Montgomery, Alabama, it was stopped by the police because it hadn't applied for a permit. In the past, such niceties had not been bothered about, but these were different days and Imperial Wizard Bill Wilkinson found himself arrested along with two hundred other Klansmen and Klanswomen. His authority was later destroyed when it was revealed that he had long been an FBI informer.

DESPERATE MODERNISATION

In an effort to modernise and go on the offensive, some chapters of the decimated Klans swapped their robes for camouflaged battledress. They claimed to be preparing for an armed showdown with radicals and went on assault courses to harden themselves. But they lost some of their identity and started to look like any other extreme right-wing organisation.

For all its spectacular displays over a period of more than a hundred years and its power to make headlines, the Ku Klux Klan has failed in its main objective of maintaining white supremacy and stopping the march to racial equality. Despite the Klan's murderous savagery, its major effect on the civil rights movement was not to halt it in its path but to hasten the triumph of its cause.

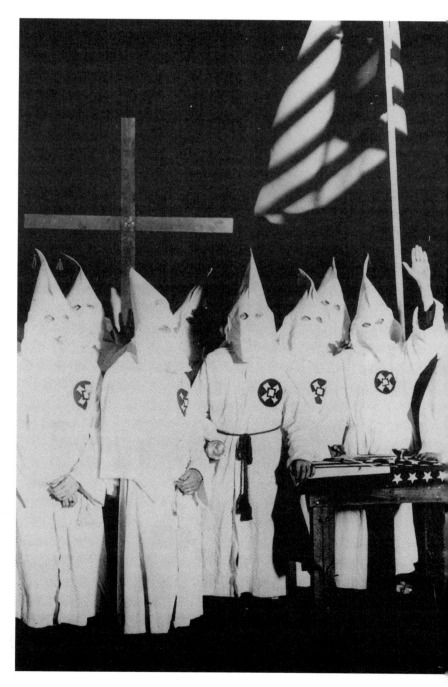

After the 1960s, the Ku Klux Klan went into a steady decline, its costumes seeming more ridiculous than frightening. Ironically, its major effect had been to stengthen the civil rights movement

Seldom can a group of people have been put through such a terrifying ordeal as befell nine nurses, all aged between 20 and 24. When one answered a knock at their door one night, she found a man with a knife and a gun who took her back into the house. He tied up the six girls who were indoors at the time and as the night wore on took them to other rooms one by one to kill them. Three others who arrived during the night were also killed. That he was caught so quickly was due to one girl who had hid under a bed and, unluckily for him, the killer failed to count up to nine.

Richard Speck

The Nurse Killer

n 1966 Chinese leader Mao Tse-tung launched his Cultural Revolution, and John Lennon, who had launched his a few years before, caused a sensation by announcing that the Beatles were more popular than Christ. The United States air force, meanwhile, lost and recovered an H-bomb off the coast of Spain. In Chicago, as elsewhere in the US, race riots were devastating the city.

But at six o'clock on the morning of 14 July, the inhabitants of East 100th Street, in the suburb of Jeffrey Manor, witnessed a disturbing sight even for Chicago. At number 2319 a girl sat screaming on a window ledge.

Neighbours came to see what had happened. The police were called and helped her away. She was Corazon Amurao who had come to Chicago from the Philippines to nurse. When the police got into the house they were appalled to find eight dead nurses in the bedrooms. They were: Gloria Davy, aged 22; Mary Ann Jordan, aged 20; Suzanne Farris, 21; Valentina Pasion, 23; Patricia Matusek, aged 20; Merlita Gargullo, 22; Pamela Wilkening, 20; and Nina Schmale, 24. Neighbours were aghast as the bodies were brought out.

After the police had finished in the house the forensic scientists took over: whoever had done the murders had apparently left plenty of fingerprints and other clues. All the women had been stabbed or strangled or both.

When the police questioned Corazon Amurao, the only survivor from the house, she revealed that the killer was a man who had said things which made her think he might be a seaman. She had seen the murderer clearly when she first answered to door to him and was therefore able to help an artist draw a detailed picture of the man who had killed her friends.

"EVERYBODY SAYS I DID IT. IF THEY SAY I DID IT, I DID IT. IF I BURN, I BURN"

Richard Speck

A FATEFUL TATTOO

In the forensic laboratory, scientists examined the finger and palm prints found in the house and on a knife which was left in one of the rooms. By midday, the description of a man was all over Chicago, including the information that he had a tattoo on his arm reading 'Born to raise hell'.

During their routine enquiries at the National Maritime Union hiring hall police discovered that a seaman named Richard Speck had been there looking for a ship going to New Orleans. Corazon remembered that the attacker had said he needed money to get to New Orleans.

The coastguards had a photograph of a Richard Speck. The sketch and the photo matched up closely. When Corazon recognised the face, the police knew that they had identified their man. At nightfall came the news that a man looking like Richard Speck had threatened a prostitute with a gun before disappearing.

Now the police had to decide whether to go public with the suspect's identity. The FBI had found a set of Richard Speck's fingerprints on their file and the scientists at the forensic laboratory worked through the night. At 4.30am they confirmed that the fingerprints on the knife matched those of Richard Speck.

The case seemed so watertight that on 16 July Chicago Police Superintendent O.W. Wilson decided to announce publicly that the suspect they were looking for was named Richard Franklin Speck.

That night, while sitting in a bar, Speck heard that he was wanted. He used the false name of B. Brian to register at the low-level Starr Hotel. Cornered and panicking, he slit his wrists with a broken bottle. Fellow guest Claude Lunsford heard him calling for help. When nobody came, Speck staggered down into the lobby. He was rushed to Cook County Hospital, but nobody yet realised that 'B. Brian' was the man wanted for the nurse murders.

The eight nurses who were murdered in their home in Jeffrey Manor, Chicago. They had been tied up in one of the bedrooms and then taken individually to other rooms in the house and killed

THE CRIME OF THE CENTURY

DAILY MIRROR, Friday, July 15, 1966   PAGE 12

MURDERED
Patricia Matuseki, 21

MURDERED
Marianne Jorden, 22

MURDERED
Nina Schmale, 21

MURDERED
Pamela Wilkening, 22

MURDERED
Gloria Davy, 23

MURDERED
Marlita Gargullo, 21

MURDERED
Valicentia Passon, 23

MURDERED
Susan Farris, 22

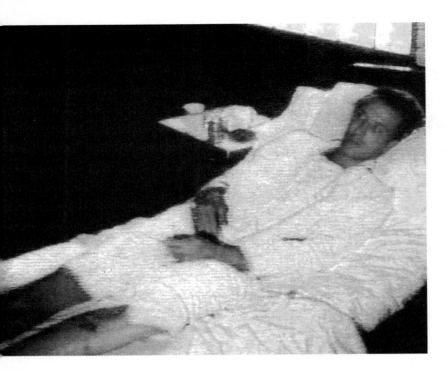

Richard Speck in the prison hospital where survivor Corazon Amurao, in her nurse's uniform, identified him as the Nurse Killer. He had slit his wrists with a broken bottle after hearing that he was wanted for murder

BLOOD-COVERED TATTOO

Then his tattoos aroused the suspicions of one of the doctors: 'This guy, he just appeared to be a fellow that I thought they were looking for because he had all these tattoos on him.'

Asked by a reporter if he'd checked the tattoos, the doctor replied: 'Yeah, that was the first thing that I looked at. The article that I read – I remember it. He had this one thing, I can quote: "Born to raise hell" on his left arm.'

Asked if he'd found it there, he said: 'Well, it was . . . the left arm was covered with blood. The other girls were working on him on the other side, throwing an IV, so I took just some regular saliva and I just washed the blood off his arm and a "B" started coming out. And I went faster and it said "Born", you know, so I went a little bit further and it said "Born to raise hell".'

A DOSSIER OF CRIME

And raise hell he had. Although he was only 24, Richard Speck had a long history of violence and 41 arrests. He was still wanted for burglary in Dallas. He had left a wife and baby daughter there, and was being divorced for cruelty. As the police brought in

more evidence, so his dossier of rape, burglary, forged cheques and robberies with violence grew. He was already the leading suspect in the burglary and rape of an elderly woman and the murder of a barmaid.

He was moved to a secure prison hospital, but denied all knowledge of killing the nurses. 'I can't remember anything,' he told the doctors. While crowds gathered outside, the prison medical team ruled that he was not sufficiently recovered to be questioned. He was under sedation and incoherent. Outside, extra police patrolled the grounds. There were two special guards in his room and he was tied to his bed by leather thongs.

However, the medics did give permission for Corazon Amurao to be driven to the hospital to identify him. Wearing her nurse's uniform, she pretended to be one of the staff of the prison hospital. Once she was out of his hearing, she whispered: 'That really is him,' and collapsed. She confirmed that she had recognised both his face and his voice.

Speck then suffered what doctors thought might be a heart attack. The prison medical director Doctor William Norcross again refused to let him go to court: 'Medically it is not thought that he is in sufficient condition to see anybody or to engage in any legal proceedings at the present time.' He thought that it might be several days before Speck would be able to go to court.

A QUESTION OF SANITY?

The police now knew that Richard Speck had been born in Kirkwood, Illinois, in 1941. One of eight children, he had a violent childhood. When he was ten he fell from a tree and was unconscious for 90 minutes. Caught in a robbery he was clubbed by a policeman. It is possible that this had injured his brain, already affected by alcohol and drugs. He regularly had blinding headaches.

It was 1 August before Speck was reckoned to have recovered sufficiently to be taken to court for arraignment. There was intense security.

The court appointed a panel of psychiatrists to decide whether he was fit to stand trial. They were not told about the head injuries he had suffered, or his long history of drug and alcohol abuse. With no money to pay for a lawyer, Speck was assigned Public Defender Gerald Getty. Getty entered a formal plea of not guilty, and made it clear that he wanted to base his defence on insanity, even though the court-appointed psychiatrists now ruled that Speck was fit to stand trial.

The prison psychiatrist was prepared to testify that Speck must have been temporarily insane at the time of the killings due to head injuries or drug use. But the defence case was not helped by remarks given to reporters by Dr Norcross.

Norcross: I don't recall it exactly but I think in general it was something to the effect of "When I awoke I saw blood in my hands. They tell me they have this evidence against me, I must have done it."

Reporter: But he did not admit that he had done it?

Norcross: No, he didn't admit he had done it. He just made vague references to the fact that if he had capital punishment that they would never get him to the chair, that he would take care of it himself.

Reporter: Do you believe that he might try to take his own life now?

Norcross: No.

Reporter: You don't think he has suicidal tendencies?

Norcross: No.

Reporter: Why?

Norcross: I just don't. It's a judgement.

The defence even tested his chromosomes for the high sex drive caused by the XYY pattern but were disappointed by the result: 'The results of both studies is that Richard Speck does not have the XYY chromosome, that he is normal in that regard. It is only XY just as any other normal person has.'

TRIAL SWITCHED TO PEORIA

Speck's lawyers applied to have the case moved from Chicago where they said an impartial jury would be impossible to find. They cited the police conference naming him as the murderer. They won their argument and the trial was transferred to Peoria, Illinois, 150 miles away. The prosecution didn't mind because Peoria was generally known among lawyers as 'the hanging county'.

2319 East 100th Street (end house on the left) in the suburb of Jeffrey Manor in Chicago where the slayings took place. Neighbours were alerted when sole survivor Corazon Amurao screamed for help from an upstairs window ledge

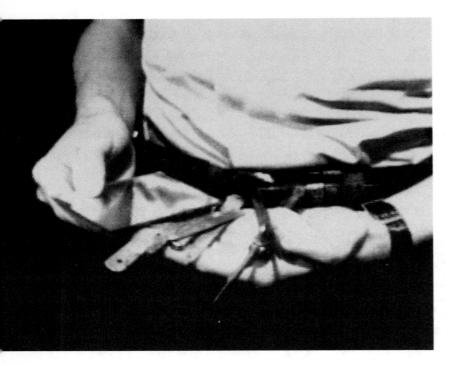

Some of the concealed weapons found during routine searches of spectators at the trial of Richard Speck, who had received death threats. Many people were carrying weapons because of the riots which were taking place at the time

Richard Speck was brought to court under heavy guard when the trial opened on 20 February 1967. To empanel a jury no fewer than 609 citizens were examined before twelve were agreed upon by both prosecution and defence.

Speck was still claiming to have no memory of the murders and seemed indifferent to his fate. When asked if he had killed the eight nurses, he replied: 'Everybody says I did it. If they say I did it, I did it. If I burn, I burn.'

When asked why he had not informed the court-appointed psychiatrists about his head injuries or drug and alcohol abuse, his reply was simply: 'They didn't ask me.'

With emotions running high, there had been death threats made to get Speck. Everyone going into the court was searched every day. Troopers often found concealed weapons which were widely being carried as protection during the riots which had convulsed the area. Indeed, it was because of these riots that Richard Speck had acquired the gun he had been carrying when arrested. He had stolen it from the handbag of a 50-year-old woman he had picked up in a bar and had taken back to his room the night before the murders took place.

Speck's refusal to admit that he was aware of the killings presented his defender Gerald Getty with a problem: he would be unable to plead not guilty by reason of insanity. Getty now decided to base his defence upon the possibility that Speck had been falsely identified and that he had in fact been elsewhere at the time.

THE PROSECUTION CASE

The four-strong prosecution team felt that it had a convincing case against Richard Speck. Led by state attorney William Martin, they prepared to document a narrative inescapably pointing the finger of guilt at one man. Judge Herbert Paschen presided as the prosecution set out the events leading up to the night of the murders.

They claimed that after Speck had gone on the run from a charge in Dallas, he fled to his sister, who lived in Chicago. When family tensions mounted, he decided to find a ship on which to work his way to New Orleans. On 10 July, his sister drove him to the Seaman's Hall of the Maritime Union, where he filled in an application form. There were no berths available at the time but he was told to go back every day in case something came up.

So he hung about, getting drunk and stoned, picking up women as derelict as himself, and sleeping in flophouses. On 12 July he was told there was a ship for him, but when he reported in, he was told he was only the reserve as a sailor with more seniority had claimed the passage. He was angry. With no money for a room, he slept rough, and next day borrowed $25 from his brother-in-law.

Speck listened impassively as his counsel read out a prosecution statement that on the next day he had pretended he had a cheque for $1,300. They claimed that Speck had seen the nurses sunbathing and had taken a room in a house on the same road where they lived. Then on the fatal night of 13 July, he fell in with some sailors who were mainlining some kind of drug from a blue bottle – he didn't know or care what – and he did the same, injecting a clear liquid into his arm.

The spectators who crowded into the courtroom heard the prosecutor charge that, giddy with drugs and drink, Richard Speck knocked on the nurses' door at around eleven o'clock at night. William Martin then called his key witness to take the witness stand and continue the horrific story.

Corazon Amurao seemed calm and surprisingly composed as she arrived at court. She repeated her identification of Speck as the man who had massacred her friends. She then took up the story of that evening at the nurses' home.

Six of the girls had been talking in one of the bedrooms when there was a knock on the door. Corazon went down and opened it.

A tall, pock-marked man was standing there. In his hands were a gun and a knife. 'I'm not going to hurt you,' he said. 'I just need your money to get to New Orleans.'

With the help of a model which was used in the courtroom, it was shown how he herded the six girls into the largest of the bedrooms and bound their wrists and ankles with a sheet torn into strips. At 11.30 Gloria Davy, another of the girls who lived in the house, returned from a date. She too was tied up in the bedroom.

The man then selected one of the girls and took her out of the bedroom. She was Pam Wilkening. The others heard her give a deep sigh. Then there was silence. They argued about whether to resist, but most thought it best not to provoke him.

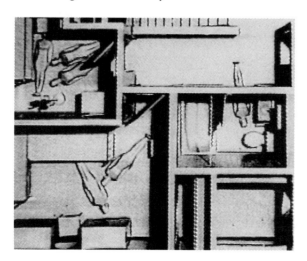

Two more girls now came home. Suzanne Farris lived in the house and she brought back a friend, Mary Ann Jordan. They were intercepted by the man, who stabbed them both and left their bodies in one of the other bedrooms. He then took Nina Schmale out of the main bedroom and strangled her.

While he was gone, Corazon rolled under one of the beds and squeezed against the wall out of sight. Now there were four girls dead and five more waiting huddled in the main bedroom.

Next he dragged Valentina Pasion away and stabbed her neck without untying her.

Corazon testified that at this point another of the Philippine girls, Merlita Gargullo, shouted: 'maskarit', it hurts, in her native tongue after she had been taken to a different room.

Now Patricia Matusek was pushed roughly into the bathroom where she was kicked and stabbed to death on the floor.

Finally, the killer returned to the bedroom where only Gloria Davy was to be seen. Corazon saw the killer tear off Gloria's jeans before taking her out. Her strangled body was found downstairs. The killer had lost count of how many girls there had been, and now left the house not realising Corazon was still under

Survivor Corazon Amurao who was described by a court reporter as 'the greatest trial witness I have ever seen'

One of the models used in court showing how Richard Speck took the women to different rooms in the house and murdered them one by one

the bed. She stayed there until 6am before she dared get out from her hiding place. Then she smashed the window screen in the front room and crawled out onto the narrow ledge, where she screamed in Filippino for help.

The prosecution was delighted with her testimony. When asked to identify the man she saw in her house that night, Corazon marched across the floor of the courtroom and pointed her finger close to Richard Speck's nose. 'This is the man!' she declared. A *Chicago Daily News* court reporter called her 'the greatest trial witness I have ever seen'.

THE DEFENCE

Detectives were sure that the files of evidence they took into court built up into an unanswerable case. But Gerald Getty, Speck's lawyer, was not beaten yet. Unable to use the defence of insanity because Speck would not confess, he started by bringing Speck's family to court as character witnesses.

Then he produced a witness to give Speck an alibi for the time of the murders: a bartender who swore Speck was at his bar from 12 to 12.30am on the fatal night. If that was the case, he couldn't have been at 2319 East 100th Street. The man said he would stake his life that it was Speck who had a hamburger at his bar that midnight. His wife backed him up.

If the jury believed the couple, a terrible miscarriage of justice would be avoided, with an innocent man condemned for what the coroner had called 'the crime of the century'.

In his closing speech Gerald Getty attacked the fingerprint evidence as being based on 'smudges', and asserted that Corazon's identification of her attacker was wrong; she had, after all, been in an extremely emotional situation and her memory could be faulty.

Finally, the talking was over. For two weeks the jury had heard horrific descriptions and seen ghastly photographs of eight murdered young women. Now it was up to them to decide whether Richard Speck was the killer responsible. A long vigil was expected. But it took this jury only 49 minutes to reach their eight verdicts: guilty, with the recommendation of death. A wave of relief swept through Chicago and the whole nation. Justice would be done.

Outside the courtroom, Chief Prosecutor William Martin was asked for his comments on the jury's recommendation: 'As I stated in my argument, it's not the function of the law to bear any hatred toward an individual but to seek to control society and to set forth some type of effective deterrent to others.'

He was asked what the most important evidence had been: 'With the post-trial motions I wouldn't want to comment particularly on the evidence. I would join Mr Stainless in saying that we all have immense respect for the courage of Corazon Amurao.'

The trial was over but the legal battles continued for defence attorney Gerald Getty. Despite the mass of evidence against his client he was determined to fight on: 'Well, all I can say is we tried this case to the best of our ability, we feel that we tried it in the best traditions of the legal profession. The jury has spoken and our only alternative now is a motion for a new trial. All cases where the death penalty is given in this state must be appealed.'

Although he had yet to pass sentence, Judge Paschen joined in the celebrations, shaking the hands of members of the victims' families and commiserating with them outside the courthouse.

The defence request for a new trial was quickly squashed. But now there came a new objection: was Richard Speck suffering from a form of epilepsy on the night of the murders? A panel of court-appointed doctors shot that down.

> "IT'S NOT THE FUNCTION OF THE LAW TO BEAR ANY HATRED TOWARD AN INDIVIDUAL BUT TO SEEK TO CONTROL SOCIETY AND TO SET FORTH SOME TYPE OF EFFECTIVE DETERRENT TO OTHERS"
>
> Prosecutor William Martin

So – was he insane? Now the fact that he killed the nurses had been proven, his lawyer could at last argue that he was legally insane at the time. Judge Paschen heard a defence psychiatrist testify that Speck had long suffered from a severe chronic personality disorder. It wasn't enough. On 5 June, Judge Paschen sentenced Richard Franklin Speck to be put to death in the electric chair.

As he had throughout the trial, Richard Speck showed no emotion.

After the sentence, the judge held a press conference: 'The death sentence was pronounced in accordance with the recommendation of the jury, and the date for execution was set for September 1, within the time allotted by the statute. There's an automatic stay of execution till final order of the Supreme Court, because the appeals in a death case are automatic.'

SPECK ESCAPES EXECUTION

The appeal led to a stay of execution when the Supreme Court of the United States ruled that jurors opposed to capital punishment had been wrongly excluded from Speck's case. Then, at the end of 1967, it called a halt on all executions in the United States.

So, on 20 September 1972, the Illinois Supreme Court commuted Richard Speck's death sentence. Two months later, he was re-sentenced to eight consecutive terms of at least 50 years each – the longest prison sentence ever handed down.

In all, Richard Speck spent 19 years in Stateville, the prison at Joliet, Illinois. He never admitted to the murders of the nurses or to any of the several other killings of which he was suspected. He was a model prisoner, content to pass his days growing fat – 200lb in the end.

So settled was he in jail that, although he was theoretically eligible, he didn't ask for parole until 1987, when he made the gesture of an application. He was not surprised when the parole board turned him down and made no further requests.

In 1991, he died in prison of a heart attack. He was one day short of his fiftieth birthday.

Throughout his trial, Richard Speck showed little interest in the proceedings, claiming that he remembered nothing of the murders. He eventually received eight consecutive sentences of 50 years, the longest ever handed down, and died in prison after 19 years during which time he had been a model prisoner

IT IS AS EASY TO BUY GUNS IN THE UNITED STATES AS IT IS
DIFFICULT FOR THE EXECUTIVE TO CURB THE RIGHTS OF
AMERICANS TO BUY THEM. EVEN INCIDENTS LIKE THAT AT
THE UNIVERSITY OF TEXAS WILL NOT CHANGE THE LAWS.
STUDENT CHARLES WHITMAN WAS AN ALL-AMERICAN
BOY BROUGHT UP BY A FATHER OBSESSED WITH GUNS, AND
HE BECAME OBSESSED IN TURN. WHEN THE PRESSURE OF HIS
LIFE AND WORK BECAME TOO MUCH, HE WENT TO THE TOP
OF THE UNIVERSITY TOWER AND WITH AN ARSENAL OF
WEAPONS SPENT 96 MINUTES KILLING PEOPLE. IT TOOK
BRAVE MEN TO END THE SLAUGHTER, BUT AS THE POLICE
CHIEF SAID, IT COULD HAVE HAPPENED ANYWHERE . . .

Charles Whitman

The Austin Sniper

n 1966 Argentina made a first abortive attempt to seize the Falkland Islands from the British. In South Korea Buddhist monks burned themselves in protest at the repressive tactics of the US-backed government of Marshal Ky, and for the first time United States aircraft bombed Hanoi. In a Chicago suburb eight nurses were the victims of a mass killing by Richard Speck.

America had not recovered from the shock of those senseless murders when in Austin, Texas, just two weeks later, an even more random mass killing took place.

The large granite and limestone tower of the University of Texas administration offices is a landmark, and its 27th-floor observation platform used to be a popular place to visit, for students, townspeople and visitors alike. It offers a remarkable view over the 232-acre university campus with its 50,000 students. On 1 August there was no hint just before noon on a hot day that death would rain down from it for the next hour and a half.

The first shot from the top of the tower ripped into the leg of a student who was cycling round the campus. Three more people fell in quick succession.

By the time the gunman had finished, he had killed 12 people at or near the tower, and wounded 30 others. Finally three policemen and a passer-by managed to storm the tower and shoot the gunman dead.

THE ALL-AMERICAN BOY

The gunman was identified as a 25-year-old architectural student, Charles Joseph Whitman, whom his friends had considered to be an all-American boy. Whitman had been born and raised in the seaside town of Lake Worth, Florida, the eldest of three sons. He was neat and hardworking, a Roman Catholic altar boy and one of the youngest eagle scouts on record.

His father was a believer in frequent physical punishment for his sons. He was also a self-confessed fanatic about firearms who boasted that he had raised his sons from babyhood to handle guns. Charles in particular grew up obsessed by firearms and became an expert shot.

At 18 he joined the Marine Corps and scored a total of 215 shooting points out of 250 to be rated a sharpshooter. However, he was often in trouble for aggressive behaviour, getting demoted from corporal to private, and serving 30 days for illegal possession of a pistol.

During his service he discovered that the military would put him through school. So he obtained a scholarship, and in 1962 was given leave to enrol at the University of Texas to study engineering. He started well, getting high grades and proving popular with fellow students.

That same year, Whitman met a student teacher, Kathleen Leissner. They married shortly afterwards. They seemed a devoted couple, although some friends sensed that she was afraid of a violent streak in her new husband.

In 1963 Whitman's grades dropped. His scholarship was removed and he had to go back to the marines. He finished his service on 4 December 1964

> **"I LOVE MY MOTHER WITH ALL MY HEART. THE INTENSE HATRED I FEEL FOR MY FATHER IS BEYOND ALL DESCRIPTION"**
>
> Charles Whitman

and returned to Austin. Now he switched to architectural engineering and began taking an unusually heavy class load as well as working long hours to fund his studies. He and Kathy lived in a pleasant house in Jewell Street, and she worked as a telephonist during the summer months with the local South Western Bell Company.

VIOLENT FANTASIES

Early in 1966, his mother left his father after years of wife-beating and moved to Austin. Charles went to fetch her, and called a sheriff's car to stand guard in case his father physically tried to prevent her from leaving. Within a few months the pressure of work, his father's constant calls to get him to persuade his mother to return, together with financial problems, drove Whitman to quit school and tell his wife he was leaving her.

His professor helped him get a partial scholarship so that he would be able to continue studying,

Charles Whitman as a child in the seaside town of Lake Worth in Florida. His father brought his three sons up to handle guns from babyhood and Charles, in particular, grew up obsessed with firearms and was an expert shot

and his bewildered wife persuaded him to start seeing a psychiatrist. Whitman admitted to the psychiatrist that he had fits of rage against family and friends, and that, like his father, he beat his wife. He also revealed that he fantasised about shooting people from the university tower.

Later, a friend, A.J. Vinicik, tried to explain what pressures might have made him crack: 'Work, scouting, schooling, studying, and so forth, there was a lot of pressure on him. He was trying to cover more ground than he was capable of doing. He was just spread out a little bit too thin.'

Kathleen Leissner and Charles Whitman leaving St Michael's Church in Needville, Texas, after their wedding on 17 August 1962. He regularly beat her and, just four years after their marriage, stabbed her to death

WHITMAN'S LETTERS

Whitman was now complaining of exhaustion and increasingly painful headaches. On the evening before the massacre, alone at home, Whitman wrote a farewell letter, saying that he hated his father with a mortal passion. He said that he loved his wife although he was going to kill her 'because I don't want her to face the embarrassment my actions will surely cause her'.

His friends Larry and Elaine Fuess dropped in as he finished typing: 'When we walked in he was typing and he told us he was typing some letters to a few friends. And we just sat down and we had a very normal conversation with him, like nothing out of the ordinary that we've ever had with him before. And he seemed to be in fine spirits. He wasn't depressed about anything; he almost seemed to be relieved and he was particularly relaxed this week.'

Nevertheless, they felt that all was not well: 'He wasn't himself Sunday night, as calm and as collected and as personable as he seemed to be. There were several things that just didn't add up to what he'd always been.'

After his friends had left, Whitman drove to the telephone company to pick up Kathy. As usual, he took her home. She evidently had no idea that anything was wrong, but some time that night, he stabbed her three times with a knife while she slept, killing her instantly.

That night Whitman drove across Austin to his mother's apartment and killed her also, by stabbing and shooting. He wrote another note: 'I have just killed my mother. I am very upset over having done it. However, I feel that if there is a heaven she is definitely there now. If there is not a heaven, she is out of her pain and misery. I love my mother with all my heart. The intense hatred I feel for my father is beyond all description.'

GETTING READY FOR THE SHOOT

Whitman spent that night preparing his weapons. The next morning he bought more so that they totalled three rifles, one shotgun, two revolvers, plus

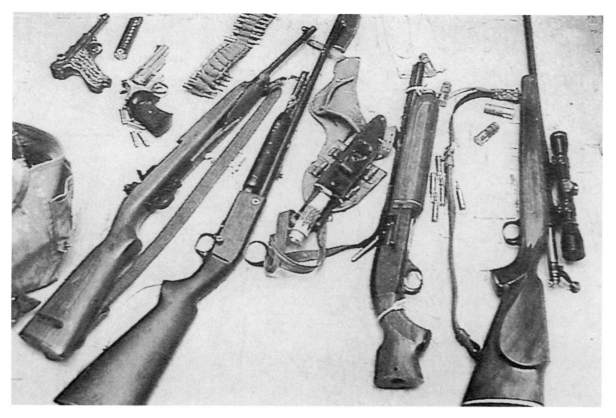

Charles Whitman's arsenal of weapons was put on display after the shootings. It consisted of three rifles, one shotgun, two revolvers, various machetes and hunting knives, together with hundreds of rounds of ammunition. In Texas, as in all but seven other US states, there were no controls on the sale of firearms

machetes, hunting knives and hundreds of rounds of ammunition. He had also collected a stock of food and water, enough to last several days.

During the morning he loaded all this into his car and drove to the university campus where he was seen by Larry Fuess: 'I saw him yesterday morning, down the library at the engineering building. I was just passing by on the way to a class and didn't have time to stop, and besides he looked unusually distraught and it just occurred to me that he had an exam coming up that afternoon and he appeared to be studying. But I stopped and had to look again, because I didn't quite recognise him. I guess now I think he was in a state of shock at the time.'

Some time after that, he put on grey overalls and loaded his equipment into a builder's trolley. He then pushed this over to the entrance to the university tower, where he was mistaken for a maintenance engineer, and so managed to take all his gear up to the 27th floor in the elevator. From there he manhandled his heavy load up three short flights of stairs to the observation deck.

The clerk who maintained the guest register, Edna Townsley, asked him what he wanted. In reply, he clubbed her with a rifle, crushing her skull.

As Whitman was making his final preparations he heard footsteps approaching. Margaret Lampourt was a tourist visiting the tower with her 15-year-old nephew, Mark, and his family. As they appeared, Whitman fired, killing them both and wounding Mark's brother and mother. Mark's father was further behind the others and took cover in an office.

THE SLAUGHTER FROM THE TOWER

Then Whitman slammed the door onto the observation platform and barricaded it with furniture. He positioned himself under the gilt-edged clock on the south face of the tower. From there he had a superb view of the campus in front of the building.

He could also see through to the shops on Guadalupe Street, and it was there that Claudia Rutt, aged 18, a promising ballet dancer, was shot down beside her boyfriend Pat Sonntag. As he turned to help her, he too was killed.

Smoke rising from Charles Whitman's gun as he fired at passers-by on the ground below. His position under the clock on the south face of the university tower offered him a superb vantage point over the campus

At first no one could understand what was happening. Then Harry Walchuk, a 39-year-old political science teacher, was gunned down as he browsed outside one of the bookstores on Guadalupe Street. Now people close to these first victims began to take cover as they realised something was wrong, but Thomas Karr also died on Guadalupe Street as he walked back from taking a Spanish exam.

Whitman spotted figures crossing the campus below. He fired, wounding a pregnant girl. Student Thomas Eckman went to help and was killed immediately with a bullet to the head. Other people who tried to help them were wounded and had to be helped away themselves.

Most of the killings happened during the first 20 minutes, while confusion reigned around the campus. People desperately tried to spot the gunman.

A Peace Corps volunteer, Thomas Ashton, was killed whilst relaxing on the roof of a building to the north of the university tower. Whitman now began moving around the observation platform picking his

targets wherever he could. He had positioned his store of rifles and ammunition so that he could cover all sides of the platform.

The fifth victim, Robert Boyer, a 33-year-old mathematician on his way to an early lunch, was hit in the back and died. By now people were beginning to realise that the shots were coming from the tower. But the difficulty was that it provided well-concealed firing positions.

Those on the ground had little chance of spotting the gunman. Shots ricocheted off the parapet, but there was little chance of hitting such an elusive target. Now attempts were being made to clear the campus as the firing continued. One of the men returning fire on the tower was traffic policeman Billy Speed. He was picked off as he crouched behind a stone railing.

As more people fell wounded, police reinforcements were moving into the area. But their chances of getting a clear shot were slim as Whitman moved from vantage point to vantage point. His prowess with a rifle kept most of them at bay.

One student, Charlotte Darehshou, was trapped behind the base of a flagpole in the centre of the campus throughout the gun battle. Whitman had a clear view of her hiding place. All she could do was crouch down and try to stay as calm as possible.

The police fired hundreds of rounds from the ground, but their efforts had little effect on Whitman, whose long familiarity with guns enabled him to pick off targets with impunity.

BODIES RESCUED

While Whitman was distracted by police fire, brave rescuers were able to recover some of the bodies on the campus. It was discovered that the pregnant girl was still alive although the bullet had killed her baby.

As the areas near the tower were cleared, so Whitman had to look further afield for his targets. Roy Schmidt was killed by a shot in the stomach at a range of 500 yards, while running for his truck. Ambulances rushed the wounded and dead away whenever they could be recovered. After an hour, the gunman was still firing from his vantage point.

AN ASSAULT ON THE TOWER

The police now realised that the distance was too great to wound or kill the gunman. While return fire was kept up a squad gathered in one of the buildings beside the tower. The policemen who made the final assault were Ramiro Martinez, who had been off duty when he heard of the emergency, George Sheppard and Houston McCoy.

As they prepared to dash across to the entrance of the administration block at the base of the tower, the police were joined by Allan Crum, one of the university's civilian employees. A 40-year-old retired air force tail-gunner, he insisted that he should go with them as he knew the building. He was given a rifle and made a deputy on the spot.

> "KNOWING THE CONDITION THE WORLD IS IN TODAY, THIS COULD HAVE HAPPENED IN ANY CITY IN THE UNITED STATES, OR ANY CITY IN THE WORLD FOR THAT MATTER"
>
> Austin's Police Chief Miles

Once inside the tower, the men took the elevator up to the 26th floor. There they met a distraught Mr Gabour, father of the murdered Mark. He tried to seize a gun and go after the killer alone. After a struggle he was sent back downstairs.

Once on the observation platform the party forced their way through the barricaded door. From the ground, other police kept firing to distract the gunman. Then Martinez and McCoy crawled one way and Crum the other.

Crum heard some footsteps coming towards him. He loosed off a blast. The footsteps retreated. He then moved round the corner but the gunman was out of sight.

Then Whitman moved round another corner into Martinez's sightline. The policeman fired and, as the sniper fired one last shot, Martinez emptied his pistol into Whitman's left side.

Whitman fell to the ground, and as he thrashed around, McCoy fired at him twice. Finally, Martinez

Student Charlotte Darehshou was crossing the campus below the university tower when the shooting began. She was trapped behind the base of a flagpole which stood in the centre of the campus grounds throughout the ensuing gun battle

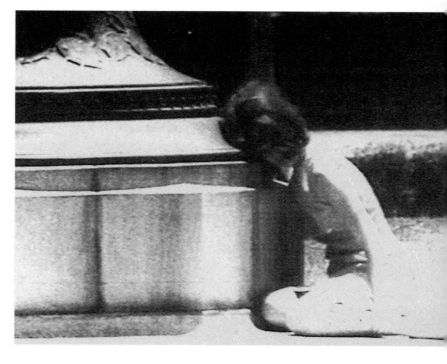

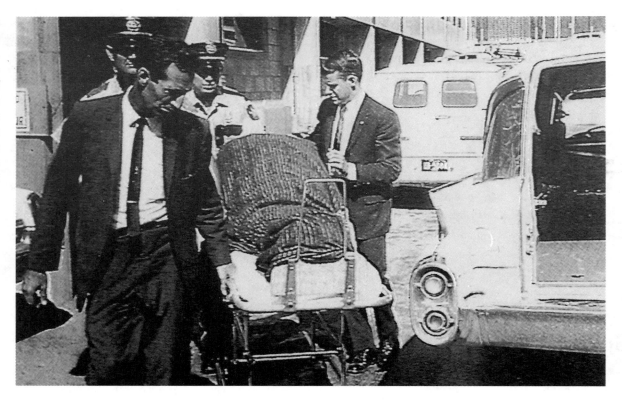

*Police taking away
the body of Charles
Whitman's wife.
Once the shootings
were over and
Whitman had been
identified, the police
went to inform his
wife and mother only
to discover that they
too had been killed*

grabbed the student's shotgun and fired point blank into his head. Medical teams quickly rushed into the building after Crum had signalled with a towel that it was all over.

Whitman was killed at 1.24pm, 96 minutes after the first shot. As his body and those of his victims in the tower were taken out, the horrified inhabitants of the city gathered to watch. People were appalled to discover that the murderer had been a student at the university, and one who at least on the surface had seemed a normal boy.

THE STORY IS PIECED TOGETHER

As staff and students began to move back into the building they were told of fresh horrors. Police had now been to see Whitman's family and discovered the bodies of his wife and mother.

Whitman's arsenal of weapons was put on display. Many people noted that in Texas, as in all but seven other US states at the time, there were virtually no controls on the sale of handguns, rifles or shotguns. More than 100 million lethal weapons were in private hands in 1966.

Whitman's father sidestepped questions as to whether his son's obsession with guns might have contributed to the tragedy: 'I am a fanatic about guns myself; I have quite a few of them. I raise my kids with guns, they know how to handle guns and know how to use guns. I was a great hunter. I spend every winter in the woods hunting, when I get a chance.'

He did not seem to make any connection between the tragedy and the obsession with guns, and Austin's Police Chief Miles was equally determined to emphasise that the massacre was a totally random act: 'One of the things that I would like to point out is that while this happened in Austin, that knowing the condition the world is in today that this could have happened in any city in the United States, or any city in the world for that matter.'

At the same press conference, Allan Crum, whose bravery in joining the police assault team had made him a national hero, described in detail how they had been able to trap and kill Whitman. When it was Ramiro Martinez's turn to speak, his hands and face showed the strain the four men had been under: 'I got to him and I saw that he was dead. Immediately there I almost collapsed from the strain. I dropped my gun on the floor there and I started waving my shotgun hollering for everybody to cease fire, that I had gotten him.'

The university's resident psychiatrist reported on Whitman's unstable state and his most persistent fantasy: 'Thinking about going up on the tower with a deer rifle and start shooting people.'

He also reported on Charles Whitman's love for his mother and his intense hatred of his father. It emerged that in his last letter Whitman had asked for his brain to be examined after death to see if there were any physical explanation for his obsessions. This led to a surprising announcement from the police chief: 'I've just been informed that the autopsy shows that Mr Whitman had a brain tumour.'

There was no medical consensus as to whether this could have caused his murderous rampage by pressing on the aggression centre of the brain. Friends were at a loss to explain why the all-American boy should have run amok. One woman friend said: 'I don't feel like that I know the Charles Whitman that they found up on the university tower. The one that I knew was kind and gentle and good and I think I'll try to remember him that way.'

For Whitman's father, however, there were no doubts: 'He was an A-student in high school. He was a young man who pushed himself tremendously in the last few months to make grades that far exceeded anything that could be . . . I think it came to the breaking point.'

But not everyone who reaches breaking point has the opportunity to go out and buy an armoury of lethal weapons . . . and then has the necessary skill, acquired through an lifetime of handling firearms, to take out his aggression by killing 14 people.

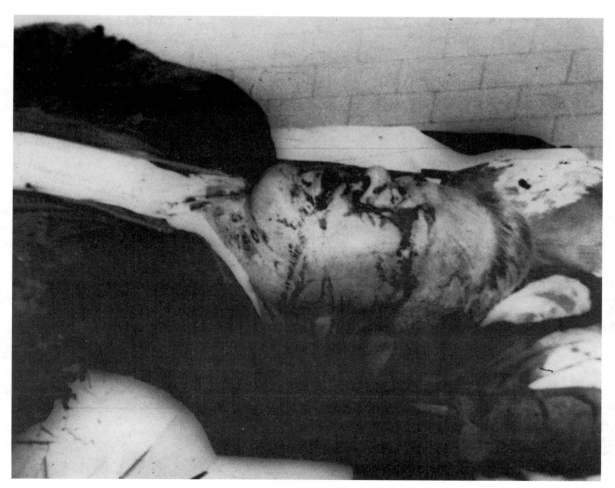

Charles Whitman on a stretcher ready to be removed from the university tower where he had spent 96 minutes shooting passers-by below. He had killed 12 people and injured 30 others as well as murdering his wife and mother the previous day

When a man is the ringleader in the killing of three policemen in cold blood and goes on the run, with thousands of police officers engaged in a manhunt and the whole public knowing what he looks like, it seems inconceivable that he will not be quickly caught. But Harry Roberts, living rough in Epping Forest, stayed at liberty for over three months.

Roberts, Duddy and Witney

The Braybrook Street Massacre

I n 1966 President Johnson inspected US troops as the Vietnam War continued. Another leader, Prime Minister Henrik Verwoerd of South Africa, one of the creators of apartheid, was buried after being stabbed to death. Things were happier in Britain as Harold Wilson led Labour back to power with an increased majority and England won the World Cup.

Soon after the Germans had been defeated by the English at football, however, there was more sombre news in the headlines as three policemen were shot down in cold blood in Braybrook Street, Shepherd's Bush, London.

Nothing rouses more anger and determination in a police force than the murder of one of its own. Perhaps because this is well-known among criminals, fewer than forty members of the Metropolitan police have been murdered in this century. But when a member has been a victim, the force does not rest until the killers have been punished.

One of the most famous occasions was in 1911, when two sergeants and a constable were killed during a raid on a jewellery shop in the City of London. The killers were anarchists who were finally cornered in Sydney Street and killed when top-hatted Home Secretary Winston Churchill brought in armed police and the army.

In 1927, the murder of PC Gutteridge in an Essex lane started another mass hunt. The gun used in the killing was found months later in the garage of a car thief, Frederick Browne. His accomplice, William Henry Kennedy, confessed to the police and both of them went to the gallows.

Then, in 1948, PC Nathaniel Edgar was shot in Southgate by a man he was questioning. As he lay dying he wrote a name in his notebook. The killer, Donald Thomas, was caught in bed with his mistress when their landlady saw his photo in the paper.

The most famous murderer of a policeman in London did not hang. Only 16 years old, Christopher Craig was too young, but his 19-year-old partner, Derek Bentley, who had shouted: 'Let him have it, Chris,' was executed. The public outcry hastened the end of hanging in Britain.

But abolition came too late for the murderer of Sergeant Purdy in 1959. He was Guenther Podola, traced while making a blackmailing telephone call. Caught and held by Sergeant Purdy, he shot his captor, and ran away. Caught through the fingerprints he left, Podola was executed at Wandsworth Prison.

THE SHEPHERD'S BUSH VICTIMS

It was seven years later when Britain's biggest ever manhunt began after the three policemen had been shot down in Shepherd's Bush. They were part of a team that had been engaged in a long hunt for a murderer of local prostitutes, nicknamed Jack the Stripper. The inquiry had ended with the suicide of the chief suspect, and now they were back on routine patrol.

In charge of the team was Detective Sergeant Christopher Head, aged 30 and unmarried. He had just been promoted to Sergeant. With him was David Wombwell who had two children and, after three years on the force, had only recently been made a temporary detective constable. The third was PC Geoffrey Fox, a father of three, whose wife later said: 'I always knew my Geoff would get killed some day.'

(t to b) Geoffrey Fox, Christopher Head and David Wombwell, the three policemen shot in cold blood in Braybrook Street in London's Shepherd's Bush

123

The three policemen were patrolling in West London in a 'Q' car, a Triumph 2000. In the vicinity there was another car, also with three men in it.

John Edward Witney, aged 36, was the owner of that car, a Standard Vanguard. He had a long criminal record, with ten convictions for petty theft. Sitting in the back was John Duddy, a 36-year-old Scotsman

Braybrook Street, which backs onto Wormwood Scrubs, the site of one of London's prisons. Locals who witnessed the three shootings assumed there had been a jailbreak

who had been convicted four times for theft. He had been working as a lorry driver until he met up with Harry Roberts, aged 30, known as a 'hard man'. He had recently been inside for some five years of a seven-year sentence for robbery with violence. In the seedy back streets of West London, he had beaten up a pensioner and cut a ring off his finger.

Roberts, the third man in the car, had been a marksman in the Rifle Brigade, and had fought in Malaya during the emergency there. The army had taught him all about guns and how to survive while living rough in the jungle. Margaret, his wife, had told the police about his crimes when he roughed her up after she refused to go on the streets for him. He vowed revenge on her.

Wormwood Scrubs, near Shepherd's Bush in West London, was where he had been imprisoned, before being transferred to Horfield Prison in Bristol.

There, he was allowed to live in a hostel and go out bricklaying. He continued with this job when he was released, but he got into debt and hurriedly left Bristol for London.

There he quickly fell in with old friends from prison and met new friends who were ready for some easy money. Among them was John Witney. They teamed up to steal metal and lead. From the pubs of London they followed rent collectors and managers of betting shops and robbed them.

John Duddy soon joined them, sporting a tattoo on his arm of a skull, with the words 'True to death'. Roberts insisted they always had guns with them, swearing he would shoot it out with the police rather than go to prison again.

AN UNNECESSARY KILLING

That sunny August day the trio found themselves in Braybrook Street, near Roberts' old residence of Wormwood Scrubs Prison, searching for a car to steal. Witney's Vanguard wasn't reliable enough to use on a job they had in mind. Witney was driving, Roberts was next to him, and between them they had a canvas bag with three guns in it.

The officers in the 'Q' car felt suspicious about the Vanguard and flagged it down. DC Wombwell walked over and peered inside. Suddenly there was a shot. David Wombwell fell, shot in the face. All he had done was to take out a notebook to write down the details of the car and driver.

Roberts told Duddy to grab a gun, and leapt out of the car. He shot at Sergeant Head, who had been questioning Witney, but missed him. Head ran back, shouting 'No, no, no!' and tried to hide behind his car's bonnet. Roberts shot him in the back and he fell in front of the car.

Duddy took aim at PC Fox, who was still sitting in the driving seat of the police car. Duddy's third shot killed him. As he fell forward against the wheel, his foot hit the accelerator. Fox's lifeless foot made the car lurch forward, running over Sergeant Head, who had still been alive. The rear wheels repeatedly crushed him. Smoke poured from the engine.

Witney, who had taken no part in the shootings, had got out of the Vanguard to see what was happening. Roberts screamed at him to get back in and drive them away. As they roared off, they passed a car. Driving it was Bryan Deacon, a security guard. Deacon shouted to his wife to take down the number, PGT 726.

A jailbreak was what the residents of Braybrook Street and the surrounding area at first assumed had happened. But the full horror of the situation soon sank in as the police and ambulances descended, and attempted to free the dead policeman trapped under the wheels of the 'Q' car.

WITNESSES FAIL TO HELP

Every resident of Braybrook Street and the people who had been on Wormwood Scrubs common were questioned by the police. One account ran: 'As far as I know there were three to six shots, I didn't really count them. You know, there was quite a few. So I ran out the front door – I was just coming to the front door as a matter of fact. And I ran over to the corner, and I could see all these fumes coming out of the car – I thought it was fumes – and I ran along and a lady came towards me, she says, "Oh," she says, "there's been someone shot."'

Everybody seemed to have seen something different and eyewitness stories improved with the telling. One boy had a particularly vivid story to tell: 'First I saw a man getting out of the car, and he was running backwards, and he tripped and the fat man in the green jumper and the beard whacked him in the head with a gun, and then someone got in the car and drove it over him.'

Detectives impatiently awaited the tracing of the car number plate. But there was a hold-up: in 1966 there was no central register of number plates,

> ## "I DIDN'T MEAN TO KILL HIM. I WANTED QUICK MONEY THE EASY WAY. I'M A FOOL"
>
> John Duddy

The 'Q' car in which the three policemen had been making a routine patrol. David Wombwell and Geoffrey Fox were both shot dead, Fox still in the car with his foot on the accelerator, causing the car to repeatedly lurch forward, crushing Christopher Head who had fallen in front of it after being shot in the back

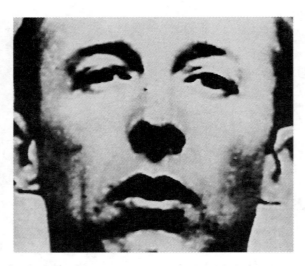

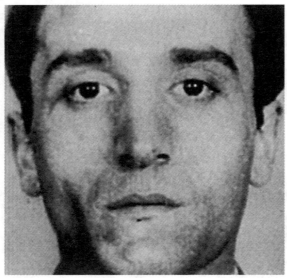

John Witney, who drove the getaway car but did not take part in the actual shootings, and John Duddy, who shot Sergeant Christopher Head. They were both quickly caught and eventually received life sentences

that he had not been anywhere near Wormwood Scrubs. But his wife let on that he hadn't said anything to her about selling the car, and that he had been out all afternoon.

By midnight Witney was in custody. Now the search began to find out where the car was hidden, and its number was broadcast. The police station became a hive of activity as evidence was carried in from Witney's flat.

Then came a telephone call. The wanted car had been spotted being driven into a lock-up garage in Vauxhall. Within minutes, the police were there. In the car they found three cartridges from the .38 Colt that had killed PC Fox.

As they towed away Witney's car to test it for fingerprints, Witney told the police about Roberts and Duddy. He showed them where the two men lived, and both buildings were raided at 5am on the Monday. But the birds had flown. They had gone first to Hampstead Heath to bury the guns, and then they had split up.

Duddy had gone home to Scotland, while Roberts had spent one night with his girlfriend, Lilian Perry, in a hotel in Bloomsbury, and then gone to buy camping equipment, including a sleeping bag. Now the hunt widened across Britain.

INITIAL POLICE CONFIDENCE

With one of the trio already in custody and charged with murder, and the other two identified, the police were confident that it would not be long before the missing pair were caught. There was a huge swell of public anger as press coverage followed every step of the hunt and reminded people of the callousness of the killings.

When the Home Secretary visited Shepherd's Bush police station, he was urged to reintroduce capital punishment for murderers of policemen. Roy Jenkins needed all his tact when faced with angry hecklers: 'I can well understand the reaction and feelings of policemen at the present time. But it would be quite wrong for me to take a major policy decision in the shadow of one event, however horrible that may be.'

and county offices closed at five o'clock. The Home Secretary, Roy Jenkins, visited the scene of the crime.

A minute search for clues was initiated around Braybrook Street and on the common, and officers from all over London volunteered to join the search. There was a sense of boiling indignation that such a Chicago-style shooting of policemen could happen on their patch, and they were pleased to be able to do something towards bringing the murderers to justice.

WITNEY ARRESTED

The car's ownership was finally tracked down to John Witney of Fernhead Road, Paddington. Detectives rushed to his basement flat. He told them that he had sold his car that day to a stranger in a pub for £15, and

As the day of the funeral of the murdered officers approached, a mountain of wreaths was sent, many of them by people who had not known the three officers personally, but who felt moved to make some gesture.

One wreath was sent by the estranged wife of the fugitive Harry Roberts. As well as flowers, money poured in for the families left behind.

Determined to catch the fugitives without delay, the police decided to enlist the help of the public again. They issued detailed descriptions and warned that the men might be both armed and dangerous. The results were not long in coming, and on Tuesday they arrested John Duddy. They found him in bed in a Glasgow tenement in the Calton district. He gave in calmly, and by that evening he was on his way back to London.

AIRCRAFT TRIP

An indication of how important the police rated the capture of Duddy was the decision to bring him back to London by aircraft. Very few criminals were given a trip in an airliner in the 1960s.

Inspector Slipper took a statement from Duddy on the plane. He reported that Duddy said: 'It was Roberts who started the shooting. He shot the two who got out of the car, and then he shouted at me to shoot. I just grabbed a gun and ran to the police car and shot the driver through the window. I must have been mad.'

It was not easy to get him off the plane without the press photographers getting a glimpse of his face and prejudicing his later identification, but the detectives managed it. At the police station, he added to his statement: 'I didn't mean to kill him. I wanted quick money the easy way. I'm a fool.'

HUGE MANHUNT

Harry Roberts was still missing. He had gone by bus with Lilian Perry to the edge of Epping Forest and there tenderly kissed her goodbye. She told the police all she knew, and they were sure he must have gone to ground in Epping Forest.

At dawn on Thursday 18 August, there began the biggest manhunt in British criminal history, as 500 policemen began searching the 6,000 acres of Epping Forest, backed up by dogs and tear gas.

Unusually for England at that time many of the police were armed. A helicopter hovered overhead, and officers from all over London and Essex volunteered to join in the manhunt. For three days, they combed the dense undergrowth for the gunman who had killed their colleagues. But they did not find him. The men directing the pursuit were soon convinced that he was not hiding in Epping Forest, after all. So they withdrew the searchers and widened the net.

The police returned several times to addresses where Roberts had lived, but they could find no clues as to where the former jungle fighter had gone. Over 6,000 sightings were investigated, most of them in London, but 160 of them in Liverpool, and over 100 in Bournemouth. Interpol was alerted in 90 countries. But still there was no sign of Roberts.

The man in charge of the hunt for Roberts, Superintendent Richard Chitty, flew to Ireland to follow up one lead that looked promising, but he soon

£1,000 REWARD MURDER

A reward or rewards up to a total of £1,000 will be paid for information leading to the arrest of HARRY MAURICE ROBERTS, b. Wanstead, Essex, on 21-7-36, 5ft. 10in., photo. above, wanted for questioning in connection with the murder of three police officers on the 12th August, 1966, at Braybrook Street, Shepherds Bush.

Information to be given to New Scotland Yard, S.W.1, or at any police station.

The amount of any payment will be in the discretion of the Commissioner of Police for the Metropolis.

J. SIMPSON,
Commissioner of Police.

The reward poster which was exhibited throughout Britain by Scotland Yard in their efforts to capture Harry Roberts, the only one of the trio who had managed to escape the police net

GREAT CRIMES AND TRIALS

returned empty-handed. A reward of £1,000 was offered on 16,000 posters. Roberts was described as slimmish with 'George Robey' eyebrows.

THE OFFICERS' FUNERAL

On the morning of 31 August, 19 days after the shootings, the road opposite the police station at Shepherd's Bush was filled with limousines. It was the day of a funeral that was as much a display of dedication as an expression of grief and sorrow.

Over 600 policemen lined the route, and crowds braved the rain of the chill day in the late summer to pledge their solidarity with the forces of law and order. As the procession wound its way through the streets of West London, a single piper played a lament in the courtyard of Scotland Yard.

A week later, on 6 September, a memorial service for the three murdered police officers was held at

Westminster Abbey. Prime Minister Harold Wilson attended, and so did most other leading politicians of the day, along with many members of the judiciary and Members of Parliament. Most of the remainder of the congregation consisted of 2,000 policemen from all over Britain.

A new sensation, the escape from Wormwood Scrubs of the spy, George Blake, pushed the murder hunt off the front pages. As Roberts had known Blake in prison, some journalists wildly claimed he had engineered the break-out.

As weeks passed without Roberts' capture, the police agreed at the committal proceedings that the trial of the two men already in custody should start on 14 November without Roberts in the dock.

A somewhat rueful Superintendent Chitty made another appeal: 'It's been a difficult investigation. The public, the police forces throughout the country and

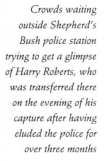

Crowds waiting outside Shepherd's Bush police station trying to get a glimpse of Harry Roberts, who was transferred there on the evening of his capture after having eluded the police for over three months

the world, have been very co-operative. All I can ask is the public will still send in these calls if they think they've sighted Roberts, because that is one way in which he might be caught.'

HIDING PLACE FOUND

Chitty's perseverance was to be rewarded. On the first day of the trial a note was passed to him that Harry Roberts' hiding place had been found in Epping Forest, after all. A farm labourer who had been looking for small game with a catapult had spied a man in a tent. It was only when the farm worker was questioned by a policeman about thefts in the area that he mentioned his discovery.

The policeman and a colleague quickly went to investigate. They found a carefully built framework of boughs and branches covered with tarpaulin and plastic sheeting. There was all the necessary equipment for a long stay.

They watched for a day and night, but nobody came back to the tent. However, the fingerprints they found there matched those of Roberts. The fox had been sighted.

A huge new search for Harry Roberts started in Thorley Wood, where his makeshift camp had at last been found. It was surrounded by policemen, many of them armed and all of them confident that this time Roberts would be caught. They moved in at dawn, sweeping the landscape, eager to find traces of their quarry.

Sergeants Smith and Thorne were looking in a hangar used for storing straw, when Smith spotted a jar of methylated spirits. On pulling the bales apart, Sergeant Smith found a primus stove. Behind another bale, he saw a sleeping bag. He gave it a hard prod with his rifle, and a sleepy, unshaven Harry Roberts emerged. 'Don't shoot,' he pleaded, 'you won't get any trouble from me. I've had enough. I'm glad you caught me.'

> "THE POLICE AREN'T REAL PEOPLE TO PROFESSIONAL CRIMINALS. THEY'RE THE ENEMY. YOU DON'T FEEL REMORSE FOR KILLING A STRANGER"
>
> Harry Roberts

As Roberts was taken into custody, police found a loaded Luger nearby. It turned out to be the one used to kill Christopher Head and David Wombwell.

The news of Harry Roberts' capture was immediately relayed to Superintendent Chitty at the Old Bailey, who went to meet the captured man that afternoon at Bishop's Stortford police station. Roberts admitted his guilt, but denied killing PC Fox.

Harry Maurice Roberts was charged with murder. That night he was taken back to Shepherd's Bush police station, just a short distance from Braybrook Street where he had gunned down two policemen.

A large crowd was waiting, hoping for a glimpse of this notorious murderer who had escaped the police net for over three months. His mother came to see him and at first failed to recognise him, all hairy and unkempt. She asked if the police had harmed him. 'No,' he replied, perhaps with sarcasm. 'They have been the essence of kindness.'

NEW TRIAL

It was decided that the trial of Duddy and Witney should be stopped, and a new one held for all three. At that trial, which began on 6 December, Roberts pleaded guilty to the murders of two of the policemen. Witney and Duddy pleaded not guilty. But all three were quickly convicted of what Mr Justice Glyn-Jones called 'the most heinous crime committed in this country for more than a generation'.

The murderers of Sergeant Christopher Head and Constables David Wombwell and Geoffrey Fox received 30-year sentences.

John Duddy died in Parkhurst Prison in 1981. John Witney was released in 1989, after 23 years. Harry Roberts, who once told a reporter: 'The police aren't real people to professional criminals. They're the enemy. You don't feel remorse for killing a stranger,' was still in prison at the end of 1993.

MARTIN LUTHER KING'S WHOLE PHILOSOPHY WAS BASED

ON PASSIVE RESISTANCE TO THE OPPRESSION OF THE BLACK

PEOPLE OF THE UNITED STATES. BUT ALTHOUGH VIOLENCE

WAS ANATHEMA TO HIM, THE BRILLIANCE OF HIS SPEECHES

AND THE SIZE OF THE DEMONSTRATIONS HE LED WERE

GUARANTEED TO AROUSE THE BIGOTS WHO OPPOSED HIM.

HE UNCANNILY FORESAW HIS END BY A SNIPER'S BULLET.

BUT WHO WAS BEHIND THE KILLING? WAS IT REALLY ONLY

A RACIST THIEF ON THE RUN FROM A JAILBREAK, OR DID

RESPONSIBILITY LIE PARTLY WITH THE FBI ITSELF?

Martin Luther King

The Assassination

There were flames and riots in the streets of Paris as protesting students came close to bringing down the French government. Russian troops invaded Czechoslovakia and snuffed out the Prague Spring uprising. United States aircraft kept up their round-the-clock bombing campaign against the communists in Vietnam.

It was 1968 and, on 3 April, Dr Martin Luther King Junior, America's leading campaigner for civil rights, arrived in Memphis, Tennessee, to lend his support to a local strike: 'Well, I don't know what will happen now. We've got some difficult days ahead. But it really doesn't matter with me now, because I've been to the mountain top. I don't mind. Like anybody I would like to live a long life – longevity has its place but I'm not concerned about that now. I just want to do God's will.'

The next evening he was dead. He had been staying at the Lorraine Motel and had stepped on to the balcony outside his room when the fatal shot came. He fell backwards, mortally wounded.

As police cars drew up, colleagues pointed to the row of buildings across Mulberry Street as the source of the shot. One of them had a window wide open. Police officers hurried round to the front of that building, on South Main Street: Bessie Brewer's rooming house. Earlier in the afternoon a man calling himself John Willard had booked in there.

The room with the window open was a bathroom. It looked directly out onto the Lorraine. The window sash had been jammed open. In the bath were footprints. The man who had paid $10 for a week's rent of room 5B was nowhere to be seen. The police soon identified him as James Earl Ray, a 40-year-old escaped convict, armed robber and man of many aliases.

> ## "VIOLENCE DISHONOURS HIM. FOR HE SOUGHT THE REDEMPTION OF MAN, NOT VIOLENCE"
>
> Colleagues of Martin Luther King at a press conference after the assassination

DR KING'S STRUGGLES

Memphis was in the grip of the garbage workers strike, which had been the reason Martin Luther King was there, to support the mainly black strikers. Only 39 years of age at his death, Dr King had first come to prominence in 1956 when he organised a boycott of segregated buses in Montgomery, Alabama. His home was bombed, but within a year, black and white passengers sat side by side on the buses.

He turned his attention to other obvious areas of segregation such as lunch counters. Amid angry scenes, some restaurant owners resisted serving black patrons. Dr King took his inspiration from the leader he most admired, Mahatma Gandhi, who had always insisted on the use of non-violent protest.

Dr King's methods won respectability for the cause of black equality. As political leaders vied for the emerging Negro votes, he and his colleagues were invited to the White House. Martin Luther King was seen rubbing shoulders with Presidents.

But it was an uphill struggle and King was frequently arrested for crimes such as 'loitering'. In 1958 he lost two ribs when a woman, hiding a gun and shouting about communists, stabbed him in Harlem. In 1960, he was acquitted of income tax chicanery.

He had quickly become a national figure, promoting the weapon of economic boycotts: 'If we're going to be free, we must refuse to spend our money in businesses and industries that discriminate against Negroes in their hiring policies.'

His thirteenth arrest came on Good Friday, 1963, when he led a march as part of the ongoing campaign against segregation in Birmingham, Alabama. He and 52 followers were determined to be arrested in order to draw attention to the campaign, and the notorious local police chief, Eugene 'Bull' Connor, said he was happy to oblige. The charge was parading without a permit.

HIS FAMOUS DREAM

On 28 August 1963, some quarter-of-a-million people participated in the Washington march. As well as the civil rights leaders, there were filmstars like Marlon Brando and Judy Garland. Before leading a delegation

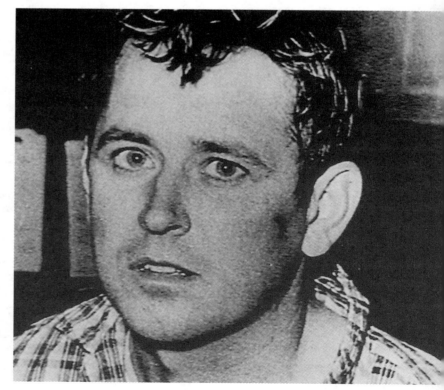

James Earl Ray was an ex-military marksman, an armed robber and an escaped convict who went by many aliases. After US authorities alerted Interpol, he was caught by British police on a plane to Brussels just over two months after the assassination

to President Kennedy, Martin Luther King made the occasion his own with one of the most enduring speeches of the twentieth century: 'I have a dream that one day on the Red Hills of Georgia, sons of former slaves and the sons of former slave owners will be able to sit down at the table of brotherhood. I have a dream. I have a dream that my four little children will one day live in a nation where they will not be judged by the colour of their skin but by the content of their characters. I have a dream today.'

In response, the following month a bomb in Birmingham, Alabama, killed four little girls at a Baptist Sunday school. Dr King returned in sorrow.

He drew attention to stubborn pockets of resistance all over the South: 'There in the midst of the darkness of Mississippi I saw that little light because of the great determination of the people themselves to be free.' In June 1964, he was arrested again when he went to Florida to demonstrate against a motel which was refusing to allow blacks to stay or eat.

But the following month, he won a great victory when President Johnson signed the Civil Rights Act, bringing into law many of the measures Dr King had campaigned for. The President invited him to the signing, and said: 'I urge every American to join in this effort to bring justice and hope to all our people.'

After the signing, President Johnson sought out Dr King's hand to shake, a symbol which some powerful figures in Washington privately frowned upon.

NOBEL PEACE PRIZE

They frowned even more that October when he was awarded the Nobel Peace Prize for his stirring fight for civil rights and adherence to the principle of non-violence. A torchlight procession in Stockholm hailed his transition to an international figure.

But violence struck again at the apostle of pacifism in the lobby of a hotel in Selma, Alabama. Dr King was registering at the previously all-white Albert Hotel when a member of the National States Rights Party hit him in the face and kicked him in the stomach. That incident, in January 1965, initiated a new wave of violence as die-hard whites saw their traditional position threatened.

Protesters at the garbage workers strike in Memphis in April 1968. Martin Luther King had gone to the city to support the mainly black workers

The passions Martin Luther King aroused meant that he faced dangers every day. In March, two weeks after militant black leader Malcolm X had been shot and killed in New York, state troopers waded into demonstrators, aborting a march from Selma to Montgomery. Later in the month, the march was restarted, this time with Martin Luther King leading it, wearing a lei from the Hawaiian contingent. President Johnson had sent 3,000 troops to keep order. By the time the marchers reached the state capital their number had grown to 25,000 people.

But in June, as marchers were battered with a club by a rider in a slow-moving truck in Philadelphia, Mississippi, a man attacked a newsreel cameraman, destroying his equipment. Dr King, who called Neshoba County the most brutal in America, voiced his protest: 'Why didn't you stop him? He ran right down the middle of the street. And he ran by the policemen, they did nothing to restrain him. They didn't arrest him, they didn't try. Now we want to know whether we're going to have police protection around here.'

Dr King went to the White House again in August 1965, when a Bill was signed ensuring federal registration of black voters. But he was cautious about the effect it would have: 'Well, I think that in some areas there will be an easing of demonstration where there is a real compliance with the 1964 Bill and with the new voting Bill, that is if it is vigorously implemented. I think in those areas, we may see a decrease in demonstrations.'

Violence still stalked the South. James Meredith, the first black person to gain a place in the state university, led a march into Mississippi. Suddenly there was a shot and he was on the ground, wounded in the back and legs. Martin Luther King rallied the marchers and led them on to finish their march.

> "I HAVE A DREAM THAT MY FOUR LITTLE CHILDREN WILL ONE DAY LIVE IN A NATION WHERE THEY WILL NOT BE JUDGED BY THE COLOUR OF THEIR SKIN BUT BY THE CONTENT OF THEIR CHARACTERS. I HAVE A DREAM TODAY"
>
> Martin Luther King

BLACK POWER

While King persevered in his non-violent approach, 'Black Power' groups were rapidly gaining influence. Many young blacks followed new leaders who preached that violence should be answered with violence, while Dr King continued to preach his message of non-violence: 'I still have a dream this afternoon. That one day segregated schools will become a thing of a dark past. White and black children will sit together in the socially healing context of the classroom. I still have a dream this afternoon.'

White extremists reacted by calling for blood. His blood. Demonstrations in the North, in Chicago, constituted a new and worrying factor for him. Although Dr King was convinced that his life was in real danger, he continued to preach restraint and to move through hostile crowds with courage. He again took his inspiration from Gandhi, who had been assassinated 20 years before: 'I think it's one of the most tragic pictures of man's inhumanity to man that I've ever seen. And I've been in Mississippi and Alabama, but I can assure you that the hatred and the hostility here, are really deeper than what I've seen in Alabama and Mississippi.'

THE KU KLUX KLAN AND THE FBI

The most obvious of Dr King's enemies were the Ku Klux Klan and other white supremacist groups. But which were the most *dangerous*? There were others who hated him no less and were more devious.

Among Dr King's enemies was J. Edgar Hoover, the founder of the FBI. Evidence later emerged which seemed to link Hoover with attempts to destroy King's reputation. When King was due to receive the Nobel Prize, he received an anonymous letter accompanying tapes recorded by the FBI which exposed a series of affairs. The letter said: 'You are a colossal

(l to r) Hosea Williams, Jesse Jackson, Martin Luther King and Ralph Abernathy on the balcony of the Lorraine Motel in Memphis on 3 April 1968. The next evening, standing in approximately the same spot and talking once again to Jackson, King was shot

fraud and an evil, vicious one. There is but one way out for you. You had better take it before your filthy, abnormal, fraudulent self is bared to the nation.'

King's weakness was that he was a loving father but an unfaithful husband, and the tapes were potentially damaging proof. 'They are out to break me,' he told a friend. The agents bugging him triumphantly reported his fears.

Simulated view through a telescopic gunsight from the bathroom window of Bessie Brewer's rooming house, the source of the shot which killed Martin Luther King. King had been standing to the left of the door with the wreath in the upper left quadrant

By 1968, when he came to Memphis to support the striking garbage workers, the harassment had intensified. He was in a constant state of concern that someone might resort to physical action against him. When fighting broke out, King thought it could be used as a cover to hurt him. He told aides: 'I've got to get out of here.' Memphis police were poised for more violence and swooped on troublemakers.

On the way to preach a sermon at the Masonic Temple, King had evidently been shaken. What he said to the congregation there later seemed prophetic: 'I just want to do God's will. And he's allowed me to go up to the mountain. And I've looked over and I've seen the promised land. I may not get there with you. But I want you to know tonight that we as a people will get to the promised land. For I'm happy tonight. I'm not worried about anything. I'm not fearing any man. Mine eyes have seen the glory of the coming of the Lord.'

The next evening, at 6.01pm, came the fatal shot on the balcony. A rifle bullet struck him on the right side of his jaw, penetrating his neck and severing his spinal cord.

The next day at a press conference his lieutenants offered this epitaph: 'Violence dishonours him. For he sought the redemption of man, not violence.' But, as his body was viewed by mourners in Memphis, there were riots all over the country, and 39 people were killed.

His wife Coretta was brave and dignified at his funeral in Atlanta. In his last brooding days, he had preached about death and made requests about his funeral. He had said: 'Tell them not to mention I have a Nobel Peace Prize or three or four hundred other awards, that's not important. I want you to say that I tried to love and serve humanity. If you want to say that I was a drum major, say that I was a drum major for righteousness. I won't have the fine and luxurious things of life to leave behind. I just want to leave a committed life behind.'

WHO KILLED KING?

Now the world wanted to know who had killed him and why. A police spokesman promised to find out: 'This evidence has received most careful scrutiny, and leads derived from it are being comprehensively followed up in several parts of the United States.'

The police quickly came up with a plausible theory. They described a racist thief who had escaped from jail a year previously and had pursued his personal demon, awaiting an opportunity to kill Dr King. At last he had found it – and the perfect spot for a sniper's nest. He had stalked his prey, seized his opportunity, scored with a single shot.

The other lodgers staying in the boarding house described him: 'He was about five ten or eleven, dark sandy hair, and a ruddy complexion.'

He had helpfully left a bundle in a doorway containing the rifle with his fingerprints on it, ammunition, binoculars and a radio. These were quickly traced to James Earl Ray, but the man himself had driven away from Memphis in a white Mustang.

JAMES EARL RAY

An ex-military marksman, Ray had escaped from a 20-year sentence in Missouri State Penitentiary by hiding in a bread truck. Two days after the shooting he abandoned his Mustang in Atlanta. Then he took a bus to Toronto in Canada. His plan was to go to Angola via Portugal.

The Canadian passport office checked recent identity photos and found his likeness under the name of Ramon George Sneyd. They alerted Interpol. British police spotted the name Ramon Sneyd on the passenger list of a Brussels bound plane on 8 June, and James Earl Ray was finally arrested. He was sent back to the United States on 19 July, handcuffed to the seat of a plane.

He was taken to Shelby County Jail in downtown Memphis, and intensively questioned. He later complained that he was pressured to plead guilty by threats that both his father and brother would be arrested as conspirators in the murder.

At Memphis Courthouse on 10 March 1969, Ray's 41st birthday, he pleaded guilty to the first-degree murder of Martin Luther King. He said nothing to dispute the charge that he was a lone gunman. James Earl Ray waived his right to a public trial and said he would accept the sentence of the court. By a previous agreement this avoided a death sentence and he was given 99 years in jail. Almost at once he regretted his decision.

Coretta King at the funeral of her husband in Atlanta. Thousands of mourners lined the streets as Martin Luther King's body was carried to Moorhouse College where an open-air service was held

CIVIL RIGHTS - CONSPIRACY
INTERSTATE FLIGHT - ROBBERY
JAMES EARL RAY

FBI No. 405,942 G

After being sentenced to 99 years in jail, James Earl Ray claimed there had been a conspiracy and that though he had bought the murder weapon, he had certainly never fired it

RAY'S NEW STORY

Ray discharged his lawyer and applied for a new trial, ready to reveal all he knew of the conspiracy that he claimed led up to the assassination. On 11 March 1969, he was moved to the state prison at Nashville. Although news reporters were waiting at the prison, he ignored their offers to speak into their microphones. If he could not get a new trial he wanted some other safe place to tell his story.

This was that he had been employed by a man called Raoul whom he met in a Montreal bar. After he had proved his competence at smuggling, Raoul gave him $700 to buy the murder gun, pretending it was part of a contraband deal. A rendezvous was arranged on South Main Street in Memphis on the day of the assassination. Ray gave the gun to Raoul, who either passed it on to the real assassin or used it himself. The tell-tale evidence of his fingerprints and the identifying serial numbers had been left to point suspicion.

In 1978 James Earl Ray was finally given the opportunity to tell his story before the House Select Committee on Assassinations. On 15 August a helicopter lifted him out of the prison on the first leg of his journey to Washington. But he found a less than sympathetic audience for his story.

Ray said that he was instructed by the mysterious Raoul to bring the gun to Memphis. He assumed it was part of a Mexican gun-running deal. It was not true that he had tracked Dr King for months as he journeyed through the South. He had not even known that Dr King would be speaking that day.

As for the firing of the shot, he said it was not him. It could have been Raoul or some other hired sharpshooter. He alleged he was nowhere near the rooming house during the shooting, but trying to get a tyre fixed at a garage. He took off when he saw the police activity.

THE FBI LETTER

After Ray was taken back to jail, the Assassinations Committee heard evidence about the anonymous letter which had been sent to Dr King. Who wrote it?

An FBI witness said: 'Well, that's a matter of dispute. It was found in the files of Mr Sullivan, who was the assistant director of the FBI and was heavily involved in these programmes. He claims that it's a plant in his files, and that someone else in the Bureau in fact wrote the document. The document which was found is a draft of the anonymous letter that was actually sent.'

When asked if there was any dispute that the letter did, in fact, come from the FBI, the witness replied: 'We've heard no dispute of that.'

This confirmation understandably upset the heirs of Dr King, such as the Reverend Robert Williams: 'Mr Hoover and his little clique that are still here should be indicted and tried for murder and when the truth, the whole truth, comes out to the American people, what J. Edgar Hoover did is going to make what Richard Nixon did look like a Sunday school picnic.'

In its findings, the House Committee concluded that James Earl Ray was the assassin, but he had not acted alone. The likelihood was that a right-wing conspiracy based in St Louis had planned the assassination, and Ray expected to get $50,000 for the hit. It absolved the FBI, but the Bureau was guilty of 'gross abuse' in its surveillance of Dr King.

TELEVISION 'RETRIAL'

Ray never got his official retrial, and remains in prison still protesting his innocence. But in 1993 one was staged for television in Memphis. Ray testified by remote camera from prison. The jury was unanimous: not guilty.

Although the mystery of Martin Luther King's death may never be solved, he left us a legacy: the lesson that, if you care enough, dreams can come true: 'So even though we face the difficulties of today and tomorrow, I still have a dream.'

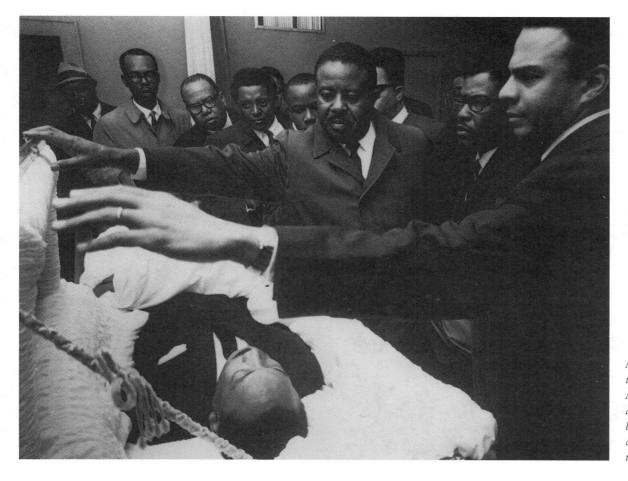

Mourners paying their last respects to Martin Luther King as he lay in state, before closing the coffin in readiness for the funeral procession

HOWARD HUGHES WAS FANATICAL ABOUT HIS PRIVACY. ALTHOUGH REPUTED TO BE AMERICA'S RICHEST MAN, AND A MAN WHO TRAVELLED THE WORLD, FEW GOT CLOSE TO HIM. HE ENTERED AND LEFT THE WORLD'S PLUSHEST HOTELS WITH HIS ENTOURAGE, SOMETIMES WITH HIS FACE BANDAGED TO AVOID IT BEING SEEN, NEVER ADMITTING HIS PRESENCE, NEVER GIVING INTERVIEWS. IT CAME AS A GREAT SHOCK THEREFORE WHEN PUBLISHERS MCGRAW HILL PROUDLY ANNOUNCED A POTENTIAL WORLD BESTSELLER: THE HOWARD HUGHES AUTOBIOGRAPHY. IT TURNED OUT TO BE A STORY IN WHICH ALL WAS NOT WHAT IT SEEMED.

Howard Hughes

Autobiography Hoax

The year 1971 saw an American lieutenant, William Calley, found guilty of murdering Vietnamese civilians, Emperor Hirohito of Japan going on his first trip abroad – to the US and Britain – and Mick Jagger marrying Bianca. At the end of that year, the sedate world of publishing also made its own little splash on the news pages.

It was on 7 December that the literary world of Manhattan was astonished by the news that reclusive billionaire Howard Hughes had agreed to tell his life story to an obscure writer named Clifford Irving, previously best known for a book called *Fake*.

A month later there was even more surprise as the legendary aviator, producer and entrepreneur protested via a sound-only press conference that the proposal was a hoax.

Irving countered from his house on Ibiza. He assured reporters that the billionaire had met him many times and the voice at the press conference was not that of Howard Hughes: 'Basically it was his money and he could do what he wanted with it. I met Howard Hughes, he talked to me, he gave me the material and I have it.'

To the question: 'Do you believe the book will still be published?' he replied: 'Oh, that's a good question. I believe it would be a crime if it's not published, because it is the autobiography of Howard Hughes and as far as I know he wants it published.'

The book was ready to go to press and it was sure to be a massive bestseller if it truly revealed the mind of one of the most extraordinary men of the century, who had suddenly disappeared from sight after a life of adventure.

At 18 Howard Hughes inherited the $10 million Hughes Tool Company, an oil-drilling business with exclusive patents. He ran it himself and, at 21, moved to Hollywood, divorcing Ella Rice, the girl he had married two years before. Soon he had become a successful movie producer, dating the stars. Among them were the glamorous Ginger Rogers; English actress Ida Lupino, whom he helped to become one of the few female directors; Ava Gardner, who, during a row, hit him over the head with a bronze statue; Jean Peters, his second wife, whom he tried but failed to make into a major star; and Jane Russell, for whom he designed a special bra when she acted in his most successful movie, *The Outlaw*, which he directed himself.

FLYING HIGH – AND FAST

But his first love was aviation and breaking records. In 1934, he flew across America in a record nine-and-a-half hours. He twice broke the world air speed record, reaching 352 miles per hour in 1935, and bettering that in a specially converted mail plane in 1937.

A year later he set his sights on the round-the-world record of 7 days, 18 hours achieved by Wiley Post in 1933. His twin-engined Lockheed landed at Brooklyn on 14 July, shattering the world record by taking only 3 days, 19 hours and 17 minutes. He and his three-man crew had travelled via Paris, Moscow, Omsk, Yakutsk in Siberia, Alaska and Minneapolis.

Howard Hughes in 1934 with Jean Harlow whom he had directed in the film Hell's Angels *four years earlier. Multimillionaire movie maker and speed flyer, the young Hughes was anything but reclusive, dating many Hollywood stars of the day*

A crowd of more than 30,000 had gathered to greet them, and Hughes and his crew were mobbed as they emerged from their aircraft. Everyone was delighted by the modesty of their new hero. Then came the official welcome and a ticker tape parade down Fifth Avenue and Wall Street, which was only slightly marred by the injury of two women, hit by a motorcycle outrider who had been struck by a heavy roll of unfurled tape. New Yorkers threw around 1,800 tons of paper, some 200 tons more than on Lindbergh.

Honoured with a Congressional medal, Hughes paid tribute to his fellow pilots: 'Any one of the airline pilots of this nation, with any of the trained army or navy navigators and competent radio engineers in any one of our modern passenger transports could have done the same thing.'

Not all his flying was as successful. He was his own test pilot, crashing four times, and was once written off for dead, emerging with a crushed chest, nine broken ribs and a lacerated skull. He was so badly scarred that he grew and kept a moustache to hide the burns.

When the Second World War broke out Hughes started a new business, Hughes Aircraft, with the aim of once more becoming a pioneer, this time with advanced flying machines. His most ambitious project was a giant flying boat more than twice the size of any other plane of its day, and more than a third larger than today's 747 jumbo jet. Because of wartime shortage of metals, he built it of wood. Hughes called it the Hercules H-4, but his detractors had other, more cruel names for it: some called it the Flying Lumberyard, others the Flying Coffin.

The name that stuck was the Spruce Goose. The big question was: would it fly? The war was over before that question was answered. In 1947 Hughes said he would prove it could. Few others thought it could ever lift off. As the Spruce Goose moved forward on the sea the thousands of spectators held their

> ## "I MET HOWARD HUGHES, HE TALKED TO ME, HE GAVE ME THE MATERIAL AND I HAVE IT"
>
> Clifford Irving

breath. At first it seemed stuck to the surface. Then it appeared to be straining upwards. It was flying! But after one mile, the Spruce Goose hit the water again, and that was the end of its flying career. The monster was put into mothballs in a hangar at Long Beach in California where, as the largest aircraft ever built, it soon became a tourist attraction.

THE AIRLINE TYCOON

Hughes was called before a Congressional committee to explain why the Spruce Goose, which cost US taxpayers a staggering $18 million, turned out a white elephant. But he shrugged it off, as he did another committee hearing the same year about his airline, Trans World Airways, and the battle with its rival, Pan American.

TWA was a triumph for Hughes. He had built it up from nothing, and made it into one of the largest airlines in the world and a symbol of American strength and technical prowess, pioneering some of the most modern airliners of the day, such as the Lockheed Constellation.

In front of the Senate he revealed some of the pressures he had been put under to amalgamate with PanAm: 'During that luncheon the Senator in so many words told me that if I would agree to a marriage of TWA with Pan American Airways and go along with his Community Airline Bill that there would be no further hearing in this matter.'

In 1966, Howard Hughes sold TWA at a profit of $500 million. But by then he had already been a recluse for many years, having disappeared into self-imposed purdah in the desert in the early 1950s.

DAYS OF MYSTERY

Hughes added to the mystery surrounding him by buying up $100 million worth of real estate among the casinos of Las Vegas, and investing $300 million in its gambling industry.

As peripatetic as he was secretive, he travelled all over the world, but it was difficult to spot him, whether he was in London, at the top of the Inn on the Park in Park Lane, or in the Bahamas, either hidden in another top-floor hideaway at the Hotel Xanadu in Nassau, or at the Britannia Beach Hotel.

Hughes ran his vast empire by remote control through a trusted accountant named Noah Dietrich. Dietrich worked closely with Hughes for 32 years, until they suddenly fell out. Then Dietrich decided to use the scribbled notes with which Hughes communicated his wishes to his executives as the basis of his own autobiography.

THE INVISIBLE MAN

Growing ever more eccentric, Howard Hughes, now believed to be the richest man in America, hid his face completely, sometimes swathed in bandages, when moving in and out of hotels. Once when a member of his entourage was asked: 'Did you see the fellow they brought out through the lobby?' he replied: 'That was the invisible man.'

The only people who ever saw his face were his five Mormon bodyguards. His bizarre lifestyle made him easy pickings for conmen, who offered false photographs, interviews and memoirs.

He could afford to pay for his privacy, and hotels guarded it strictly:

Reporter: We were told that you didn't have Howard Hughes up there. Who was that fellow up there in your Presidential suite?

Hotel Employee: We don't give out that information. Howard Hughes is not here.

Reporter: That isn't Howard Hughes?

Hotel Employee: No.

Reporter: Well, who is it?

Hotel Employee: That we don't give out.

RICH PICKINGS FROM PUBLISHER

It was not surprising that many people suspected another scam when they saw the headlines about Hughes' proposed autobiography. But McGraw Hill could argue that Clifford Irving was a known author who had arrived with letters in Howard Hughes'

handwriting confirming that he would collaborate with them in the production of the book.

Irving produced further letters from Hughes urging publication and expressing surprise at any delays. He claimed to have had more than 100 meetings with the recluse, and it was not surprising that McGraw Hill executives, led by publisher Albert Leventhal, grew increasingly excited by the prospect of such a massive coup.

They had few doubts about signing a contract with Irving and Hughes, and they accepted instructions, apparently from Hughes, to send cheques to Clifford Irving for sums which eventually totalled more than $600,000.

Irving himself received an initial $25,000 advance, and the remaining money was paid in cheques made out to H.R. Hughes. These were soon cashed.

One of the many letters which Clifford Irving produced for publishers McGraw Hill, purportedly written by Howard Hughes himself, urging the swift publication of his autobiography and expressing his astonishment at the needless delays

Clifford Irving and his wife Edith leaving New York's Chelsea Hotel on their way to court in February 1972. Using the stolen identity card of Helena Rosencrantz, her first husband's wife, Edith was able to cash cheques made out to H.R. Hughes

A MYSTERY WOMAN

On 13 May 1971 a flight landed at Zurich Airport. On board was a woman wearing a wig and dark glasses. She quickly made her way to the offices of the Swiss Credit Bank in Bahnhof Strasse. There she opened an account in the name of Helga Rosencrantz Hughes.

Swiss banks are famous throughout the world for their discretion. There seemed no reason to query the woman's Swiss passport and identity card or her relatively modest deposit of a thousand Swiss francs. Over the next seven months the account fluctuated as large American cheques from the publishers McGraw Hill were paid in and the lady withdrew equally large sums of cash.

By early December Helga Rosencrantz Hughes had withdrawn all the money in the account, in cash, leaving the bank holding photostats of the McGraw Hill cheques, which she had countersigned on the back: H.R. Hughes. The signatures on the cheques matched the one she had signed on her original bank account signature card.

THE LONG-DISTANCE INTERVIEW

On 7 December McGraw Hill announced the forthcoming publication of the book and almost immediately Howard Robard Hughes denied any part in it. On 7 January 1972, he gave his first press conference in 14 years: by telephone from Nassau to an audience of seven selected journalists in a conference room at the Sheraton Universal Hotel in Los Angeles. They sat fascinated as his voice emerged from the loudspeaker on a table in front of them, pointing out how fantastic the whole affair was.

Reporter: I take it, sir, that you do not know a man named Clifford Irving then?

Hughes: No, I never saw him. I never even heard of him until a matter of days ago when this thing first came to my attention.

Reporter: You think that it's possible that there has been a man going round representing himself as Howard Hughes and has duped this author?

Hughes: Duped the author?

Reporter: Yeah – into thinking he was talking to Howard Hughes.

Hughes: No, that doesn't seem possible to me. I mean, it seems to me that the author has ample motivation for doing this thing without being duped.

Reporter: I understand he got paid $300,000 advance for the book.

Hughes: That's what I've been told and that's what we're trying to run down because that's the one thing that I don't understand here. In other words there's got to be a bank record somewhere of this transaction. It is so fantastic and so, I don't know, beyond the bounds of anyone's imagination that I simply haven't any idea what . . . Well, obviously the motive for Irving could be money.

Reporter: Thank you very much, sir.

Hughes also signed two affidavits rejecting the book's authenticity. All seven of the questioners had met him in the past and all agreed that it was Hughes' voice. A recording was rushed to a laboratory where Dr Laurence Kersta compared it with a recording of Hughes' voice at a Senate sub-committee hearing in Washington: 'From the result of our analysis this afternoon it must be my opinion that it indeed was Howard Hughes' voice.'

PUBLISHERS STAND FIRM

But Irving and his publishers still insisted theirs was the genuine article. Returning to the United States with his wife, Edith, and their son, Irving asked reporters if McGraw Hill and Time Life would conceivably have parted with such massive sums unless they were certain they were buying the real thing.

Publisher Harold McGraw backed Irving unconditionally at a press conference, producing cheques with apparently genuine endorsements. To him, the evidence seemed irrefutable: 'Personally handwritten letters, personally signed contracts, endorsed cheques which you've just seen, and then the manuscript itself, edited in his handwriting on a good many of the pages.' Handwriting experts backed him up.

But by the end of January 1972 serious doubts were creeping in, and Irving emerged from New York's Chelsea Hotel to confront sceptical reporters who were asking if it were true that the Swiss Credit Bank had called in the police and that McGraw Hill had suspended publication of the book. Events were now speeding up, and on 31 January two Grand Juries were called to see if there was fraud.

THE WHOLE EDIFICE COLLAPSES

The Irvings were called to testify before the Grand Jury. Then on 10 February McGraw Hill admitted they had been fooled. It was a hoax. Separately, Edith was accused by the Swiss police of passing herself off as Helga R. Hughes.

Now it emerged that when Irving had said he was with Howard Hughes, he had really been off with other women. One of them was scuba instructress Anne Baxter, who did little to back up his story. The other was the singer and Danish Countess Nina Van Pallandt, of Nina and Frederick fame, whose evidence was damning. A reporter outside asked her: 'Did you talk to the Grand Jury about your visit to

Once the hoax was exposed by Hughes, Clifford Irving faced both Grand Jury and Internal Revenue Service investigations. The various women he had actually been with at the times when he was supposedly meeting Hughes did little to back up his story

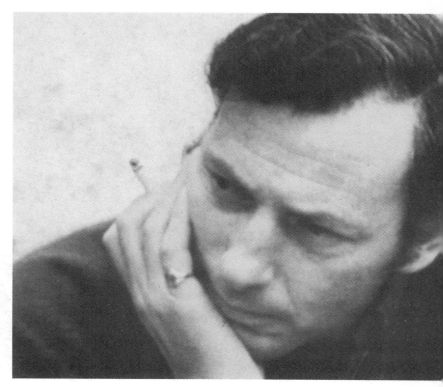

Mexico with Clifford Irving and did you confirm to them what you said in Europe which was that he never saw Howard Hughes?' Nina replied: 'Not in my presence, no.' Pressed further, she declined to be more specific.

Worse was to come as the source of Irving's basic information was revealed to be Stanley Meyer, a Hollywood wheeler-dealer. He had supplied Irving with a draft of Noah Dietrich's memoirs about his years with Hughes. With the Dietrich diaries to work on, Irving and his friend Richard Suskind got the inside information they needed to produce the authentic looking manuscript which bamboozled McGraw Hill.

Charges were immediately filed, and these were spelled out by Assistant District Attorney Robert Morvillo: 'Investigation conducted by the office of the District Attorney of the office of New York and the office of the United States for the Southern District of New York. Indictments were filed in both the state courts and in the federal courts today charging Mr and Mrs Clifford Irving and Mr Richard Suskind with crimes in connection with the so-called authorised autobiography of Howard Hughes.'

HOW IRVING DID IT

Reporters listened intently as the two prosecutors spelt out where Irving had got the model for his forgeries of Howard Hughes' writing: 'After seeing the "Dear Chester Bill" letter in its entirety in *Life* magazine he realised that his first effort in simulating the writing of Mr Hughes was faulty and on subsequent occasions he redid it.'

The two prosecutors then went on to detail the precise method Irving and Suskind had used to give their manuscript such apparent authenticity: 'In July and August on the isle of Ibiza a book was written in tape-recording sessions between Mr Irving and Mr Suskind. What would happen is that on one day Mr Irving would pretend that he was Mr Howard Hughes and Mr Suskind would ask him certain questions based upon their research and on the next day Mr Suskind would pretend that he was Howard Hughes and Mr Irving would ask him questions based upon their research and then those tape recordings were transcribed. The book that was eventually given to McGraw Hill was a transcription of conversations between Clifford Irving and Howard Hughes.'

Robert Maheu, a former employee of Howard Hughes, leaving the New York federal courthouse after testifying before the Grand Jury that he had never met Clifford Irving and was not the source of information for the 'autobiography'

The hoax had gained worldwide publicity, but reporters were anxious to know whether financially it really had been such a big fraud. In his answer the prosecutor broadly stated why he thought people had found this particular case so fascinating: 'Well, because there is an indictment still pending and there hasn't been any plea, I can't give you too broad an answer with regard to that. But I can say in our securities fraud unit, on a daily basis we get crimes of a much greater magnitude in the area of security swindles, market manipulations and things like that. I think this particular case just has a combination of factors which makes it irresistible to follow.'

The game was up, and on 6 March the Irvings confessed that their proposed *Autobiography of Howard Hughes* had been a fraud.

They also revealed the way in which they had been able to cash the cheques which McGraw Hill had thought were going to Howard Hughes. It was indeed Edith Irving who had gone to Zurich to open the false bank account at the Swiss Credit Bank. She had stolen the identity card of her first husband's wife Helena Rosencrantz to justify the initials. Once the account was in place with an apparently authentic signature she had no trouble paying in and withdrawing large sums.

The Swiss Credit Bank claimed to recognise her: 'The cashier who made two or three of the payments to her remembered her quite well.'

THE PUNISHMENTS

The couple and Richard Suskind pleaded guilty to attempted fraud and agreed to collaborate fully with the authorities who in return promised leniency. Clifford Irving received two-and-a-half years and Suskind six months. Edith Irving was released having been awaiting sentence for two months, but she still had to stand trial in Switzerland.

> **"I THINK THIS PARTICULAR CASE JUST HAS A COMBINATION OF FACTORS WHICH MAKES IT IRRESISTIBLE TO FOLLOW"**
>
> Assistant DA Robert Morvillo

Clifford Irving was freed after serving 17 months of his sentence and, finanacially, he appeared to have profited little from his attempt at fraud: 'I'm broke. I need a job in the sense of a publisher and I need a place to stay for my family.'

He had agreed to pay back all of the money that remained from the advances he had been paid, and publishers McGraw Hill were able to reclaim the rest from their insurers.

Edith was given a second prison sentence of two years by the Swiss authorities. Although there was a joyous public reunion between Edith and Clifford upon her release, the Irvings' marriage was soon over.

Clifford Irving moved back to America from Ibiza to write a book about the scam he now liked to look on as a practical joke. He continued to project his undoubted charm in new directions and, during an interview at his rented house in Connecticut, he philosophised about his motives: 'Well, W. Somerset Maugham says money is the sixth sense that enables us to enjoy the other five.'

Less than four years later on 5 April 1976, Howard Hughes, the man who had enabled Irving to try to realise his dream of massive wealth, died of a stroke in his private jet.

Distant relatives shared his fortune, and Clifford Irving seemed resigned to being known forever more as the man who failed to get a share. An interviewer began by asking him: 'Have you ever been introduced without anybody mentioning the word fraud or hoax?' His reply: 'No, I never have, and it's one of my ambitions that that will happen.'

It is an ambition unlikely to be fulfilled. But his book about the hoax did top the bestseller lists. The man whom Irving had gambled would never expose him never did write his autobiography, but the exploits of Howard Hughes were so extraordinary that they did not need one in order to live on.

WHEN PATTY HEARST, AN HEIRESS FROM THE RICH NEWSPAPER-OWNING FAMILY, WAS KIDNAPPED, IT SEEMED THAT THE KIDNAPPERS, WHO CALLED THEMSELVES THE SYMBIONESE LIBERATION ARMY, WERE MAKING UNUSUAL DEMANDS, LIKE REQUIRING FOOD TO BE DISTRIBUTED TO CALIFORNIA'S SIX MILLION PEOPLE ON WELFARE. BUT WHEN PATTY WAS CAUGHT ON SURVEILLANCE CAMERAS LEADING AN ARMED ROBBERY ON A BANK, THE AFFAIR TOOK ON SOME EVEN STRANGER TWISTS. THERE WAS TO BE AN AMBUSH, A BLOODY SHOOT-OUT AND A BLAZING HOUSE BEFORE THE CASE WAS CONCLUDED.

Patty Hearst

The SLA Kidnap

The biggest news of 1974 was the resignation of Richard Nixon as President of the United States after the Watergate scandal. There was satisfaction in Britain as Harold Wilson returned to Downing Street as Prime Minister, and surprised applause at the United Nations as the PLO leader Yasser Arafat addressed the world.

There was surprise too when on 15 April surveillance cameras at the Hibernia Bank in a suburb of San Francisco recorded a robbery. For one of the female robbers looked familiar. She was Patricia Campbell Hearst, the heiress who had been kidnapped nine weeks before.

She had been born into luxury, daughter of Randolph Hearst, owner of the newspaper empire which included the *San Francisco Examiner*. His father, newspaper magnate William Randolph Hearst, had been the model for Orson Welles' film *Citizen Kane* and had built the legendary mansion, San Simeon, which Randolph Hearst subsequently gave to the state of California.

When Patty Hearst was a 19-year-old student at Berkeley University, she moved into an apartment on

Bienvenue Street with her fiancé, Steven Weed, a lecturer at the university. On 4 February 1974 two people broke into their apartment, hit Steven Weed, grabbed Patty, and stuffed her into the boot of their car.

An eyewitness said: 'I heard a scream and then I heard what were gun shots and I looked out the window and then all I saw were the sparks of the gun going off and I hit the floor.' Asked whether she had heard the girl who was being taken out say anything, she replied: 'Well, I heard her pleading, "Please no, not me," or words to that effect.'

By the time Steven Weed came round, Patty was imprisoned in a cupboard. Her parents waited at home in the elite suburb of Hillsborough: 'We sit by the phone, and we answer them and we just hope that whoever has our daughter will turn her loose. They haven't killed anybody yet, they haven't injured anybody terribly seriously, nobody is crippled for life or anything like that. I just hope that they don't go any further and I hope that they will return our daughter to us safely.'

TAPED MESSAGE

Radio station KPFA received the first message from the little known terrorist group, the Symbionese Liberation Army, and a tape from Patty: 'I had a few scrapes and stuff, but they washed them up and they're getting OK, and I caught a cold but they're giving me pills for it. I'm with a combat unit that's armed with automatic weapons, and there's also a medical team here. These people aren't just a bunch of nuts, they've been really honest with me. But they're perfectly willing to die for what they're doing.'

There was a warning from the leader of the SLA, the self-styled Field Marshal Cinque: 'Whatever happens to your daughter will be totally your responsibility and the responsibility of the authorities which you represent. If they and yourself violate these, her life and the blood of that will be upon your hands only.'

Recognising their daughter's voice, the Hearsts awaited the kidnappers' demands. Her father said: 'I believe she's safe, I believe that they are taking good care of her and I believe these people are sincere.'

Demands soon came: first, free two captured SLA men, Russell Little and Joseph Remiro, and then distribute $70 worth of food to each of California's six million people on welfare.

Hearst protested this would cost $400 million, far beyond even his means. His daughter's voice on another tape, which was found in a luggage locker, modified the demands: 'Dad, Mum, I'm making this tape to make you know that I'm still OK and to explain a few things, I hope. They had every intention that you should be able to meet their demands, they're not trying to present an unreasonable request, it was never intended that you feed the whole state. So whatever you come up with basically is OK and just do it as fast as you can and everything, everything will be fine.'

Patricia Hearst with her former fiancé Steven Weed. Her kidnappers knocked him unconscious and then abducted Patty from the couple's home in Berkeley

Field Marshal Cinque – by now identified as escaped convict Donald DeFreeze – added some chilling rhetoric of his own: 'You do indeed know me, you've always known me: I'm that nigger you've hunted and feared night and day. You know me, I'm the wet back, you know me, I'm the spic. Yes indeed, you know us all and we know you: the oppressor, murderer and robber – and you have hunted and robbed and exploited us all. Now we are the hunters that will give you no rest and we'll not compromise the freedom of our children. Death to the fascist insect that preys upon the life of the people.'

Patty's father hurriedly launched the 'People in Need' programme, funded with $2 million of Hearst money. A thousand volunteers attempted to distribute food but there was chaos, fighting, and widespread pilfering. Later distributions were better organised but in Oakland a full-scale riot erupted and 36 people were arrested.

On 3 April, a new Patty tape was received. Much of it was unintelligible, but she called her parents racists and proclaimed that she had joined ranks of the Symbionese Liberation Army. Only now was she freed from her cupboard prison.

CHANGE OF NAME AND TONE

Allegedly brainwashed, misinformed, abused, raped and cowed, she announced that she was adopting the name of Tania and becoming an active member of the gang. The next day another tape confirmed her decision: 'I'm joining the forces of the Symbionese Liberation Army, and fighting for my freedom and the freedom of all black people.'

Convinced by her captors that she had been abandoned, she posed with a gun in front of their flag and made a further attack on her family: 'And I would never choose to live the rest of my life surrounded by pigs like the Hearsts.'

> "I'M JOINING THE FORCES OF THE SLA AND FIGHTING FOR MY FREEDOM AND THE FREEDOM OF ALL BLACK PEOPLE"
>
> Patty Hearst

As the news made headlines worldwide, Patty agreed to take an active part in violent acts with the other members of the gang. These members were: 28-year-old Donald DeFreeze, an escaped prisoner who called himself 'General Field Marshal Cinque Mtume'; Nancy Ling Perry, called 'Fahizah', aged 27, a former topless dancer; William Wolfe, aged 22, who called himself 'Cujo', son of a rich doctor; Camilla Hall, codenamed 'Gabi', aged 24, daughter of a Lutheran minister; Patricia Soltysik, who called herself 'Zoya', ex-Berkeley student and writer of Patty's tape-recorded messages; Angela Atwood, known as 'Gelina'; and William Harris, codenamed 'Teko', ex-member of the Marine Corps and husband of Emily Harris, born Schwartz, now codenamed 'Yolanda'.

To test her, the gang took Patty on their next exploit – the armed raid on the Hibernia Bank. She later claimed that she was covered by guns the whole time. Eyewitnesses said she shouted at them: 'The first person who moves gets his head blown off!' and 'Get on the floor – we're not fooling around.' She convinced both the gang and the FBI that she was now a genuine member of the SLA, and the FBI issued a warrant for her arrest.

Patty's next tape insisted that she had acted of her own free will: 'I was positioned so that I could hold customers and bank personnel who were on the floor. My gun was loaded and at no time did any of my comrades intentionally point their gun at me.'

The FBI printed thousands of posters. Their effect was to confirm Patty in her sense of isolation and ostracism from the world she had known. The following month, two of the gang, Bill and Emily Harris, stole some socks from Mel's Sporting Goods store in South Central Los Angeles. When the clerk tried to stop them Patty Hearst shot 30 rounds from an automatic rifle from the getaway van parked across the street.

HEADQUARTERS ATTACKED

No one was hit, and all three escaped in the van but didn't realise that it had got a parking ticket that morning. This clue soon led the police to 1466 East 54th Street, which they were sure must be the headquarters of the SLA. They surrounded it with a 374-man task force including a battalion of paramilitary SWAT officers. It grew into the biggest operation ever mounted in the history of the California police. They were determined to get the gang – alive or dead.

At 5.44pm, they issued a loud-hailer warning, which was ignored. So they decided to smoke out the gang – which they now assumed included Patty Hearst – with tear gas, and gave the occupants of the house one last warning. Then they alerted all forces for the final attack, convinced that they faced a ruthless and well-armed enemy.

The demands for surrender brought a barrage of bullets, and in the next 40 minutes over 6,000 shots were exchanged. The gang had clearly decided to die rather than surrender. As police fired more tear-gas canisters, Nancy Ling Perry came out shooting. She was cut down in a fusillade of police bullets.

The others hacked their way into the two-foot crawl space between the ground floor and the foundations. Then the house caught fire. At this stage, the police didn't know who or how many were in there. Overhead, helicopters prepared to swoop.

As the heat grew unbearable, Camilla Hall attempted to crawl out of the ventilation shaft. A police marksman put a bullet through her forehead.

NO PATTY

As the flames died down, the police began a body count. Willie Wolfe, Angela Atwood, and Patricia Soltysik had been burnt to death; Nancy Ling Perry and Camilla Hall had been shot; Donald DeFreeze had put a bullet in his brain. But where were Patty Hearst and the Harrises?

The following week the police put what was left of the SLA's arsenal on display. They had discovered that Patty Hearst and the Harrises had not been at the house at the time of the raid, and now both the police and the FBI vowed to track them down. They charged Patty with committing 20 crimes, two of them carrying life sentences.

Patty Hearst caught on surveillance tape during a robbery at the Hibernia Bank in San Francisco. She later claimed that she had been forced to take part and that she was covered by guns the whole time

But the fugitives seemed unrepentant. On a tape sent to a radio station, Patty eulogised her dead comrades. She stated that life was very precious to her, and that she would never surrender.

Now she fled east across the United States with the Harrises. Meanwhile, the FBI tried to adapt photographs of Patty to show what she would look like in various disguises. These subsequently turned out to look little like the reality.

For a while Patty and the Harrises lived in a remote farmhouse in Pennsylvania which was later discovered by the FBI. Despite hours spent attempting to clean their fingerprints before they left, there were enough remaining to link them with the house. While there they ran four miles every day with weighted kit, to toughen up. Patty was in charge of training several new recruits in the use of firearms. Once she was in a car crash; the three sheriffs who rescued her didn't realise who she was.

They fooled their neighbours too. One later described them as: 'People that we came to know vaguely. There were two men and two ladies, and the story they told us was that they were people from New York, I believe, and they were a sports writer and his associate, secretary and proofreader. One girl was Chinese, the other was a redhead.'

They returned to California where they robbed two banks: at one of them Emily Harris accidentally killed a customer.

PATTY'S ARREST

Then, in San Francisco, more than a year after the rest of the SLA had been killed, an FBI agent, acting on a tip-off, burst into an apartment at 625 Morse Street. In the kitchen he found two women. One of them was Patty Hearst.

When arrested, Patty gave a clenched fist salute and listed her occupation as 'urban guerrilla'.

Outside a nearby house, the two Harrises were arrested on their way back from jogging. 'Yolanda' ran away but was easily caught. 'Teko' gave in without a struggle. All three were formally charged on two counts of bank robbery and the use of a firearm to commit a felony.

Patty Hearst giving a clenched fist salute to the press as she was driven away after her arrest. At first she was defiant and listed her occupation as 'urban guerrilla' but once she realised that her parents still loved her, she quickly lost her SLA persona

Ex-marine William 'Teko' Harris and his wife Emily 'Yolanda' Harris who were caught with Patty. They both received eleven-year sentences, later reduced to just three years, despite Emily having killed someone during a bank robbery

At first, Patty seemed defiant. But she quickly lost her 'Tania' persona when she found that her parents still loved her and showed their happiness on television. When asked if Patty had been glad to see them, her mother replied: 'She was. We told her we loved her and hugged her and kissed her. We are eternally grateful to the FBI and the San Francisco police for bringing Patty in safely.'

A STORY UNFOLDS

As the arraignment proceedings began in the federal courthouse in San Francisco, Patty haltingly told her family a story of brainwashing that at first seemed incredible – how she had been held for weeks in a cupboard until she was so disorientated and desperate that she would accept almost anything that her captors told her.

American opinion was divided when her lawyer Terrence Hallinan announced her defence at a press conference. It was that Patty had been completely robbed of her free will: 'She remained in this closet with her hands bound, blindfolded and no lights on. The closet was hot and extremely uncomfortable.

When the blindfold was removed she felt as if she were on an LSD trip: everything was out of proportion, big and distorted.'

The suggestion that she had been drugged was later denied by Patty. Her lawyer continued: 'After an interminable length of time which seemed to her to be weeks, she was released from the closet and seated with the gang of captors who were at that time discussing the robbery of a bank. And she was instructed by them that she must accompany them to the bank, that she must allow herself to be photographed by the bank camera and in addition that she must announce her name aloud so that everyone would know that she was participating in the holdup.'

Patty and her first lawyer disagreed over tactics, and within a week he was replaced by the famous and flamboyant F. Lee Bailey. But even he couldn't get her out on bail.

The prosecution case was in the hands of the chief US attorney for Northern California, James R. Browning Jr, who announced that his line would be that Patty participated willingly in all the holdups. Her trial opened on 4 February 1976.

On 1 February 1979, having served most of her sentence, Patty Hearst was granted clemency after her parents appealed to President Carter

THE TRIAL

Jury selection took five long days. The defence was keen to have ex-military men who would appreciate the power of brainwashing. The prosecution wanted women, and the final jury had seven. But finding an unprejudiced twelve was hard. When Judge Oliver Carter asked the pool of potential jurors if any had not heard of the case not a single hand was raised.

The defence team argued over whether Patty should go on the stand. Finally she agreed, but Bailey instructed her not to answer questions which would incriminate her. This risked alienating the jury but did conceal her presence at the bank robbery where a customer had been killed.

The prosecution produced a string of witnesses who testified that she had been acting of her own volition, but under orders from her erstwhile captors. James Browning seemed utterly confident. When asked if he were apprehensive at the start of the trial, he replied: 'Not at all, not at all, we're looking forward to getting started.'

F. Lee Bailey, on the other hand, seemed ill-at-ease and unhappy. His strategy that she had been an unwilling victim was undermined by the Harrises,

who were allowed to give a string of interviews claiming Patty had been a keen, loyal member of the SLA.

Under cross-examination, Patty couldn't really explain why she hadn't run away when she had the opportunity. The best she could come up with was that she had been afraid that both the SLA and the FBI would come after her.

Under constant pressure from the press, Patty's parents began showing the strain which would eventually lead to their separation. When asked what she thought of her daughter's testimony, Mrs Hearst said: 'I thought they asked her everything except who her kidnappers were. It's perfectly obvious that the government and the FBI have no interest in bringing her kidnappers to justice.'

F. Lee Bailey's instructions to his client to refuse to answer questions about her year on the run meant 42 defiances of the judge's rulings. The psychiatrists he questioned were repetitive. And his closing argument seemed muddled.

A QUICK VERDICT

Sequestered throughout the trial, the jury spent only one night considering their verdict while just one of their number held out. Their quick decision caught everyone by surprise.

So, on 20 March 1976, Patricia Hearst returned to court to hear the jury find her guilty of armed robbery and the use of firearms to commit a felony. Patty was not surprised at the verdict.

Sentencing was delayed for six months while the authorities waited to see if she would testify against other members of the SLA. She did.

While Bailey pleaded Patty had already been brutalised, vilified, tortured, molested, punished, convicted and incarcerated, the prosecution argued for a heavy sentence on the grounds that she had shown no remorse. Judge Carter had died since the trial and was now replaced by Judge William H. Orrick. He sentenced her to seven years in the penitentiary.

Her mother assured her that the fight for her freedom would go on and an appeal was launched to the Supreme Court. On 26 July she was back in court, ready to testify about the shoot-out at Mel's Sporting Goods store on behalf of the prosecution against Bill and Emily Harris. But Emily and her husband presented no defence so Patty was not needed as a rebuttal witness.

Emily was angry at Patty's betrayal, as she saw it. She and her husband each received sentences of eleven years, but these were later reduced to just three by a community release board.

Granted bail of $1 million, Patty had lived with her parents at Hillsborough, near her childhood home. But, on 24 April 1977, the Supreme Court rejected her appeal and instructed her to report back to the federal prison at Pleasanton to complete her remaining sentence.

Her parents were understandably dismayed at what had happened, and her father stated: 'This is one thing I've always heard and . . . really I think it annoys me. It is that this girl, because she comes from a wealthy family, presumably, and an influential one, should be given . . . and should be treated like anybody else. Now we hope to God she had been treated like anybody else. If she was anybody else I wish the SLA had treated her like anybody else because if they had treated her like anybody else she never would have been kidnapped. And I wish the government and the press and everybody else had treated her like everybody else, because if they had treated her like everybody else I believe today she would be free.'

PATTY FREED EARLY

Many people were now feeling this, and public opinion had swung back in favour of clemency. Her parents appealed to President Jimmy Carter and finally, on 29 January 1979, only five months before Patty would be eligible for parole anyway, she was granted clemency. At 8am on 1 February 1979, she walked to freedom with her bodyguard, Bernie Shaw. There were rumours going round that they had begun a relationship while she was on bail.

> "IT'S PERFECTLY OBVIOUS THAT THE GOVERNMENT AND THE FBI HAVE NO INTEREST IN BRINGING HER KIDNAPPERS TO JUSTICE"
>
> Patty Hearst's mother

Jubilantly, she greeted the press waving the commutation paper. Asked what was the first thing she would do when she got home, she said: 'To have breakfast with my family and friends. And I'm going to go there now and thank you all so much. Bye bye.'

At last Patricia Campbell Hearst was back home with her family. Her long years of many kinds of imprisonment were over. She seemed philosophical about her ordeal: 'I think that I've gotten a lot stronger, a lot more self-confident. I take a lot of things in stride that make other people fall apart.'

Two months after her release Patty married her bodyguard, Bernie Shaw. Speaking of her sensational period as an urban guerrilla, she recently said: 'That girl was someone else.'

Patty Hearst with husband Bernie Shaw, her former bodyguard whom she married two months after her release

JIMMY HOFFA WAS A BRILLIANT LABOUR LEADER AND UNION ORGANISER. HIS MEN IN THE TEAMSTERS UNION WERE PREPARED TO OVERLOOK SOME OF HIS BEHAVIOUR BECAUSE HE DID WELL FOR THEM. THAT BEHAVIOUR, IN PARTICULAR, LED TO VERY CLOSE LINKS WITH THE MAFIA, INTO WHOSE ENTERPRISES WERE INVESTED MILLIONS OF DOLLARS OF TEAMSTER FUNDS. ONE WHO WOULD NOT OVERLOOK THIS CONNECTION WAS SENATOR ROBERT KENNEDY. THE TWO MEN WERE AT WAR. BUT WHEN HOFFA SET OFF FOR A LUNCH APPOINTMENT ONE DAY AND WAS NEVER SEEN AGAIN, IT WAS NOT KENNEDY WHO WAS SUSPECTED OF FOUL PLAY. WHAT DID HAPPEN TO HOFFA?

Jimmy Hoffa

His Disappearance

The United States finally admitted defeat and pulled out of South Vietnam in 1975, and the Vietcong drove in triumph into Saigon. President Ford had little to say to newsmen about the defeat while the discredited aides of his predecessor, the disgraced Richard Nixon, tried to show a brave face to the world about their prison sentences.

America's most charismatic labour leader and union organiser, Jimmy Hoffa, was fighting to get his old job back as President of the Teamsters Union. On 30 July 1975 Hoffa set off for a lunch appointment at Max's Red Fox Restaurant near Detroit. He was spotted leaving the restaurant parking lot in a car. Then he went missing, and no trace of him was ever seen again. There was a nationwide search, all in vain. His disappearance remains a mystery.

Controversial and corrupt, gutsy and abrasive, the 62-year-old Hoffa had made a lot of enemies as President of the Teamsters.

Born in Brazil, Indiana, in 1913, Jimmy Hoffa was left fatherless at the age of seven. He quit school early to help support his mother and brothers. The young Hoffa got a job unloading food, and joined the

International Brotherhood of Teamsters, Chauffeurs, Warehousemen and Helpers. By the age of 18, he had been elected a local official. He called a strike, just when a load of strawberries had to be moved into cold store. Management caved in immediately.

Hoffa had discovered his vocation: union organiser. He proved a fearless recruiter and negotiator. The 1930s were a rough time for labour relations in the United States. Organisers were killed, cars were bombed and strikes often turned violent. Hoffa's brother was among the victims of a shooting that occurred during one of these strikes. Troops were sometimes called in, and management and unions used the Mafia to intimidate each other.

Hoffa threatened to move his members into the rackets. Then he came up with a deal: the Teamsters wouldn't get into crime if the Mob wouldn't interfere with his Teamsters. The Mob agreed to this, and gave a rake-off on the extra profits that resulted. Jimmy Hoffa had found his formula for success: cash and connections for him, jobs and security for the members of Detroit Local 299.

He married 18-year-old Josephine Poszywak, whom he had met when they picketed the laundry in which she worked. The couple soon had a daughter, then a son.

He worked long and hard for his members and to develop his own powerbase. Soon his talents were nationally recognised. The gutsy 5ft 5in organiser was sent to help members wherever a tough, no-holds-barred approach was needed.

In 1942, exempt from military service because his union work was considered vital to the nation, James Hoffa created a unified Michigan Conference of Teamsters. As the Second World War ended, Hoffa was re-elected President of Local 299.

The massive economic surge which the United States experienced after the Second World War gave the Teamsters an immensely powerful position, and Hoffa became chief negotiator of all Teamsters in the central United States. By 1956 he was in a position of national power, and was being courted by businessmen and politicians at home and abroad. In Israel he

met Prime Minister Golda Meir and personally donated large sums to found a children's home.

Hoffa's own house, in a back street in Detroit, bought for $6,800 in 1939, was just a place to sleep. Working a 20-hour day he had reached the No 2 spot in the Teamsters, and was heir-apparent to the ageing Dave Beck, nominal President of the union. It was Hoffa who controlled the members – and the money.

THE KENNEDY VENDETTA

But his links with the Mob landed him in 1957 in front of the Senate Select Committee on Improper

Labour leader Jimmy Hoffa testifying at the Labour Rackets Hearings in 1957. Despite evidence of links between the Teamsters and the Mafia, Senator Robert Kennedy was unable to make any charges stick to Hoffa

Jimmy Hoffa (right) campaigning for the Presidency of the Teamsters Union in September 1957. Despite his dubious connections with the Mafia, he won by a massive majority

Kennedy: Did you say: 'That SOB, I'll break his back'?

Hoffa: Who?

Kennedy: You.

Hoffa: To whom?

Kennedy: To anyone. Did you make that statement after these people testified before the Committee?

Hoffa: I never talked either one of them from testifying.

Kennedy: I'm not talking about to them. Did you make that statement, here in the hearing room after the testimony was finished?

Hoffa: Not concerning them, far as I know of.

Kennedy: Well, who did you make it about then?

Hoffa: I don't know, I may have been discussing somebody in a figure of speech.

Kennedy: Well, who did you make the statement – whose back were you going to break?

Hoffa: I don't even remember it.

Kennedy: Whose back were you going to break, Mr Hoffa?

Hoffa: Figure of speech. I don't even know who I was talking about and I don't know what you're talking about.

Kennedy grilled Hoffa 18 times and attempted to jail him for planting a stooge inside the Committee staff. Kennedy was appalled by the evidence which emerged of links between the Teamsters and the Mafia. He had earlier gone after Dave Beck, going into great detail to prove his links with organised crime. As a result, in March 1957 Beck was convicted of grand larceny for income tax evasion, false tax returns and misuse of union funds.

But Jimmy Hoffa was harder to pin down. The jury at his trial just couldn't agree, and he went free. So, with Beck discredited and fighting to stay out of jail, Hoffa made his move to win the No 1 spot. That year, 1957, he stood for President of the union, and was the popular favourite. The members felt that, however dubious his connections, he had their interests at heart, and that he was a tireless and successful negotiator for them.

Labour and Management Activities, popularly called the McClennan Committee. Robert Kennedy, the Committee's chief counsel, now declared a lifelong vendetta against Hoffa. On television he attacked the union official, often supported by his brother, the future President, who was on the Committee and sat beside him. The following is a typical sample of an exchange between the two men.

HOFFA WINS PRESIDENCY

He walked away with the Presidency, winning with 1,208 votes against 453 for his combined opponents. But immediately there were problems. A court order was obtained which restrained Hoffa from taking office until various questions raised by the McClennan Committee had been answered.

Then the AFL-CIO, the national federation of labour unions, decided that the racketeering charges against the Teamsters were bringing the rest of the labour movement into discredit. George Meany, the federation's President, led the drive to oust the Teamsters, and at its national conference in December 1957 over two-thirds of the delegates voted to expel the Teamsters. Hoffa shrugged off the news: 'The AFL-CIO didn't build us and they won't weaken us.'

He plunged into a flurry of activity, and pushed through the first national freight haulage agreement. The Teamsters became the largest labour union in America, partly by poaching other unions' members. These either didn't know or didn't care that not all Hoffa's methods were legal. Among the union's more dubious activities were extorting money from companies by threatening strikes or even bodily harm and bribing government officials.

Hoffa got an infamous Mafia chief, Anthony Provenzano, known as Tony Pro, made head of New Jersey's 14,000 Teamsters. Sadly, Tony's union work in Hoboken was interrupted by a seven-year sentence for extortion. It was just one example of the way in which the Teamsters and the Mafia had become intertwined at local level.

INVESTING IN THE MOB

The massive growth of the Teamsters during the 1950s gave Jimmy Hoffa control of a ballooning fund of union dues and pension contributions. Not for him

the banks or traditional investments. He poured the money into potentially much more lucrative real estate investments in Las Vegas and Florida, projects which were firmly controlled by members of the Mafia.

> "THE GOVERNMENT DELIBERATELY HID EVIDENCE; THE GOVERNMENT DELIBERATELY USED THE COURT TO HYPE EVIDENCE; AND THE GOVERNMENT HAS DELIBERATELY LIED, UNDER OATH"
>
> Jimmy Hoffa

Many of the decisions were made by Hoffa alone, and few other officials in the Teamsters had the authority or the knowledge to question him. In all, it is estimated that more than $50 million of Teamster money was siphoned into the crime syndicate's boomtown of Las Vegas. Kickbacks and secret loans became commonplace and many of these were never repaid.

By 1960 these activities had raised so many questions that Hoffa was spending much of his time going to court to answer charges arising from what he regarded as Robert Kennedy's personal vendetta against him. He was using nearly a hundred lawyers – all paid for by the union.

In 1962, Jimmy Hoffa exploited his re-election as President of Local 299 to show how solidly his members were behind him. For the first time since 1937 he faced a challenge. Every weekend he flew back from whatever part of the country his duties as union President had taken him to in order to campaign for his seat: 'Bobby Kennedy won't win this election, don't worry about it. We're gonna win it and that's all there is to it.'

There was little doubt that he enjoyed both the backing and friendship of many of his members. He had always made a point of being accessible to them, and now they returned his trust. For most of them he was the leader who had vastly improved their pay and working conditions, and they were not too worried about how he had achieved this as they went to the polling booths. Outside observers confirmed that the election was run totally honestly, and Hoffa won by 3,615 votes to 208.

But Bobby Kennedy, now Attorney General, was still on his trail. First came a charge for assault by a disgruntled Teamster aide. Then Kennedy put his quarry on trial for widespread bribery with union funds. The defence carted filing cabinets into court to counter each charge as it came up.

Hoffa was unrepentant – and confident: 'Since we don't know which witness or which loan is going to be discussed during the course of the day, we're forced to bring to the courtroom all of our files, to be in a position irrespective of what witness or what loan. We can immediately reach in the file and have access to the information to defend ourselves.'

Despite their President's courtroom troubles, the Teamsters flourished. The membership was largely divided between those who didn't believe the charges and those who didn't care. In the event, the government decided not to proceed with the assault charges, and the bribery case soon collapsed with a hung jury.

Hoffa's greatest threat came when a former mental patient tried to shoot him in court with an air pistol.

But this good luck did not last. The government brought new charges that Hoffa had bribed jury members to ensure that the trial would collapse. It then charged him again with diverting huge sums of money from the union's pension funds. Hoffa fought back: 'I have an affidavit in my possession signed by a former employee working for Walter Sheriden who in return works for the Justice Department, Bobby Kennedy, where he states emphatically they will never rest until they put Hoffa in jail, even if they have to trump up charges.'

When a reporter asked if he thought he would be in jail as a result of the trial, he replied: 'Not if I get a fair trial, and I have not received a fair trial here. The government deliberately hid evidence; the government deliberately used the court to hype evidence; and the government has deliberately lied, under oath.'

Jimmy Hoffa and Frank Fitzsimmons (right) taking their oath of office after their election in July 1966. Although Fitzsimmons, as Vice President, was only supposed to take over as President for the duration of Hoffa's imprisonment, in fact he connived with Nixon to keep Hoffa out of power for good

Teamsters Union President Jimmy Hoffa being questioned by the press in March 1967 shortly before he reported to the US District Court in Washington to begin his prison sentence for jury tampering. He had spent three years appealing but the conviction was upheld

HOFFA GOES TO JAIL

These assertions failed to impress. In March 1964 Jimmy Hoffa was found guilty of jury tampering. He received an eight-year sentence. Then in July he was found guilty of the conspiracy and fraud charges as well. His sentence was a further five years in jail.

Hoffa vowed to fight on and attacked his old enemy: 'I have been sentenced. I will appeal. I am not guilty, and I say to the millions of members of organised labour, have heed. Because those who'll fight for you and fight to win, will find that out of this conviction the zeal of Attorney General Robert Kennedy will be to destroy you unless you give in.'

He walked off to begin his struggle to stay out of prison. He remained President of the union, appointing his friend Frank Fitzsimmons Vice President on the understanding that, if imprisoned, he would take over again when released.

Over the next two-and-a-half years, Hoffa and his attorneys fought to keep him free. They accused the government of unconstitutional activities such as unauthorised wiretapping and the use of perjured witnesses, and they claimed that the charges had been trumped up as a result of the personal vendetta between Jimmy Hoffa and Robert Kennedy. But in December 1966 Hoffa's last appeal failed and his convictions were upheld.

On 7 March 1967, journalists mobbed the President of the Teamsters Union as he reported to the US Courthouse in Washington. Jimmy Hoffa was going to jail. It was a day he had thought he would never see. Now, with the handcuffs on his wrists covered by his raincoat, he entered Lewisburg Jail, swearing that he would not have to serve his full sentence of 13 years.

The years behind the grim walls were to prove bitter and humiliating. Once inside he found that he was not getting any special privileges. But much of the membership stayed loyal, and a Teamsters local sent an airplane greeting on every Valentine's Day, his birthday. A long streamer carried a message reading: 'Birthday Greetings, Jimmy Hoffa'.

He remained the nominal President for the first four years, but Frank Fitzsimmons soon stopped paying much attention to orders coming from Lewisburg. The hand-picked stooge found that he enjoyed his new power, and started looking for ways to turn his temporary job into a permanent one.

While Hoffa's attempts to get parole were turned down, Fitzsimmons was strengthening his links with Nixon, who was grateful for the support of a man with two million voting members, and such substantial funds. Nixon told Charles Colson, his Presidential assistant, to do anything he could to be helpful. Colson and H.R. Haldeman discussed Hoffa's release on terms favourable to Frank Fitzsimmons. They told junior counsel John Dean to draw up a document commuting Hoffa's sentence in such a way that Fitzsimmons could not be challenged by him. First Hoffa resigned the union Presidency. Then they wrote in a condition, which he didn't know about, that he couldn't take any further part in union affairs until 1980.

Finally, on 24 December 1971, President Nixon commuted James Hoffa's sentence. After four years and ten months, Hoffa was a free man. He seemed genuinely ignorant of any limitations on his release. When a reporter asked if there were any prohibitions placed upon his activity as far as getting back into labour management was concerned, Hoffa replied: 'I won't know that until I'm in Detroit on Monday and talked to the parole officer, who under the rules of the release from prison, will outline the conditions that I'll work under. I don't know.'

He was also tactful about the abilities of his supposedly temporary successor. When asked by reporters if he were satisfied that the union was in good hands in the hands of Mr Fitzsimmons, his answer was: 'Frank Fitzsimmons and I have been friends for over forty years. Frank came from off the truck when I first hired,

> ## "I SPENT ALL OF MY LIFE GETTING CONDITIONS, WAGES AND HOURS FOR WORKERS IN THIS COUNTRY. AND I STAND ON MY RECORD THEN AND NOW"
>
> Jimmy Hoffa

as I came out of a warehouse. He's an excellent administrator, knows the insides of the team and union just as well as I do and does an excellent job and I'm sure will continue to do so.'

This cloud of goodwill was quickly blown away when Jimmy Hoffa discovered that he had been legally castrated. Fitzsimmons and the White House had made sure he would never work in the union again. He seemed totally amazed: 'Not until I was on the street, and in St Louis, Missouri, some several hours later, did I know there was a 1980 restriction.'

Back at home in his lakeside cottage, Hoffa discovered that it wasn't only the White House which preferred Fitzsimmons as union President. The Mob had found 'Fitz' much easier to control, and Hoffa now started making veiled threats in his constant phone calls to former colleagues as to what he might reveal in order to get reinstated.

Meanwhile, Fitzsimmons was safeguarding his own position by donating $1 million to Nixon's re-election fund.

Hoffa's attempts to force the White House to publish the confidential documents relating to his release and the conditions imposed upon him failed. So did his attempt to have the Presidential limitation on his activities ruled unconstitutional.

There was a rash of violent incidents – the car of Frank Fitzsimmons' son was blown up, and supporters on both sides were physically attacked. Hoffa had also lost the friendship of Tony Provenzano by failing to back him in a pension scam. Provenzano was now a sworn enemy and dedicated to stopping Hoffa getting back into the union.

THE RED FOX RESTAURANT

So it was foolhardy of Hoffa to agree to go alone to a meeting at the Red Fox Restaurant in Bloomfield Township 15 miles northwest of Detroit. This was apparently with Provenzano or some of his Mafia colleagues to discuss making peace.

Jimmy Hoffa's last known movements were described by his son James P. Hoffa: 'He left for an appointment at Max's Red Fox Restaurant at approximately 1.30pm Wednesday, 30 July 1975. He called home at approximately 2.15pm. We have not heard from him since.'

Hoffa had called in at a limousine company on his way to the Red Fox. There he mentioned that he was meeting Tony Provenzano and a colleague. He was seen waiting in the car park looking angry. In his call to his wife he said that he had been stood up. The last sighting of him was driving off in a car with three men. A nationwide search followed, with hundreds of leads and reported sightings being followed up, but nothing was found.

The FBI became involved in the case on 3 August because kidnap demands were received. All of these proved false.

James P. Hoffa indicated one possible cause for his father's disappearance: 'It's difficult to imagine anybody having a motive to hire my father or abduct him and I would think that there must be some relationship back to the union, although I cannot name names and I really don't know names.'

One name which he may have had in mind was Charles O'Brien, Hoffa's foster son. 'Chuckie', as he was generally known, had been brought into the Teamsters by Hoffa but had then defected to Frank Fitzsimmons. O'Brien disappeared on 1 August and his union colleagues seemed perplexed by his behaviour. When asked by a reporter if it were normal for a man not to show up at work and not to call his boss to let him know why, an official replied: 'If you know Mr O'Brien, anything is normal.'

When O'Brien eventually reappeared after five days he had a perfectly clear explanation: he had gone to Memphis to spend time with his new bride, and then on to Washington for a business meeting with Frank Fitzsimmons. He seemed equally perplexed by his foster father's disappearance when interviewed: 'I came down here to visit my family and I get a phone call saying that I'm missing and it was blown into a proportion that I nearly came back to Detroit and made myself available to anybody that was involved in the case that wanted to talk to me.'

Tony Provenzano and his Mafia associates were interviewed but all had formidable alibis.

For the FBI the Hoffa case is still officially open, but their belief is that he never left the car he was seen driving off in, at least while still alive. One of the more popular theories has it that the three men seen in the car with Hoffa were Mafia executioners who shot or garrotted him as they drove along. His body was then supposedly stuffed into an oil drum and buried deep in a dump that had served as a Mafia cemetery before.

Since his disappearance and assumed murder, Jimmy Hoffa has been recognised as a brilliant labour leader whose links with crime were the downside of a ruthless dedication to his members. As he said: 'My philosophy is very simple. The working man of America is being short changed every day in America. And I spent all of my life getting conditions, wages and hours for workers in this country. And I stand on my record then and now.'

Like Faust he made a pact with the devil. Like Faust he paid the penalty.

Jimmy Hoffa outside Lewisberg Jail where he served nearly five years. Whilst his imprisonment and presumed murder by the Mafia point to a life of crime and conspiracy, Jimmy Hoffa has long been recognised as a brilliant labour leader

THERE WAS NO DOUBT ABOUT WHO HAD KILLED BOTH THE

MAYOR OF SAN FRANCISCO AND ONE OF THE CITY'S MOST

PROMINENT SUPERVISORS. IT WAS ANOTHER SUPERVISOR.

WHAT WAS IN DOUBT WAS HOW MANY OF THE CITY'S

POPULATION SECRETLY APPROVED OF THE KILLINGS. FOR

THE MURDERED MEN WERE ASSOCIATED WITH THE LARGE

AND INFLUENTIAL GAY COMMUNITY – SOME THOUGHT

TOO LARGE AND INFLUENTIAL. AND WHEN THE KILLER WAS

GIVEN A LIGHT SENTENCE ON THE GROUNDS THAT HIS

MIND HAD BEEN DISTURBED BY EATING JUNK FOOD, MANY

THOUGHT THAT JUSTICE HAD BEEN MANIPULATED. EVEN

THE KILLER COULD NOT LIVE WITH THE SCANDAL.

Dan White

The City Hall Killer

Prime Minister Begin of Israel and Egypt's President Sadat signed a peace accord in 1978, and Italy hoped for peace as members of the terrorist Red Brigades were brought to trial. There was ecological tragedy as the *Amoco Cadiz* ran aground off the coast of France, spilling oil into the English Channel, and personal tragedy in New York as veteran tightrope walker Carl Wallenda failed in his attempt to cross a busy street.

There was tragedy in San Francisco, too, when on 27 November, Dianne Feinstein, a city official, broke the news that both Mayor Moscone and Supervisor Harvey Milk had been shot and killed. The rumour was that an ex-supervisor, as city councillors are called in San Francisco, had shot both men and was roaming the streets with a loaded revolver.

San Francisco, home of the Golden Gate Bridge, cable-cars and Dirty Harry and famous for its gold rush and earthquakes, had become, during the 1970s, the place to which hippies and gays travelled from all over America to put flowers in their hair.

At least 100,000 homosexuals had settled down in the Castro district. Some estimates reckoned there was nearer 200,000. Whichever, it was a significant part of a city of 700,000 people, and enough for them to have elected their own supervisor. The man they had chosen was both loved and hated. His name was Harvey Milk, and he was the man who, that fateful day, was murdered alongside the mayor.

The man who fired the fatal shots soon gave himself up to the police. His name was Dan White and he had represented an Irish Catholic working-class area of the city. The accused was 32 years old and had served in Vietnam. He was well-known and well-liked.

Flowers were laid on the steps of City Hall. But while many mourned, others gloated. Dan White had been both a fireman and a policeman and, although the flags were dutifully lowered, many in both forces felt that the politicians had courted disaster – Mayor George Moscone by imposing an out-of-town police chief on the city, and Supervisor Harvey Milk by his

aggressive homosexuality. In the police station, White was treated more like a hero than a prisoner.

PROUD TO BE GAY

Dan White and Harvey Milk had both been elected on the same day. They couldn't have been less alike. Harvey Milk was Jewish and a New Yorker. Noted for his humour, he had only come to San Francisco in 1969. He opened a camera store on the main thoroughfare of the homosexual district, Castro Street, and set about becoming the community's leader.

Harvey had campaigned hard for his election, standing on a platform of improving the rights of gays and other minorities in the city. Once in office he showed that he cared about broader issues as well. He got wide publicity when he highlighted the dangers of dogs fouling the parks by apparently stepping on some muck. Actually it was a replica which he had planted himself.

Supervisor Harvey Milk (left) and San Francisco Mayor George Moscone in April 1977 at the signing of the city's Gay Rights Bill. They were both found shot dead in their offices at the City Hall

Dan White being taken for questioning at San Francisco's Hall of Justice on 27 November 1978, the day of the shootings

Proud to be gay, Milk had marched to the inauguration with his arm around his lover, Jack Lira. Later, on Freedom Day, he made a speech, proclaiming: 'Gay people, we will not win our rights by staying quietly in our closets. We are coming out!'

In his pocket he had carried an anonymous postcard. It read: 'You get the first bullet the minute you stand at the microphone.' His answer was: 'If a bullet should enter my brain, let that bullet destroy every closet door.'

Milk was openly supported by Mayor Moscone. Watching with a mixture of disgust and disbelief was Supervisor Dan White. He had been the only member of the Board to have voted against holding that year's Freedom Day parade.

UPHOLDER OF AMERICAN VALUES

Ex-cop Dan White was a proud man, too. Proud to be called working class. He was an athlete and a staunch defender of what he saw as traditional American values. In the fire service, he had won fame and a medal for saving a mother and child. He was invited to run

for elected office. He campaigned against turning a local Catholic school into a youth campus for juvenile delinquents and won handsomely. But his success meant he had to resign from his $18,000-a-year job as a fireman. Supervisors at City Hall were paid less than $10,000 a year, and he found he couldn't support his family on that.

White was forced to ask rich businessmen to settle his election expenses – and they expected some quid pro quo. Out of place in the wheeler-dealer world of politics, White was soon disillusioned. As he said: 'It's the first time in my life I did not have confidence in the decisions that were made by my peers.'

Unlike his adversary, Harvey Milk, White was not a political animal. He felt isolated by the mayor, who wanted the youth campus that Dan had pledged to fight against. So, on 10 November 1978, only one brief year after his election as supervisor, Dan White decided to resign. He told the press that neither his family nor his constituents were being properly looked after, so he thought he ought to concentrate on earning a living.

But his financial backers were upset when they heard, and pressured him to retract his resignation. Five days later, he attempted to. But the resignation was officially registered, so all he could do was to go to Mayor Moscone and ask to be allowed to be reappointed. He thought he had got the mayor's agreement.

THE POLITICAL MAYOR

George Moscone was a 15-year political veteran, a lawyer who had been a state Senator. He had fought a rough, tough campaign to become mayor of San Francisco, and had won with only a two per cent majority. From the start of his term of office, he was fighting the next election. He liked to keep everybody happy, but now he wasn't sure if it was necessary to placate Dan White's backers.

He thought he might get more political mileage out of appointing someone else to the post that Dan White had vacated, someone keen on the youth campus, for instance. Someone, perhaps, whose appointment might win more favours from Harvey Milk and the other key supervisors.

Besides, Moscone had just had a severe political setback when the Reverend Jim Jones, leader of a religious sect, had killed Congressman Leo Ryan in Guyana. Moscone had earlier made the bad mistake of appointing Jim Jones a housing commissioner. He explained: 'I appointed somebody who had a reputation as a peacemaker in this city, who had worked with poor people and people in frustration whose reputation was that you do not resort to violent means, you deal with reason and persuasion.'

There had been little reason about when Jones had Congressmen Ryan shot during a fact-finding tour. Later Jones had persuaded 912 of his followers – many of whom were from San Francisco – to commit suicide. Congressman Ryan's funeral took place on 22 November, only twelve days after Dan White's resignation, and George Moscone was aware that, politically, this was a highly sensitive time for him.

> ## "IF A BULLET SHOULD ENTER MY BRAIN, LET THAT BULLET DESTROY EVERY CLOSET DOOR"
>
> Supervisor Harvey Milk

Dan White wanted his job back, and there were rallies for and against the resigned supervisor happening under the mayor's window. White appeared on TV seemingly optimistic about his chances of persuading the mayor. He announced: 'When I leave the studio here I'm going right to the city attorney's office and I am very confident that I will be reappointed to my job.'

ENCOUNTER IN CITY HALL

However, on 27 November, Dan White heard from a reporter that George Moscone had chosen someone else. He set out immediately for City Hall. He had decided to confront the mayor – and the supervisor who was ruining him and his city.

In the pocket of his best suit were extra hollow-nosed bullets for the loaded gun he was carrying under his coat. He avoided the metal detector at the front door by climbing through a window – since fitted with bars – and walked down a corridor in the basement. He told police later that he had no intention at that stage of killing anyone, but that may be just the way he remembered it.

During an interview while awaiting trial, Dan White stated that he shot the two men when he realised he was not going to be reappointed to his position and that it was the first time in his life he had not had confidence in the decisions of his peers

Dan White going to court where his lawyers did not dispute his guilt but claimed that he was suffering from manic depression and therefore was not fully responsible for his actions

White went up the steps to the mayor's office, and in answer to his question, George Moscone confirmed he was going to appoint someone else. 'Why?' Dan screamed. 'Weren't you even gonna tell me?' George invited Dan into his parlour to have a conciliatory drink. 'Maybe we can help out . . .' he began, but Dan pulled out his gun and shot Moscone in the chest and the shoulder. The mayor crashed on to the floor. As he lay there, Dan carefully shot him twice more, in the head, severing the brain stem.

White then ran down the corridors until he reached Harvey Milk's office. He shouted at Milk: 'What the hell are you doing to me, my name, my family? You cheated me!'

Dan shot Harvey five times: in the stomach, in the chest, in the back, and in the head. He hurried back down the corridor and out of the building. He drove to a phone booth to ask his wife to meet him at a church. With her, he gave himself up.

It was left to Dianne Feinstein, now acting mayor, to break the news: 'Both Mayor Moscone and Supervisor Harvey Milk have been shot and killed. The suspect is Supervisor Dan White.'

WHITE EXPLAINS

As the bodies were being brought out of City Hall on trolleys, Dan White was in custody at police headquarters, trying to explain why he had killed Mayor Moscone. He said: 'I got kind of fuzzy and my head didn't feel right. He was talking and nothing was getting through to me. It was just like a roaring in my ears. He was going to lie to the press and tell them I wasn't a good supervisor and that people didn't want me. Then I just shot him.'

As for Harvey Milk's death, he said: 'He started smirking because he knew I wasn't going to be reappointed, as if to say "too bad!" I got all flushed and hot and I shot him.'

Appalled as she was by the murders, Dianne Feinstein spoke compassionately about Dan White: 'Supervisors are not paid very much. Dan has a newborn baby, had opened a new business, and had to mortgage his house.'

As the bodies of Mayor George Moscone and Supervisor Harvey Milk were taken from the coroner's office to funeral homes, a shocked calm settled over the city of San Francisco. The office where Milk was killed was sealed by the police. On the mayor's door was a bunch of flowers.

However, the gay community reacted angrily. Living as he had with threats, Harvey Milk had left a message to be broadcast if he were assassinated. He said: 'Don't be angry or go crazy in the streets. Do something positive in my memory, come out in the open, speak out for homosexual rights.'

A memorial service for the Catholic Moscone and Jewish Harvey Milk was held at City Hall. It was attended by thousands. Acting Mayor Feinstein delivered the eulogy: 'And if our spirits are numbed, tomorrow's future can be a bright one. Though we feel sorrow we must avoid the spirit of bitterness and recrimination; remorse must not beget revenge.'

Joan Baez led the singing as they lay in state together, the Catholic and the Jew, the family man and the homosexual, mourned by all who believed in the rule of law.

His grieving family saw Mayor Moscone buried with full honours. 'So we ask God why? We believe that George's death has not ended but merely changed, and that he has overcome death.'

The gay community held its own wake, with the lighting of a symbolic candle. There were positive speeches, as Harvey Milk had requested: 'Thank you George, thank you Harvey, thank you for living your lives, we celebrate your life and what you did for us.'

SUPPORTERS OF WHITE

But there were many people in the city who, while not approving of his method, felt that Dan White had acted for the good of the greater community. Within the ranks of the guardians of law and order there was a division of loyalties. They all knew and liked Dan White. And they watched with distress when District Attorney Joe Freitas announced murder charges and his determination to see a fair trial: 'In order to ensure that there be no violation of the full rights entitled to this defendant, and other defendants.'

When potential jurors arrived for selection, they found security tight. Liberals were screened out by both the defence and the prosecution, which had to be seen to be aiming for the death penalty. So the final jury wound up as twelve working-class people with a majority of Catholics – Dan White's sort of voters, not George Moscone's or Harvey Milk's.

THE TRIAL

The trial of Dan White began on 1 May 1979 with agreement on both sides that White had climbed into City Hall with a .38 Smith and Wesson, commonly called a 'Chief's Special', and killed the mayor, finishing him off with shots to the head. White had then reloaded, gone to the office of Harvey Milk, and shot him dead, too.

Dan White's lawyer didn't dispute the killings, but said that White was suffering from a mental illness: manic depression.

The key defence witness was Dr Marty Blinder, often called as a local expert in cases of diminished responsibility. Impressively erudite, yet popular in his language, Blinder convincingly portrayed Dan White as depressive, stressed out by what he saw as widespread corruption in City Hall. He described White as dazed and confused, committing the murders 'as if he were in a dream'.

The jury at Dan White's trial was told that the junk food White had eaten on the day of the killings had impaired his reasoning to the extent that he could not have premeditated the murders, despite all the evidence to the contrary

Encouraged by the skilful questioning from the defence counsel, Douglas Schmidt, Blinder diagnosed White's condition as having been aggravated by consuming junk food and bingeing on candy. All these factors taken together, he claimed, would impair a person's ability to premeditate.

The jury was so impressed and so relieved to have found a justification for going easy on Dan White that it voted for the mildest possible verdict: voluntary manslaughter.

News of the verdict quickly spread. One of the leaders of the homosexual community commented on the radio: 'This means that in America it's all right to kill faggots.'

GAY PROTESTS

Normally peaceful gays suddenly looked dangerous. Hundreds of them descended on City Hall, to be met with police batons. Frustrated in their efforts to storm the building, the demonstrators turned their attention to the cars the police had arrived in. By the end of the

night, 120 people had been injured and 60 arrested. Eleven police cars had been burnt to twisted metal, and the official estimate of damage was $1 million.

Now *two* inquests took place: was the riot avoidable and how did the 'Junk Food Defence' succeed?

Distinguished psychiatrist Lee Coleman made a detailed study of the testimony and went public to attack the jury's decision: 'The jury heard Dan White had something wrong with his brain chemically, and therefore was incapable of wanting to kill somebody. They heard that he wasn't even focusing his eyes at the time he finished off each man with two more shots to the head from close range. They heard that it was only the twinkies and the cokes, and without those the two men would still be alive. This testimony had to confuse the jury.'

All Dr Blinder could do in response was repeat his court testimony: 'He was a perfect superguy, and the loss of his job, his wife losing her job, lack of income, no sleep, getting more and more depressed, eating garbage, made him finally unable to tolerate it.'

The usually peaceful gay community of San Francisco reacted violently to the light sentence given to Dan White, stating that the judgement virtually condoned the murder of gays. 120 people were injured and 60 arrested during the protests

Dr Coleman queried how diminished White's responsibility really was: 'A person doesn't take extra bullets, avoid the front entrance metal detector, finish off each man with two extra close-range shots to the head after wounding them, if he doesn't plan to kill and intend to kill.'

Then, on 3 July, Dan White was sentenced to a maximum of seven years, eight months in jail. Dr Coleman's view that the jury had been over-influenced by the psychiatric evidence was backed up by Dr Jay Ziskin, a leading psychologist and lawyer: 'The forensic psychiatrists in my opinion had misled the judiciary, the legislature, the general public into believing that they had the capacity to accurately assess somebody's mental state a month prior to ever having seen him, when in fact there is no scientific evidence which will support that contention.'

There were attempts to try Dan White again under federal law, as happened in the 1990s when the Los Angeles police officers were acquitted of beating Rodney King. 'We'll get our justice. They've won the battle but they haven't won the war. We'll have our day in court and that's all we want.'

But on this occasion federal proceedings were not allowed to take precedence over a decision made at state level. Federal prosecutors accepted that there was no legal justification: 'We regret very much that we don't have the opportunity to prosecute. But that personal feeling of not being able to do it doesn't in any way change my opinion that the decision reached was the correct one.'

Dan White served five years, one month and nine days. Mayor Feinstein hoped it would be a quiet release: 'In five years there's time for people to put their feelings to rest and I believe that a good deal of that has already taken place. So I don't anticipate any major problems. I think there will be some vocal demonstrations, and every evidence we have at this point indicates that they will be peaceful.'

> **"THIS MEANS THAT IN AMERICA IT'S ALL RIGHT TO KILL FAGGOTS"**
>
> Reaction of one of the gay community's leaders to the jury's verdict

They weren't. There was still a great deal of anger within the gay community and among others who felt that justice had not been done.

During his term of imprisonment, Dan White had fathered a baby on a conjugal visit: proof, said protesters, that jail had not been any great hardship for him and that his crimes had not been adequately punished. Not all the protesters showed the tolerance they demanded from others: 'We are historically a city of joy, creativity and diversity. Dan White was a racist, sexist Johnny-come-lately from Southern California who tried to steal that from us.'

A threat to Dan White's life seemed real enough as protestors voiced their opinions: 'I think his life is in danger wherever he goes in the state,' said one. Another said: 'I honestly hope somebody gets him as soon as he gets out, and I've never wanted anybody to be injured in my life.' A less vengeful protestor said: 'Oh God, there's no way he would survive an instant here. I just hope that no one ever finds out where he is.'

They didn't need to. Just a year after his release, on 21 October 1985, police cars and an ambulance raced to Dan White's home. San Francisco's police chief broke the news: 'Dan White has apparently committed suicide. He was found in his car today at about ten minutes to two. There is a hose leading from the exhaust pipe into the car. There was a note left on the windshield of the car to his brother, apologising for putting him through the ordeal of finding his body, and there were some other personal notes, one to his wife, and one to his mother.'

By this time, Dan White was separated from his wife, and drowning deep in a wave of the depression that had already cost the lives of George Moscone and Harvey Milk. Mayor Dianne Feinstein had the last word: 'There is the hope that this is the end of what has been a very sad and tragic chapter in San Francisco history.'

THE SCARSDALE DIET HAD DEDICATED FOLLOWERS IN

MANY PARTS OF THE WORLD, SO IT WAS SENSATIONAL

NEWS WHEN ITS INVENTOR, THE CHARMING DR HERMAN

TARNOWER, WAS SHOT FIVE TIIMES BY HIS MISTRESS WHO

WAS JEALOUS AT FINDING HERSELF SUPPLANTED IN HIS

AFFECTIONS. WHEN IT WAS KNOWN THAT HIS KILLER WAS

THE RESPECTED HEADMISTRESS OF A TOP GIRLS' SCHOOL,

AND THAT SHE HAD WRITTEN HIM A TEN-PAGE LETTER

BEFORE DRIVING TO HIS HOUSE TO LEAVE HIM DYING IN HIS

BLOOD-SOAKED PYJAMAS, THE TRIAL WAS AWAITED WITH

GREAT INTEREST. WAS HER DEFENCE MISMANAGED?

The Scarsdale Shooting

As 1980 opened, Soviet troops poured into Afghanistan following their Christmas Eve invasion. Jimmy Carter lost the battle for the US Presidency to Ronald Reagan. There were explosions in both Britain and the United States as the SAS recaptured the Iranian Embassy from terrorists in London and as Mount St Helen erupted Stateside.

In Westchester, an exclusive county north of New York where the rich and famous of Manhattan take their ease, gunfire disturbed the peace, sparking a story that held the attention of women worldwide.

Five shots rang out on the night of 10 March 1980 at the home of Dr Herman Tarnower, famous for inventing the Scarsdale Diet. Inside he lay dying, as the police were called. Outside, they arrested a suspect named Jean Struven Harris.

Dr Tarnower was rushed to a hospital, and at 11.58 he was declared dead. The international success of his bestselling book ensured widespread publicity, which grew as it emerged that the arrested woman was his longtime mistress, famous in her own world as the head of a prestigious private girls' school. She was 56 and divorced. He was 68 and unmarried.

THE RISE OF DR TARNOWER

The son of a New York hat manufacturer, Herman Tarnower graduated in 1933. He began his career in the centre of New York, specialising in heart disease after serving his residency at Bellevue Hospital. In 1938 he moved to Westchester General Hospital, where he set up the cardiology department, ahead of his time in prescribing diets for his patients.

In 1941, Herman's career was interrupted when Japanese carrier aircraft attacked the US fleet without warning at Pearl Harbor, bringing the United States into the Second World War. Among the crowds of volunteers, Dr Herman Tarnower was in the forefront and Washington soon commissioned him to serve in the US Army Air Corps.

He spent a successful war, and when the planes carrying the atomic bombs took off, General Douglas MacArthur assigned Major Herman Tarnower to the Atomic Bomb Casualty Survey Commission. As the deadly mushroom cloud formed over Nagasaki, his Commission prepared to study the effects of the blast on the people who lived there.

He was on the first plane to land at Nagasaki after the Japanese surrendered. The destruction made a lasting impression on him, turning him from a hawk into a dove when discussion about war came up. Seventy thousand people died in the first blast, and Herman Tarnower realised that many times that number would be the victims of radiation sickness in the years to come.

So impressed was he with Japan that back home he built himself a house with a strong Japanese influence. He also built – and owned – a medical centre for Scarsdale in the same style. At first housing four doctors, it rapidly expanded until nine specialists shared the premises. The affluent of Westchester made it – and him – a great medical and financial success.

Outside his work, Tarnower believed in having a good time. A highly eligible bachelor, he took an endless succession of women on tropical trips, but never allowed himself to get too involved with any one of them. The game parks of Africa were favourite hunting grounds. He shot several animals and had their heads mounted for display. Some women complained he did the same with them.

THE FAMOUS DIET

When a publisher discovered Tarnower's one-page diet notes for patients, he convinced him to compile *The Scarsdale Diet*. Tarnower explained its success: 'To summarise why it works: it's simple, it's safe, it's satisfying and it's effective.'

He promised a loss of a pound a day by cutting out fat, butter, bread, alcohol and cream, and became an instant media celebrity appearing on America's top chat shows. In a society where being slim ranks almost as high as being rich, Tarnower seemed to have discovered the secret of both. Three million copies of his book were sold grossing $11 million.

He displayed a relaxed charm as he revelled in the publicity, working it like a professional: 'Low fat cottage cheese, with a spoonful of low fat sour cream, lots of walnuts and fresh fruit, and fruit that you want. And if you try it Merv, if you try it, you'll be addicted just as I am, no doubt about it. And don't get off to Tuckerhoe, go right to Scarsdale.'

Jean Struven Harris, headmistress of the exclusive Madeira School with an entry in the Washington Social Register, was nicknamed 'Integrity Jean' at the school where she worked. In reality, she was living off 'speed' and desperately unhappy

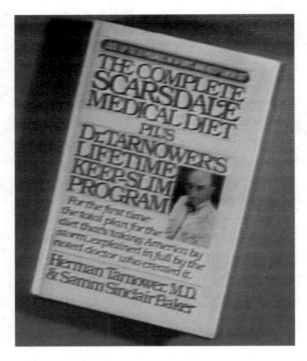

Dr Herman Tarnower became world famous for the Scarsdale Diet, appearing on many top chat shows. Jean Harris had helped him research and write the book

THE DOCTOR'S FRIEND

His first acknowledgement was to a friend who had helped with the research and writing of his bestseller. These special thanks went to Jean Harris, school teacher, historian, socialite, and mistress of Herman Tarnower for the past 14 years.

The mother of two grown-up sons, Mrs Harris had reached the peak of her profession. As headmistress of the exclusive and expensive Madeira School, she was in the Washington Social Register.

But although she presented a confident face to the world, inside she was in turmoil. While she carried out her duties with conviction, she was living off Dexedrine, better known as 'speed'. This made her schizophrenic and liable to burst into fits of anger. Ironically, just before she stepped into the spotlight of world news, she upset her Board by expelling four girls' for smoking pot.

Nicknamed 'Integrity Jean', she lived a secret life of desperate passion for the doctor, who was notorious for a succession of casual affairs. With her family grown up and living away, she felt very much alone, and was only too aware that Herman Tarnower, generally known as Hy, had got himself a new mistress, one who was a serious rival.

Lynne Tryforos had been taken on as his administrative assistant. But she was soon in his bed. There followed a bitter struggle, and the last straw came when Lynne placed a small ad in the *New York Times* which read: 'Happy New Year Hy, Love Always, Lynne.' It appeared while Hy and Jean were holidaying in Miami and caused a huge row.

A CRIME OF PASSION

Finally, Jean Harris snapped, and on 10 March at her house on the school campus in McLean, Virginia, she wrote a ten-page letter to her lover, collected her gun, and drove through the rainy night to his house.

When she was arrested, she reportedly told the police: 'I shot him. I did it.' She explained that she had come in the hope that he would kill her. She wept: 'He wanted to live. I wanted to die.'

Later the next morning, Police Chief William Harris made a statement to the press: 'She made certain admissions which I wouldn't know if you would call a confession or not.'

Asked whether she had admitted shooting the doctor, he said: 'She admitted that she shot him.'

When the story broke, the papers had a field day and sent an army of reporters to dig for dirt. Nowhere was the scandal more shocking than at the Madeira School. The school's President had to announce the news: 'On behalf of everyone at the school, I want to say that we are most distressed to learn of unfortunate events affecting Mrs Harris, the headmistress.'

A search of the doctor's house had revealed signs of a violent quarrel. In the bathroom was Lynne's négligé. In the garden was a box of her curlers that Jean had thrown out, shattering a window.

THE LEGAL FIGHT BEGINS

Jean Harris was arraigned at Harrison Town Court on 13 March 1980. She was released on a bail of $40,000 which was put up by her brother and sister. Then, on 26 March, she was charged with second-degree murder and two counts of criminal possession of a pistol. Eight months later, her trial began in White Plains, New York.

Spurning a plea bargain, she pleaded not guilty and prepared to fight. She chose as her lawyer a flamboyant criminal attorney named Joel Arnau. He took the line that the shooting had happened accidentally while Tarnower was trying to stop Jean Harris from committing suicide.

If Arnau could get her off she would inherit the $220,000 left to her in Herman Tarnower's will. If she were found guilty of his murder she would lose it. Lynne Tryforos and family had been left the same amount. The trial lasted three months and provided a daily soap opera for the eager press.

Prosecutor George Bolen painted a lurid picture of a woman blinded by jealousy. She had tolerated a string of casual lovers in the past, but now she was faced with a real rival. The jury – eight women, four men – were told that she wrote a suicide note and then collected her .32-calibre gun.

The prosecution described how the first bullet went through Tarnower's hand, proving that he was trying to shield himself, and ended in his chest.

Harris had told the police that she had left the house to get help. But they noticed she had taken her gun and coat with her. She had also told them that she only produced the gun to commit suicide in front of Tarnower, but he came at her and grabbed it.

Upstairs, the doctor was left on his knees, dying in blood-drenched pyjamas.

Next came the defence's opening statement. The shooting was just a 'tragic accident', and Arnau tried to deflect press questioning.

A total of 93 witnesses gave evidence. The lines of spectators were so long that they were allowed in for only one hour each. Here was a chance to glimpse into the passionate lives of the rich and famous.

MRS HARRIS TAKES THE STAND

At last came the witness they were all awaiting: the outwardly upright headmistress, forced to reveal the details of her affair in open court.

She insisted that she had never intended to harm the doctor. Her explanation was that he had pushed

Jean Harris outside court in White Plains, New York, in December 1981. The trial lasted for three months and provided a daily soap opera for the eager press and public, many of whom sympathised with her

her hand. Away and down. 'I pulled the trigger with suicide in mind. Hy fell back and I got up and ran.'

The public who were listening so avidly had various views: 'I sympathise completely with her, but she certainly didn't pick the right way to solve it,' said one. 'I think I would have the courage to quit the relationship myself,' said another, while a third asserted: 'I'm in complete sympathy with her, I think she got a raw deal.'

When cross-examined by Prosecutor Bolen, Jean Harris said she had planned to sue Lynne Tryforos when the new mistress cut up $1,000 worth of her clothes. Bolen encouraged her to blacken Lynne, and Jean Harris obliged with such descriptions as dishonest slut, lacking taste, and added: 'a whore is a whore is a whore'. But all this venom went to show just how much she hated her rival and provided a motive for premeditated murder.

THE LETTER

To her embarrassment, the ten-page letter Jean Harris had written to Dr Tarnower on the day of the shooting was permitted to be read out at the trial. In it, she

complained that he seemed to prefer the company of a vicious, adulterous psychotic to her: 'You made me feel like a piece of discarded garbage, jeered at, old and pathetic. I stay at home while you make love to someone who has almost destroyed me.'

The effect of the letter was to reinforce the impression that here was a woman who felt angry and slighted enough to kill. The prosecutor followed up this theme, and as the jury listened intently, Bolen asked: 'Isn't it true you intended to kill Dr Tarnower and then kill yourself? Because if you couldn't have him nobody else would?'

She replied: 'No.'

The 'Scarsdale Letter', as the press christened it, had been mailed by Jean Harris on the morning of the crime and had not reached the doctor's house until after he was dead. The talk among spectators was not whether she was guilty but how long she would have to serve in jail.

In his closing address, Prosecutor George Bolen hammered away to the jury on one single point: that finding the négligé in the bathroom had set off in Jean Harris a passionate rage that ended in the firing of five

Jean Harris adamantly refused to plea bargain, maintaining that Tarnower had been shot and killed accidentally while trying to prevent her committing suicide

White Plains, N.Y.

Jean Harris being taken to prison after receiving her 15-year sentence. The press were fascinated with the spectacle of 'Queen Jean' getting her comeuppance

bullets. Three of these bullets had gone straight into Herman Tarnower's defenceless body.

In his final address to the jury, Jean's attorney portrayed her as a deeply disturbed woman who had wanted her lover to kill her. He concluded: 'There is no evidence that Jean Harris ever intended to kill Herman Tarnower. This suicidal, sick woman was obsessed with dying. That's why she's not guilty of murder.'

As Jean Harris stumbled out of court, dazed by the press attention she was getting, the wait for the verdict began.

VERDICT AND SENTENCE

For eight days and nights the mostly blue-collar jury wrestled with the evidence. They knew that a guilty verdict would mean jail for Jean Harris for a minimum of 15 years. Finally they sent word to Judge Russell R. Leggett that they were ready.

And on 28 February 1981, Jean Harris was found guilty of second-degree murder and unlawful possession of a gun. Judge Leggett told the jury: 'The evidence substantiates the verdict,' and announced that sentencing would be in a month's time.

Mrs Harris was then taken away to Bedford Hills Correctional Facility. In protest, she began a partial hunger strike. She said that she would rather be dead than in jail.

The press pursued Harris to jail, fascinated by the spectacle of 'Queen Jean', as they now called her, getting her comeuppance. Being ordered about wasn't easy for her to take. Tired and desperate, she wrote sadly in her diary: 'It is a new experience for someone who has lived in a world where logic and decency still play some role, to wake up in the clutches of correctional officers.'

On 20 March 1981 Jean Harris was taken back to court for sentencing. There she heard Judge Russell Leggett pronounce that she was to be imprisoned for the minimum term of 15 years.

In a dignified and desperate plea, she responded: 'I did not murder Herman Tarnower. I loved him very much. For you to arrange my life so that I will live in a cage is not justice but a travesty of justice. No one feels his loss more than I do.'

Although the sentence ruled out the possibility of parole, many people expected an early release. But it was not to be. Gradually she got used to her new surroundings, hoping against hope that, one day, the truth, as she saw it, would prevail.

A FRANK INTERVIEW

Her two sons, David and James, were frequent visitors, and there came a day when she was allowed to give a remarkable interview to cameras. 'There are many people outside who think I either died five years ago or was let out five years ago. A lot of people are surprised that I'm still in here,' she said.

She tried to account for the severity of the sentence she was given: 'They said I was the absolute picture of Buchenwald when I came in. I don't know where they got that opinion and they were happy to see me go because also it proved a point: it isn't just poor black women who go to prison, it's middle-class white women who go to prison too.'

She gradually came to terms with the iron bars and, having been there so long, became a senior figure in the jail: 'Two young women who had just come in

> ## "IT PROVED A POINT: IT ISN'T JUST POOR, BLACK WOMEN WHO GO TO PRISON"
>
> Jean Harris

were walking in back of me a couple of days ago and I heard one of them say to the other: "That's Jean Harris, she's been here a long time." And I had been here a long time.'

She agreed that her long experience of being the one to give orders had made her less than a model prisoner: 'No, I haven't been a model prisoner. I think of myself as a model prisoner: I essentially mind my own business and I don't steal things and I don't lie and cheat and sleep around and do any of the things that go on around here all the time. But: I talk back. My mother used to call it impudence and I guess I'm still impudent sometimes when I say what I think to the people who are pulling my strings.'

Once she settled down she devoted herself to the prison parenting service, helping young women learn to be mothers.

She wrote a book about her case called *Stranger in Two Worlds*, and she gave the royalties to the prison nursery where she worked.

Did she learn from the experience? She said: 'I think so. Unfortunately that is a poor way to become worldly, I don't recommend it to anyone. I don't want anyone to think that I'm lucky to have been here, but I'm lucky to be learning. I mean, if you stop learning, you stop really existing.'

A MISHANDLED DEFENCE?

Looking back, what was it that went wrong with her defence? 'I should have plea-bargained I suppose, and I didn't, but I had very bad legal advice.'

Her lawyer Joel Arnau was adamant that she wouldn't take his advice and enter the defence of extreme emotional disturbance: 'She was a woman who was used to giving orders, not taking them. She did what I thought no client should do, and that is she ruled out defences that would have helped her.'

Judge Russell Leggett was equally forthright: 'She was just naive in refusing to allow her attorney to plead extreme emotional disturbance.'

Jean Harris during a televised interview from prison. She talked openly about Herman Tarnower, her drug addiction and its role in the murder, and the surprising severity of her sentence and how she eventually came to terms with it

He called the shooting a crime of passion that should never have been so severely punished: 'Most of them would have been smart enough to say, hey, I'm caught with the smoking gun, I'll plead extreme emotional disturbance and they would have been out.'

Joel Arnau had no doubts about her reasons: 'She had a greater fear than being convicted. She had a fear that they would find that there was something wrong with her mentally and that would affect her teaching career and you could not get her off that.'

Her own view was: 'I should have had a stronger lawyer who didn't listen to me I guess, who said, look shut up and sit down and I'll tell you what we're going to do, you're not going to tell me what to do.'

Whatever the reason for her plea, the result was a tragic error which put her away for an unnecessarily long time.

What would the judge have given her if she had agreed to accept a plea bargain? Leggett said: 'Had Jean been convicted of manslaughter because she acted under extreme emotional disturbance, her sentence would probably have been no more than a minimum of four and a maximum of twelve years. She has done more time as a minimum out of that than I would have given her as a maximum.'

Further mitigation should have come from evidence about the drugs she was taking. But this was never offered at the trial: 'It was like to me a little white pill which I found out from my lawyers is called speed on the streets.'

And who had prescribed these drugs? Doctor Herman Tarnower, the doctor she trusted above all. The effect that the drugs might have had on her mental state was never discussed at the trial, nor was the reason why they might have been prescribed: 'For overwork I guess and for exhaustion. Hy said, "Well here, take some of this, it'll pep you up. I take it sometimes myself."'

She was convinced that the drugs played a vital role. 'Not just in Hy's death but in my life. During those years it was just I was constantly being told calm down, and I wanted to bite them and they'd say calm down, because I couldn't calm down.'

Also never asked at the trial was the question of whether she was addicted not to drugs but to her doctor: 'I suppose you could make a case, yes I think he became an addiction. I guess he did.'

Mario Cuomo, Governor of New York, turned down appeals for clemency three times. Yet virtually all the participants in her trial, including the jury, favoured her release after ten years in prison. Jean Harris seemed resigned to her fate: 'I'm being treated as though I was one of the most dangerous, vicious women in the state of New York.'

Jean Harris with her lawyers Joel Arnau (right) and Bonnie Steingart (centre). She had refused to take their advice and enter a defence of extreme emotional disturbance, though she later accepted that she should have done so and that this was indeed the case

Then, unexpectedly, early in 1993, Jean Harris was released. It was her 13th year of captivity and she was due to have an operation. She said of the news: 'It was a doctor who called me who had just been on the phone to Albany to the Governor, and he said I'm calling to tell you that the Governor is granting you clemency and he wanted me to tell you before you went in for your operation.'

In her earlier interview she had seemed to have the last word about the man who had caused such turmoil in her life: 'I think you should think Tarnower was a very interesting man who had I don't think a very good sense of values. He was very self-centred, but whatever he was I found it very appealing. I was very much in love with him.'

BLACK FAMILIES IN ATLANTA, WORRIED AND FRIGHTENED,

GREW ANGRIER AND ANGRIER OVER A PERIOD OF NEARLY

TWO YEARS FROM MID-1979 AS A LONG SUCCESSION OF

MURDERS OF BLACK CHILDREN CAME TO LIGHT. THERE WAS

A STRONG FEELING THAT THE AUTHORITIES WERE NOT

PUTTING THE EFFORTS INTO CATCHING THE KILLER THAT

THEY WOULD HAVE HAD THE VICTIMS BEEN WHITE. BUT

THEN THE POLICE WERE REINFORCED, FBI AGENTS CALLED

IN, A SPECIAL SURVEILLANCE WAS KEPT ON KEY LOCATIONS

IN THE CITY. FINALLY, THERE WAS A SPLASH FROM A BRIDGE

AND THE POLICE FELT THAT THEY HAD THEIR MAN.

Wayne Williams

The Atlanta Killer

The Pope came close to death when he was gunned down in Rome in 1981. The British rejoiced in the wedding of Prince Charles to Diana Spencer in St Paul's Cathedral and there was general relief with the arrest of Peter Sutcliffe, who had murdered thirteen women. In the US the return of the Iran hostages made a triumphant opening for the Presidency of Ronald Reagan.

In the city of Atlanta, however, events of a more local nature were causing panic. By May, 26 black children had been murdered over the previous two years. Most were boys between the ages of seven and fourteen, and most had been strangled. The police, who had seemed powerless, were now reinforced and keeping watch on key locations. One was the Jackson Parkway Bridge over the Chattahoochee River.

In the early hours of 22 May, policemen on the watch there heard a splash and found a car stopped near the bridge. Its driver was a 22-year-old black man named Wayne Williams. In the car, the police found some rope and a bloodstain on the front seat. But this was not enough to detain him, and they had to let him go.

A CATALOGUE OF KILLINGS

The police investigation had begun in July 1979 with the discovery of the bodies of two teenage boys. Edward Smith Jr, aged 14, had been shot. Frogmen who found his body in the river found another body nearby, that of 13-year-old James Evans, who had been asphyxiated. They had gone missing from their homes in Atlanta earlier in the week.

These bodies didn't attract much attention at the time. Inquiries were routine and ineffective. There seemed to be few clues for the police to go on. Patrolmen were alerted, but this didn't stop the disappearance in October of another 14-year-old, Milton Harvey, who had wandered from home and whose skeletal remains were found the following month.

The disappearance of nine-year-old Yusef, son of civil rights worker Camille Bell, raised the alarm.

She described what had happened: 'I went down and the lady who lived next door to us then asked could he go to the store for her. He went to the store and he didn't come back.'

On 8 November, Yusef's strangled body was found hidden under the floor of an abandoned school. Civic leaders were understandably horrified: 'There is something sick about people who would snatch out the lives of little children.'

Then came a girl, 12-year-old Angel LeNeer, found tied to a tree, raped and strangled on 10 March 1980. One day later, ten-year-old Jeffrey Mathis disappeared, and eight days after that, Eric Middlebrook, aged 15, was found bludgeoned and stabbed to death. When three more children died or disappeared, their parents formed a committee in an attempt to stop the slaughter. They demanded that police commitment

Wayne Williams was convicted of murdering Jimmy Ray Payne (bottom row, column 3) and Nathaniel Cater (next row up, column 2). No one was ever charged with the murders of the 26 children

Mayor Maynard Jackson during a television press conference where he announced a reward of $100,000 for information leading to the arrest of the Atlanta Killer. 20 children had been murdered before this action was taken

children. I know you're in a bad spot, but that's the price you pay when you're on the other side.'

The city's officials were under intense pressure. Friction grew when some claimed that the killer must be white. But as the murder toll grew, others said that only a black person could have won the confidence of so many black children to be able to abduct them.

PRESSURE INCREASES ON OFFICIALS

Frustration was becoming apparent within the police department, too. Mike Edwards, head of the criminal investigation unit, walked out after an argument over policy: 'A missing child is really not considered a crime, so at that time we had a number of children counted missing that were not handled by homicide. And in order to recognise a problem you have to put the two together.'

Phone-in programmes kept the pressure on figures such as Public Safety Commissioner Lee Brown, who was accused of being slow to react to the situation: 'I would like to know why so many black kids have had to die before anyone got really interested in wondering what happened to them. A bunch of them died before anyone got interested. This is because they are black kids.'

Brown defended his office: 'From our perspective we became concerned when we had the death of the first black child. Anytime there's a child, or any person, who loses their life, it's a very serious matter. We have devoted – even before establishing our special task force – literally thousands of investigative hours attempting to resolve the case.'

The twelfth victim of the elusive killer was Clifford Jones, aged 13. He disappeared on 20 August and was found strangled the next day. His mother said she had no reason to worry about letting him out alone: 'I didn't know – and there's nobody around here killing up no black kids. If I had known that, I'd have never let my baby out of the house. If I had known, my baby'd probably be alive today, instead of being dead. He'd be alive, if I had have known – if they had put out a warning before, my baby would have been alive today.'

be increased, which consisted at that time of only five officers: 'There is someone in this city who is picking up boys, black, between the ages of eight and twelve. Little boys on the streets are not safe alone anymore.'

Racial overtones were introduced when police were accused of making too little effort because the victims were black. The task force was housed in a tiny basement room in the city police department. A sergeant and four helpers had only six phones for thousands of calls a week.

Tension increased when a boiler exploded in a day-care centre killing four small black children and a teacher. It seemed like an accident, but some parents refused to believe that the explosion wasn't linked to the missing and murdered children.

A spokeswoman attempted to speak for them: 'How many children are gonna have to lose their lives, before you, Mayor Jackson . . .' The reaction of the mention of the mayor drowned her words, but she carried on: 'You know, you're not hearing us, you're saying you're concerned. Well I'm concerned. Everyone here is concerned. You know, we don't want to see you on TV and we don't want to see you in voting time, we want to see you now about our

The police task force was increased to 25 officers, stretching the department's resources and budget to breaking point. But, despite the alert and all the warnings, young black boys still continued to disappear from the streets of Atlanta.

During the fall and winter of 1980 the killer appeared to have claimed five more victims. By the spring there were 20 unsolved murders.

At last, the city and the nation took resolute action. Atlanta put up a reward of $100,000. Mayor Maynard Jackson went on television: 'Somebody, somewhere out there, knows what we're looking for, knows who's doing this insane series of acts and attacks on our children. A hundred thousand dollars will shake that information loose.'

Boxing champion Muhammad Ali increased the reward by a further $400,000.

FBI AGENTS JOIN THE HUNT

Firemen volunteered to join the police in their door-to-door search for information. So did a psychic who claimed to have helped to solve 14 murders. The regular police were supplemented by 35 agents from the FBI, who were permanently stationed in the city. Twenty thousand people were interviewed face-to-face and another 150,000 by telephone.

George Bush, then Vice President, announced federal aid of $1½ million. 'We hope that this infusion of federal assistance will end the suffering for the families and the trauma for this city, and indeed the trauma for the entire country, because as I say it's national.'

A new spirit infused the searchers, who were determined to track down whoever was shaming their city. A rumour spread that the murders were part of a Ku Klux Klan attempt to exploit already fraught racial tensions. An eleven o'clock curfew was imposed on all black children aged fifteen and younger. Vigilante patrols appeared on the streets.

Atlanta's Mayor Maynard Jackson launched a 'safe summer' programme with visits to recreation centres which had been opened to provide closely supervised activities for children between the ages of six and 15. Eight thousand children enrolled on the first day. The mayor gave them a message: 'Have fun, have a good time, stay safe.'

But the authorities knew that nobody was safe yet. By 22 May six more children had gone missing to add to the 20 known victims.

Then the murders stopped – after the splash heard on Jackson Parkway Bridge. The cops had had to let Wayne Williams go because they had no cause to hold him. But they followed him, kept him under observation, and started looking into his background.

WILLIAMS: BRIGHT YOUNG MAN

Wayne Bertram Williams, then 23 years old, was an only child. His parents had lavished love and attention on him.

Williams was bright, energetic and ambitious. At the age of 12, he had built and set up his own radio station. Among those he interviewed on it was Congressman Andrew Young: 'At the time I remember being extremely impressed that a 13-year-old kid would have a neighbourhood radio station. He had a pretty professional looking layout.'

After this Wayne became a freelance cameraman, selling film to local television stations. Jim Rutledge, a local producer, remembered him: 'When I first met Wayne he came in with his film camera and had a

Despite a large reward and sustained police action, together with a 'safe summer' programme of supervised activities for children and a curfew for under-15s, six more children became victims of the Atlanta Killer

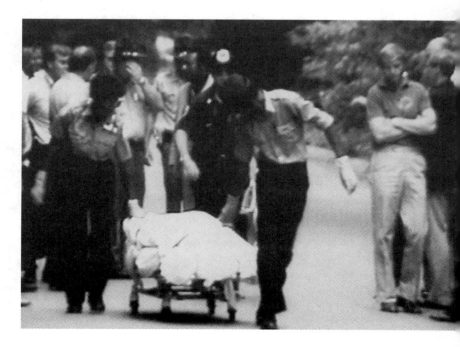

After hearing a splash near a bridge police questioned Wayne Williams who was nearby, but although they found a piece of rope and a bloodstain in his car it was not sufficient to make any charges. They did, however, keep him under constant surveillance when a body was washed up near the bridge two days later

shot of an accident. It was terrible footage but it was the idea that he had something and he was energetic.'

Williams put flashing lights and a police radio in his car, and was arrested for impersonating a police officer. Next he set up as a musical impresario and leafleted schools, saying he was looking for young black talent to join a group he called Gemini, after his astrological sign.

THE INVESTIGATORS CLOSE IN

Two days after the encounter on the bridge, the body of Nathaniel Cater was washed up nearby. A 27-year-old known homosexual, he was older than the other victims but undoubtedly killed by the same hand.

After the splash, Wayne Williams had told the police who flagged him down that he was returning from a musical audition. He said he had not stopped on the bridge itself. But examination at the Georgia state crime lab found that fibres from Williams' home and car apparently matched fibres on Cater's body.

However, the evidence was still not enough to arrest Wayne Williams and he was allowed to stay free, under surveillance. The net tightened after a witness said he had seen Williams and Cater at a movie theatre, hand in hand, just before Cater disappeared.

Now FBI agents were digging deeper into his past, discovering an interest in boys and youths that he claimed was purely to do with his music business.

Williams seemed to enjoy the media attention, and categorically denied any involvement in the abductions or killings. But, with further investigation into his recent past, police found many suspicious links to the victims. At least one had auditioned for him at a local recording studio.

Williams had used a diner for a mailing address. Two of the victims turned out to be customers of it. He had also frequented gay bars and known cruising grounds for Atlanta's homosexuals. Once, in 1978, he had been an eyewitness of a fatal shooting at 1.20am.

Wayne Williams was also well-known to have a vicious streak in his character. Despite his parents' financial support of his various schemes, he had been seen punching his father for not giving him enough money. One witness claimed to have seen Wayne slapping his mother as well.

The efforts to link Williams with as many of the victims as possible took police to a housing project in southeast Atlanta where he had distributed handbills, recruiting kids for a talent show he organised. One of the administrators recalled: 'He came to the office and asked us to distribute letters and to recruit kids for his talent show. He was a talent scout, and he was to develop their talent and put them in contact with the major companies and so forth.'

On 3 June the police questioned Williams for twelve hours, but still couldn't pin any of the murders on him. They were forced to let him go at 3am, hiding under a paper bag in the back seat of a car.

Never shy of the press, Williams recorded an interview on the condition that his face wouldn't be filmed or photographed. He described police efforts to make him confess: 'They openly said: "You killed Nathaniel Cater and you know it and you're lying to us." They said that, and they said it on a number of occasions.'

Now he was under constant observation from both the police and the media. He led police on a chase past the houses of their superiors, and got five tickets for traffic violations. To tease the police that he might fly away, he made inquiries about chartering an aeroplane.

ARRESTED AND CHARGED

These games were brought to an end on 18 June 1981, when the law struck at last, and he was arrested and charged with the slaying of Nathaniel Cater. Bail was refused, and two days later, a judge referred the case to a Grand Jury.

Now began an all-out effort to link him securely with the other murders. This involved more minute searches of his house, taking hairs from his dog, and attempting to match any of these with hairs and fibres found on the bodies. Police upset his family by smearing fingerprint powder, cutting holes in their carpets, and stripping their beds.

Homer Williams, Wayne's father, protested bitterly about his son's treatment: 'Why, why would you just pick a person for convenience?'

Now a Grand Jury had to decide if there were a prima facie case to answer on the indictments chosen by the District Attorney: Nathaniel Cater, whose body Williams was suspected of throwing into the river on the night the splash was heard, and Jimmy Ray Payne, who was fished out of the same river about a mile downstream, three weeks before.

Payne had been reported missing after he failed to turn up for a job interview. The police found a witness who claimed that he had seen Jimmy Ray Payne with Wayne Williams.

Wayne Williams remained confident throughout his trial that the evidence against him was insubstantial and that he would not be convicted

THE LAWYERS GET TO WORK

Upset by a wave of what they regarded as prejudicial publicity, Wayne's lawyers went to court with his parents and asked that any Grand Jury influenced by such adverse publicity be disqualified.

Williams was brought from jail for his bond hearing. He promised that if he were granted bail he would remain in Atlanta and not attempt to influence witnesses.

The opposing lawyers took their argument on to the streets. District Attorney Lewis Slaton was asked if Williams might flee: 'Well, I think it's possible.'

Defence attorney Mary Welcome took a different view: 'There's no reason to fear him at all. He hasn't committed any crime. There has been no quote that he has committed any crime.'

Despite the defence attorney's apparent confidence in Williams, the judge ruled that there would be no bail or bond. And he promised to poll the Grand Jury if he felt that publicity had influenced any decision they came to. The Grand Jury gave the go-ahead to proceed with the prosecutions.

The Fulton County district attorney announced the decision with some relief: 'Count number one: causing the death of Jimmy Ray Payne, by asphyxiating him with objects and by means which to the Grand Jury are unknown. Second count: accusing Mr Williams of the murder of Nathaniel Cater.'

Lee Brown, the public safety commissioner in Atlanta, promised to keep investigating into the cases of the 26 murdered children: 'The tragedy we've been experiencing for the last two years, it's not over. We have made one arrest; we have 26 cases where we have not charged anyone. Our task force shall continue to work full speed ahead and even faster at this time until we can successfully bring closure to all of the cases.'

Lewis Slaton was asked whether there had been pressure for an arrest: 'I will say that pressure or politics did not figure into the timing at all.'

> "NOBODY SAW ME KILL ANYBODY. ALL YOU GOT IS A BUNCH OF HEARSAY MESS"
>
> Wayne Williams

THE TRIAL BEGINS

Wayne Williams' trial for the murders of Nathaniel Cater and Jimmy Ray Payne began on 5 January 1982.

The prosecution relied heavily on the hairs and fibres taken from his house and car in police searches.

The results of those searches came with the testimony of Larry Petersen, a microanalyst at the Georgia state crime lab. He stated that fibres and hairs found on the bodies matched those on the floorboard of Williams' car, and may have come from carpets on the floor of his bedroom and from other rooms in the house, from a spread on Wayne's bed and a bathmat. There were also some similar to hairs from the family dog.

Mary Welcome scoffed at the forensic evidence: 'I think that any one of you, under the circumstances, could have killed Nathaniel Cater, because I'm sure that all of you have fibres in your hair of some sort that may match some of the fibres that were found.'

With the case going badly for them, the prosecution asked Judge Clarence Cooper to allow the introduction of evidence linking Williams with ten of the other murders. This would 'reveal a bent of mind', promised Assistant District Attorney Joe Drelay, adding that all the other victims had fibres and hairs on their bodies that matched those found in the house and car. And in some cases there also were eyewitnesses who could place Williams with the victims.

The prosecution made its plea to introduce the additional testimony after the judge had sent the jury out of the courtroom. Defence counsel Alvin Binder objected to evidence being presented about crimes with which Williams was not charged. But Judge Cooper ruled that he would allow the new evidence. It was a turning point in the trial.

Testimony about Williams' sexual leanings was given by a 15-year-old boy who said he was picked up by Williams at a shopping centre during the summer of 1980. Williams invited him into his car with the promise of a job, but then made sexual advances.

Asked to identify the man who propositioned him, the boy pointed to the accused, saying: 'I can't forget his face. It makes me sick.' He said he ran from the parked car when Williams said he had to get something out of the trunk.

Wayne Williams took the stand for three days. He denied meeting any of the victims or that he was a homosexual. He claimed that he had been set up and was totally innocent.

About the night he was picked up on the bridge, he claimed he had a perfectly good reason for stopping: 'When I crossed it I stopped on the other side of the bridge, because I was trying to find the sheet of paper I had the number written on before I got to the telephone. I stopped maybe about ten or fifteen seconds.'

But under cross-examination, Wayne seemed to change from a quiet middle-class youth to a street-wise smart guy, confirming the prosecution's contention that he was a Jekyll-and-Hyde figure. Goaded by the prosecutor, Williams screamed: 'None of the witnesses saw me on that bridge. Nobody saw me throw anything off that bridge.'

He went on: 'Nobody saw me kill anybody. All you got is a bunch of hearsay mess.' And he burst into tears as he left the witness stand.

After nine weeks and 200 witnesses, Williams was led out and the jury of eight blacks and four whites retired on 27 February. Only twelve hours later they returned with their verdict: guilty on both counts of murder. The general opinion was that they had been convinced not by the evidence but by the fact that the murders had ceased when Williams was arrested. Judge Cooper sentenced Wayne Williams to two consecutive terms of life imprisonment.

With great relief, jubilant investigators closed the files on the killings and Safety Commissioner Lee Brown made it official: 'With the conviction of Wayne Williams we have reviewed all of the evidence that's present today, and as a result we've cleared 23 cases.'

In other words, the official view was that Williams had committed all the crimes. This was confirmed when reporters asked District Attorney Lewis

Slaton if Williams would be charged with any of the other murders: 'We don't have any present plans of bringing any further indictments in Fulton County.'

Wayne Williams was taken away to jail for life twice over. Slaton was confident that the Atlanta Killer had been caught. The case was closed: 'The evidence showed that there were 13 killings in five months in 1981. At that time we identified the defendant. There has been no other killing since that time that fits the pattern.'

STILL DOUBT PERSISTS

Was justice really done? A new team of attorneys prepared an appeal. A distinguished committee which included author James Baldwin, TV producer Abby Mann, civil rights specialist James Kunstler and Harvard Law School's Alan Dershowitz claimed that police withheld evidence of a Ku Klux Klan suspect.

Dershowitz appealed: 'Let's have a fair fight, let's have a true scientific test and let the chips fall where they may without any loaded dice.'

But despite these brave words, the appeal was unsuccessful and Williams' two life sentences were confirmed by the Georgia Supreme Court in 1983. Wayne Williams remains in jail, and may well be there for the rest of his life.

With the help of evidence linking him to ten of the murdered children, Williams was convicted of killing two men who were found in the Chattahoochee River near the Jackson Parkway Bridge. No more Atlanta Killer-style murders took place after Wayne Williams' arrest

DENNIS NILSEN WAS A 'KNIGHT IN SHINING ARMOUR'
ACCORDING TO NEIGHBOURS, A KINDLY MAN WHO HELPED
RUN A JOBCENTRE. BUT THE DISCOVERY OF HUMAN FLESH
BLOCKING THE DRAINS AT HIS BLOCK OF FLATS, FOLLOWED
BY ITS MYSTERIOUS OVERNIGHT DISAPPEARANCE, LED TO
HIS BEING REVEALED AS ONE OF BRITAIN'S MOST PROLIFIC
SERIAL KILLERS. THE MAN WHO HAD LEARNED TO CARVE IN
THE ARMY'S CATERING CORPS PUT HIS EXPERTISE AND A
LARGE BLACK COOKING POT TO GRISLY USE – BUT ONLY
AFTER HE HAD CLEANED AND DRESSED THE BODIES, AND
KEPT THEM AWHILE FOR COMPANY.

Dennis Nilsen

The Kindly Killer

United States forces were dying in a suicide bomb attack in the Lebanon and thwarting a communist takeover in Grenada. British Prime Minister Margaret Thatcher visited the Falkland Islands, scene of the previous year's war with Argentina. On a more peaceful note, Poland's Solidarity leader Lech Walesa was given an ecstatic reception on his release from detention.

But the biggest story of 1983 for the residents of Cranley Gardens, in the North London suburb of Muswell Hill, was what came to light in February when the tenants of the flats comprising number 23 complained that their lavatories wouldn't flush.

What Michael Cattran, a drains cleaner, found when he came to investigate the manhole outside the flats led him to call his supervisor. 'I think there's human flesh in there,' Cattran reported.

But when Cattran returned with the supervisor next day he had a bigger shock, and a more sensational story. The matter blocking the drains had mysteriously disappeared. They called the police who found a few traces which, when checked by pathologists, were confirmed as being human.

A tenant told the police she had heard Dennis Nilsen, another tenant who occupied a top-floor flat, going up and down the stairs during the previous night.

When Nilsen came home from work Detective Chief Inspector Peter Jay was waiting for him. He told Nilsen that human remains had been found in the drains. Nilsen put on a show of being surprised but was told by the Chief Inspector to 'stop messing about'. In the front room of Nilsen's flat, Jay asked: 'Where's the rest of the body?' After a few moments' hesitation, Nilsen replied: 'In two plastic bags in the wardrobe next door.'

Nilsen was arrested immediately. In the car taking him to the police station, Jay asked: 'Are we talking about one body or two?' Dennis Nilsen replied: 'Fifteen or sixteen.'

DENNIS NILSEN, MASS MURDERER

Over the next few days the police began to build a picture of Dennis Andrew Nilsen, who had casually claimed so many victims.

Born on 23 November 1945 in the coastal town of Fraserburgh in Scotland, Nilsen was the son of a Norwegian soldier who came to Scotland after the German invasion of Norway and married a local girl, Betty Whyte. The marriage was not a happy one and the couple soon divorced. Dennis rarely saw his father and lived with his mother's parents.

His grandparents were very strict and instilled in him a sense of guilt for any pleasurable feelings. At the age of six, when he was shown his grandfather's dead body, love and death seem to have merged in his mind and his fascination with death began.

At school Nilsen admitted to being confused by the feeling of attraction he got for other boys and this added to his sense of being different. He left school as soon as he could.

In 1961 be became a soldier, joining the Catering Corps in 1964. Still obsessed with death, he told how he photographed a friend lying in a field as if killed in battle. With the Catering Corps he learned butchery and became an expert carver. He travelled to many parts of the world, including West Germany, Aden,

where he cooked for prison guards, and the Gulf where he volunteered for an Arab regiment with British officers, the Trucial Oman Scouts. Then, with the Argyll and Sutherland Highlanders, he went to Cyprus and he stayed with them when they moved to Ballater near Balmoral in 1970 where he cooked for the Queen's Guard. His army career continued until, on being sent to Northern Ireland, he became so disillusioned with the army that he decided to leave.

Ex-Corporal Nilsen, so hard up that he sold his general service medal for £8, had various jobs during

Michael Cattran beside the manhole at Cranley Gardens in North London where he discovered human flesh. He had been called out to check the drains when tenants complained that their toilets would not flush

the next few years. These included spells as a security guard and as a member of the Metropolitan police force where, he said later, he resigned because he was unhappy arresting homosexuals. In March 1974 he joined the Department of Employment and, based at a JobCentre, he was conscientious and prepared to work long hours. Despite being a keen trade unionist, he won promotion to executive officer.

Nilsen used to walk his dog at Highgate Cemetery where he could indulge his obsessions – for death and his hero, Karl Marx, who is buried there. At home he was becoming even more fascinated with death and necrophilia, putting on elaborate death makeup and watching himself in the mirror.

THE FLAT OF HORROR

In 1975 he met a 20-year-old named David Gallichan, whom he called 'Twinkle', and together they moved

> "ARE WE TALKING ABOUT ONE BODY OR TWO?" "FIFTEEN OR SIXTEEN"
>
> Dennis Nilsen's reply to police at the beginning of the investigation

into a flat in Melrose Avenue, Cricklewood. After two years, Gallichan left and, feeling deserted and lonely, Nilsen's fascination with death intensified. He later admitted that some of the young men he started picking up after Gallichan's departure never left the flat in Cricklewood.

Nilsen found no difficulty in picking up young men in the London pubs where homosexuals gather – whether they were looking for company, money, or just a bed for the night.

After his arrest, although trying to be helpful to the police, he found he couldn't remember all his murders. He said he *thought* the first one had been an Irish teenager at Melrose Avenue on 30 December 1978. He didn't want the boy to leave, so first he strangled him with a tie, then, when unconscious, he drowned him in a bucket of water. After cleaning the body, Nilsen dressed it in fresh underpants and lay in bed with it. A week later he put it under the floorboards.

This first anonymous victim was to set the pattern, but for the time being it satisfied Nilsen for almost a year. Then, in December 1979, he went to the Princess Louise in High Holborn where he met Kenneth Ockenden, a 23-year-old tourist who was due to fly back to Canada the following day. As before, the departure of his companion of just one night was resented by Nilsen so, as Ockenden listened to music on headphones, Nilsen strangled him with the cord. He then took photographs of the body before reluctantly disposing of it.

Nilsen was astonished at the ease of it all. Nobody suspected him and, over the next 20 months, he claimed to have killed at least ten more young men. Nearly always he got them drunk, strangled them with a tie, took a bath with the body and then made love to it.

The lights of Soho's amusement arcades attract crowds of runaways and young male prostitutes. It was in such an establishment that Nilsen picked up

After leaving the army, where he had trained as a butcher and become an expert carver, Nilsen joined the Metropolitan police. He eventually resigned because he was unhappy arresting homosexuals

The house on
Melrose Avenue in
Cricklewood where
Dennis Nilsen lived
in the ground floor
flat which, he said,
was handy for the
disposing of bodies.
He estimated that he
had probably killed
a dozen men here

Billy Sutherland, a 27-year-old Scotsman with a girl-friend and child in Scotland, but who went with men for money. Nilsen said that, as far as he could remember, the two of them went on a pub-crawl round the West End. He said that he hadn't particularly fancied Sutherland, and only took the man home because Sutherland had said he had nowhere to go.

Sutherland's mother, who lived in Edinburgh, reported that he had gone missing after travelling down to London to look for work but, as there were forty other men on the police list of missing persons with the same name, it was not surprising that one more Billy Sutherland would not easily be found in the big city.

POLICE REJECT ACCUSATION

In November 1980, Nilsen had a lucky escape. His victim of the night, Douglas Stewart, woke up from his drunken stupor to find himself being throttled. He put up such a good fight that he escaped and ran away. Stewart reported the incident to the police but

they dismissed his accusation as being a tiff between gay lovers, rejecting it as a 'domestic quarrel'.

Malcolm Barlow, a man who had spent much of his life in hospital, was the last person to die in the flat in Melrose Avenue, Cricklewood. Nilsen had found him slumped against his front wall and had called an ambulance. When Barlow was released from hospital he came back to thank the kind man who had looked after him. This time he was strangled and stuffed under the kitchen sink – there was no more room under the floorboards. Nilsen then decided to move.

After his move to Muswell Hill at the beginning of 1982, Nilsen went on killing until his almost deliberate lack of caution allowed him to be arrested.

After his arrest the police took Nilsen back to the first flat in Cricklewood and asked him to show them where and how he had disposed of the bodies. While a small army of policemen dug up every inch of the garden, he happily demonstrated to detectives how he had managed to get rid of all the other incriminating evidence. His butchery training, he told them, had

The kitchen of 23 Cranley Gardens in Muswell Hill. It was here that Dennis Nilsen 'kindly' cooked meals for some of his victims before cooking the victims themselves in the large pot on the stove

come in useful for cutting off the heads, removing the organs and dissecting the torsos. Once it was dark, he put plastic bags containing the insides of his victims into a gap behind the fence where they were soon eaten by scavenging animals. He then built a bonfire on which he put the limbs, either stuffed in suitcases or wrapped in pieces of carpet. Then he burnt the lot, putting some old tyres on top to disguise the smell. He said that, in all, three bonfires were made.

With the press crowded outside, Nilsen showed the police where he had found a skull still intact and smashed it with a rake into tiny pieces. Then he had carefully crushed those and other bones that wouldn't burn with a garden roller.

To help with the search, the police had drafted in cadets, and a detective reported on the finds they had made so far: 'We found a small piece of a jaw and some teeth attached to it in the rear garden of the premises at Melrose Avenue. And this morning I found quite a large consignment of human bones, in

particular a large piece of thigh bone in the region of about six inches.'

Asked if the bones would make identification easier, he replied: 'Obviously the more we find must assist the pathologist in his subsequent findings.'

Finally, on 12 February 1983, Dennis Nilsen was remanded in custody at Highgate Magistrates Court. He was sent to Brixton Prison as a Category A maximum security prisoner. This meant being confined to his cell except for half-an-hour's exercise each day.

At first, he was represented by a local solicitor, but later discharged him, preferring to speak for himself. Nilsen claimed that his co-operative attitude should have earned him some privileges. When these weren't forthcoming, he refused to empty his slop bucket and got 56 days punishment for assaulting an officer. He appealed against wearing a prison uniform and, to this at least, the magistrates *were* sympathetic.

By now, Nilsen was detailing the murders in his second flat, in Muswell Hill. Being on the top floor, he told the police, it wasn't as handy for getting rid of bodies as the flat in Melrose Avenue, from which he had moved because the landlord had given him a thousand pounds to do so. But for this the crimes might never have been discovered.

After settling into his new flat, Nilsen started trawling the streets of Soho once again, looking for attractive young men that nobody would miss. It helped, too, if they weren't very strong and well-nourished. Nilsen told of how he had chosen badly with one victim, John Howlett, a former Guardsman. Howlett turned out to be tough and fought back. When Nilsen discovered that his victim was still breathing, he dragged him to the bath and drowned him. He then cut up the body in the bath, after which he threw away some of the larger bones

> ## "THE MOST EXCITING PART WAS WHEN I LIFTED A BODY AND CARRIED IT. IT WAS AN EXPRESSION OF MY POWER"
>
> Dennis Nilsen

and flushed the heart and lungs down the lavatory. Finally, in a large black cooking pot, now in Scotland Yard's Black Museum, Nilsen rendered down the head, hands, feet and ribs.

THE FEELING OF POWER

Nilsen later recalled: 'The most exciting part was when I lifted a body and carried it. It was an expression of my power to have control. The dangling elements of limp limbs was an expression of passivity. The more passive, the more powerful I was.'

But the end was drawing near. Nilsen brought home 28-year-old Graham Allen from Glasgow, cooked him an omelette, and then strangled him. It was Allen's remains that eventually blocked the drains at Cranley Gardens which led to the police being alerted.

The bathroom at Cranley Gardens where Dennis Nilsen liked to take a bath with his victims' corpses and then have intercourse with them. Afterwards, he would cut up the bodies and flush their organs down the toilet

However, before this discovery there was one more victim. Stephen Sinclair was another Scottish drifter who had grown up in institutions, mental hospitals and Borstals. He had never had a real home and, by 1983, when he met Nilsen, he was a drug addict, begging for enough money to stay in cheap hostels. The killing took place only a few days before Nilsen was arrested. Sinclair, the last victim, was therefore fresh in Nilsen's mind when he was arrested and was the subject of a vivid memoir Nilsen wrote in prison about how he had met and disposed of him.

On the night of 26 January 1983, Nilsen took Sinclair home. He plied him with drink and drugs and soon Sinclair had passed out in an armchair. Nilsen wrote: 'This was something I had to do. I thought of all that potential, all that beauty, and all that pain that is his life. It will soon be over.'

Nilsen had only one tie left. He lengthened this with a piece of string, put it round Sinclair's neck, and pulled tight. 'I spoke to him. "Stephen," I said, "that didn't hurt at all. Nothing can touch you now."' Two weeks later the police found some of Sinclair's dismembered body wrapped up in newspaper in a teachest.

When his neighbours downstairs heard that Nilsen had been arrested, they couldn't believe he had done anything wrong. 'A wonderful man, a knight in

> ## "A MIND CAN BE EVIL WITHOUT BEING ABNORMAL"
>
> Judge Croom-Johnson

Tarpaulins covering the back garden of Dennis Nilsen's first flat in Cricklewood while police dug in search of more bodies. Nilsen described how he would sometimes leave the insides of his victims here for scavenging animals and then burn their limbs on a bonfire

shining armour' was how two girls who lived on another floor, Vivienne McStay and Monique Van Rutte, described him.

ANONYMOUS VICTIMS

At Hornsey police station a special unit was established to trace as many of the victims as possible. But, despite the co-operation of Scotland Yard's missing person's bureau and their fingerprint records, only seven of the victims, of the total of fifteen that Nilsen was suspected of killing, were identified by the time of the trial.

The Medical College of London Hospital joined in the task of trying to identify the remains that had survived Nilsen's attempts to destroy the evidence. By piecing together a jigsaw of teeth, bones and other

fragments, they scored a notable success in putting a name to one victim, Graham Allen, from his dental records alone. This identification came too late to be included on the charge sheet at Nilsen's trial.

It took eight months for the crown prosecutors to build up their case. In the meantime, there were appearances in court for remand and applications to choose lawyers. Dennis Nilsen chopped and changed between using a solicitor and defending himself. He was examined by psychiatrists, for both prosecution and defence.

Observers noticed how he appeared to have shrunk from the robust, tall figure he had seemed when first charged. He now had a thin, almost wizened physique. But he seemed in good spirits and was happy to give photographers a 'V-sign' through a police van window.

Meanwhile, forensic experts examined every square inch of the two houses where the bodies had been disposed of. Some clues were discovered to help identify the victims but, in the end, more than half of them remained unnamed.

THE TRIAL

As the trial approached the charges were restricted to six counts of murder and two of attempted murder.

A selection of Dennis Nilsen's murder tools including knives, the large cooking pot in which he rendered down parts of his victims' bodies and the knotted piece of string and tie with which he strangled his last victim, Stephen Sinclair

Dennis Nilsen being taken to court from Brixton Prison where he was held on remand. There was never any question of his guilt, just of how much responsibility he had over his actions at the times of the murders

Ralph Saeems was Nilsen's final choice of solicitor, and he advised Nilsen not to plead guilty, but to go for a verdict of not guilty due to diminished responsibility. So the task of Allan Green, the prosecuting counsel, was now to prove to the jury that Nilsen knew that what he was doing was wrong at the time that he did it.

Nilsen's trial finally began on 10 October 1983 in Court No 1 at the Old Bailey. There was no conflict over whether or not he had committed the horrific murders: the only difference of opinion was whether he was sufficiently abnormal at the time as to substantially reduce the acts to manslaughter.

That is what his defence team attempted to argue. The main point at issue was the legal definition of that word 'substantially'.

Prosecutor Allan Green detailed all 15 killings, including those Nilsen *wasn't* charged with, to show how calculating he had been. Among the first witnesses to face Nilsen were three men who had got

away from him. Douglas Stewart said that he found his legs bound to the chair he had fallen asleep in. He fought loose and fled.

Paul Nobbs, a student, had made an approach to Nilsen in a Soho pub. At Nilsen's flat, he had drunk so much that, when he woke up in the morning, all he could feel was a hangover. During the day, he went to University College Hospital where a doctor found his eyes 'popping out' and deduced that he had been the victim of strangulation.

Carl Stottor was a female impersonator. He later gave a graphic description of his ordeal: 'I fell asleep. I woke up and he was strangling me. I passed out. Actually I thought that I'd got caught up in the sleeping bag which he'd warned me about, and I thought he was helping me out, but he wasn't. Anyway I passed out from that and I remember vaguely hearing water running and being carried and I felt very cold. And then I thought in the bath that he was trying to drown me.'

Stottor survived because Nilsen changed his mind. Stottor awoke thinking it was all a bad dream.

When the turn of the defence came, it relied on the evidence of two psychiatrists to show that Dennis Nilsen was not responsible for his actions. Dr James MacKeith testified that he had a severe personality disorder. Dr Patrick Gallway testified that Nilsen was schizoid, paranoid and irrational. This seemed to fit closely with the testimony of the prosecution psychiatrist, Dr Paul Bowden, that Nilsen had told him that the killings gave him a sense of power.

There were no more witnesses and, after the prosecution and defence counsel had made their final pleas, the jury listened to the judge's summing up. He talked of evil. 'There are evil people who do evil things,' he said. 'A mind can be evil without being abnormal.' Mr Justice Croom-Johnson added: 'There must be no excuses for moral defects.'

However, two of the jury members were unable to come to a decision as to the degree of Nilsen's responsibility. The judge accepted a majority verdict of guilty. Dennis Nilsen was sentenced to life imprisonment on 4 November 1983, the judge recommending that he should serve at least 25 years.

Nobody knows exactly how many people were killed by Dennis Nilsen – by his own confession he is Britain's worst serial killer. In the end, only seven of his victims were ever identified by the police and the anonymity of the remainder is a chilling reminder of how just how easy it is in modern society for drifters and runaways to become lost in a big city, and for their murder to go unnoticed.

Some of the bones found in the garden of Nilsen's flat in Cricklewood. Despite the efforts of police and experts at the Medical College of London Hospital, less than half of the victims were identified

THE RELEASE OF A PICTURE IN AUGUST 1985 CAUSED

PANIC IN LOS ANGELES. MANY PEOPLE DISCOVERED FOR

THE FIRST TIME, AND MANY OTHERS HAD THEIR SUSPICIONS

CONFIRMED, THAT FOR SIX MONTHS A SERIAL KILLER HAD

BEEN AT LARGE AMONG THEM, PERPETRATING A STRING OF

HIDEOUS SLAYINGS DURING THE NIGHT. THERE WAS A RUSH

ON SALES OF LOCKS, ALARMS, GUARD DOGS AND GUNS.

BUT THE PICTURE SOON DID ITS WORK, AND A SATANIC

CHARACTER FOUND HIMSELF FACING OVER 60 CHARGES

OF SERIOUS CRIMES, INCLUDING 14 MURDERS. BIZARRELY,

HIS ONLY CONCERN SEEMED TO BE WHETHER HE WOULD

EVER SEE DISNEYLAND AGAIN.

Richard Ramirez

The Night Stalker

Two world leaders celebrated anniversaries in 1985: Ronald Reagan a 74th birthday and Margaret Thatcher a tenth as leader of Britain's Conservative Party. Soviet leader Mikhail Gorbachev and his wife Raisa impressed Paris with their charm during their first formal visit to the West. A lesser world figure, Madonna, married Sean Penn.

The people of Los Angeles probably cared little about these events, however. By August 1985 the city was in the grip of terror.

A killer had been stalking his victims through the city at night for more than six months and the police had finally released a photofit. A cadaverous face now stared out from posters all over the city.

It was known that the same man was responsible for at least a dozen brutal murders and scores of attacks ranging all over the vast city. All police units were on full alert. Every possible sighting was given special priority. 'Suspect described as a male, dressed in black. Suspect considered armed and dangerous, stop and hold for prints.'

A public announcement by Los Angeles County Sheriff Block did little to calm the apprehensions of the local population: 'Nobody knows where this individual may strike next.'

Headline writers vied to come up with a name to match the fear that swept through California. People interviewed by the media gave their views: 'I can't tell you how I feel. I am just scared to death' and 'If I hear strange noises now I go out and bring my gun. The police might not be there in time.'

Soon even the police were calling the killer the 'Night Stalker'.

DIARY OF DEATH

The wanted man's first known killing took place in Rosemead, on 17 March: two women were gunned down in the house that they shared. Hawaiian-born Dayle Okazaki was shot through her forehead in the kitchen. When her friend Maria Hernandez came home, the killer was waiting. He fired but her car keys deflected the bullet. She begged the gunman not to shoot again; amazingly he ran off leaving a baseball cap with the logo of the rock band AC/DC on the floor of the garage.

That same night in Monterey Park a law student, Tsa-Lian Lu, was shot dead.

Ten days later in Whittier, Vincent and Maxine Zazzara were shot after their house had been broken into. She had also been stripped, slashed, stabbed and had had her eyes gouged out. A footprint made by a large-size Avia track shoe was found outside.

The same print was at the next killing, six weeks later, also at Monterey Park, on 14 May. William Doi was shot through the head. He managed to phone for help before collapsing. He died in the hospital.

Detective Frank Salerno, who had helped to track down the Hillside Stranglers eight years before, was determined that interdepartmental confusions should not hinder the hunt for what seemed to be a serial killer. A task force from all police departments concerned was now set up.

At Monrovia, on 1 June, the killer struck again, bludgeoning an 83-year-old woman to death. This time a new element was introduced: he drew Satanic symbols on the woman's thigh and the walls of her home with lipstick.

Vincent and Maxine Zazzara were shot dead in their home and Maxine's body was mutilated. Police found a footprint which linked these murders to others in the Los Angeles area, confirming that they had a serial killer on their hands

In Arcadia, on 27 June, Patty Higgins, a school teacher, was found in her house with her throat slit. First, like other victims, Patty had been beaten. Four days later, also in Arcadia, 75-year-old Mary Cannon was found with her throat slashed. She, too, had been beaten before being stabbed.

At this stage, the police were still reluctant to admit publicly that there was a serial killer: 'Well, on two of the females, they did have their throats cut. And some of the other victims, they were bludgeoned. But as I say there were some similarities, and they do have some dissimilarities, that the investigators have told us.'

The rampage continued with another vicious assault in Arcadia, followed on 7 July with two separate attacks in Monterey Park. In the first, a grandmother, Joyce Lucille Nelson, was battered with a blunt instrument, and then strangled. Later that same night the Stalker broke into the home of a nurse. He tried to rape her but couldn't.

In Sun Valley, he struck again twice on 20 July. Max and Lela Kneiding were both shot while asleep in their beds. Max died instantly, but his wife was savagely slashed.

While detectives were searching there, news came that another couple, the Khovananths, had also been attacked. The husband had been shot in bed, and both his wife and their eight-year-old son raped.

Even after the Night Stalker savagely assaulted another couple on 6 August, the police spokesman, Joe Garza, remained cautious: 'We don't want to create any paranoia. Yes, there have been a few incidents here recently, and most people should just use the basic security principles. In other words, when you go to bed make sure your windows and doors are locked, even if it's warm, maybe investing in an air conditioner instead of leaving your windows and doors open for ventilation.'

FRIGHTENING SKETCHES

Two days later the police got the break which finally enabled them to act. On 8 August, Elyas Abowath was murdered in his bed and his wife was savagely assaulted. But she survived her ordeal and was able to tell the police how her assailant had made her swear upon Satan that there was no money in the house. She was also able to give an excellent description of a young man with a scraggy body and a cadaverous face, with rotting teeth and spiky hair. It brought into focus all the other descriptions which the police had been given.

Now they released their sketches of the killer they believed was responsible for at least 14 murders and countless burglaries, slashings, assaults and rapes. Worried that they would start a panic that they couldn't control, they had waited until they could issue a detailed description before revealing that they had a task force already in the field.

The police were soon inundated with calls from people volunteering information. But despite police precautions, hysteria swept Los Angeles: 'I bought several more locks for my windows and doors because this is really scary. I mean you would think in a nice neighbourhood like this it couldn't happen, but I guess it happens everywhere.'

Terror had come in off the streets and into people's bedrooms. Although most of the doors and windows through which the Night Stalker had entered his victims' homes had been open, Valley residents naturally reacted with trepidation. How could they really be sure that he wouldn't break in tonight? They

Police sketches of the Night Stalker who was believed to be responsible for at least 14 murders and numerous burglaries, stabbings and rapes. The police waited until they had a detailed description of the suspect before releasing any pictures for fear of starting a widespread panic

trembled as dusk fell over the mountains. Sales of alarms sky-rocketed, hardware stores ran out of bolts, locks and padlocks. Neighbourhood Watch groups sprang up all over, while existing ones found that they had a rush of volunteers. Areas where the Stalker had already struck were deserted at night. He could be around any corner, as a resident warned: 'Get an alarm system. Our neighbours here, they got a couple of shepherds and they're going to give us a shepherd. It's really bothered us, a lot of us.'

The price of guard dogs suddenly doubled and gun stores reported record business, as citizens armed themselves: 'I have grandchildren. They come to stay. Should I sit by and watch them get killed, or should I try to save them?'

Citizens who never before felt the need, took to the shooting galleries and learned to defend themselves. Self-defence classes were packed, and the Guardian Angels found that their services were in extraordinary demand.

THE STALKER MOVES ON

The photofit picture brought an unprecedented flood of information which had to be followed up by an overstretched force. Many officers felt almost overwhelmed by the public reaction: 'In 11 years I've never seen anything like it. More people are afraid, they're scared.'

Los Angeles was getting too hot for the Night Stalker. He moved north to San Francisco, where he struck again. On the night of 17 August, he broke into the home of Peter and Barbara Pan in Lake Merced. He shot them both in the head, ransacked the house and scrawled the words 'Jack the Knife' and some Satanic symbols on the wall.

Shocked neighbours of the couple heard one of the first policemen on the scene describe what he had

> "THESE ARE HORRIBLE CRIMES. MANY INVESTIGATORS WHO WENT TO THE SCENE HAVE DESCRIBED THEM AS SOME OF THE MOST GROTESQUE THAT THEY HAVE SEEN IN THEIR EXPERIENCE"
>
> District Attorney Ira Reiner

found: 'They're an elderly oriental couple, the man approximately 69 years old, the wife approximately 64 years. The man is dead. The wife was taken to County Hospital in serious condition. The last we know is she is still alive. There is evidence of an opened door and an open window on the ground level, that somebody got in that way.'

It was swiftly established that the .22-calibre gun used was the same as that used in two of the Valley killings, and a pentagram drawn on the wall was also similar, but detectives remained cautious: 'Because of certain similarities between a murder case in our city and the serial murders in the Los Angeles area, investigators from both jurisdictions are meeting to determine if the cases are related.'

It was not long though before they were forced to agree that the same killer had been at work. Mayor Dianne Feinstein offered a $10,000 reward for information: 'Someone that will go into a home at night and will kill, and kills at random . . .'

San Francisco was now as alert as Los Angeles. But the Night Stalker's compulsion to kill was still unsated. So he headed for a new area where he could strike unexpectedly: Mission Viejo, 50 miles south of Los Angeles. On 24 August the Stalker broke into the home of William Carns. Shot in the head, Carns survived with brain damage. Then the Stalker raped Carns' girlfriend, boasting: 'I'm the one they're writing about' and forcing her to say 'I love Satan'.

This time, the police were swift to admit the link: 'We were notified by our homicide investigators at the scene that they have found evidence that does make us believe that it was the Night Stalker.'

FINGERPRINT CLUE

The raped girl had noticed that her attacker drove off in an orange Toyota. Only an hour earlier, a car of the same description had been reported to police by an alert teenager who thought it was being driven suspiciously. When the Toyota was found abandoned in the Rampart area two days later, it was tested for fingerprints by two new methods.

Superglue was put in a saucer and placed inside the sealed car. As the fumes from the glue rose they coated every surface, turning all marks white. Then a laser beam was projected on to all the fingerprints which had shown up and scanned them. They were photographed and checked against all convicted criminals in California.

A computer quickly isolated a suspect with key characteristics. Another one blew it up, and California Attorney General John van de Kamp was able to announce a name: 'It took just three minutes to identify ten possible suspects. Richard Ramirez was number one on the list.'

Sheriff Block released the name and picture of Richard Ramirez to the media, and within hours they were on the front page of every newspaper in the Los Angeles area. As well as every police officer, every citizen was on the lookout for the 25-year-old persistent offender who had been in and out of prisons all of his life, and had now apparently turned to murder for pleasure – or to serve Satan.

Unaware that he had been identified as the prime suspect, Richard Ramirez calmly walked into a shop where he saw his own face in the newspapers. He ran for two miles trying to steal a getaway car but was eventually caught and beaten by angry citizens

THE LIFE OF A CRIMINAL

Ricardo Leyva Ramirez was born in El Paso, Texas, on 28 February 1960. America's largest border city is a hotbed of smuggling, drug abuse and other crime.

From an early age Ramirez was a drug user and a thief, with the nickname of Ricky the Klepto. Local police knew him as a regular at juvenile detention camps, and then reform school. To them the news that Ramirez had moved on to more serious crime was no surprise.

Not all his neighbours shared this view, though: 'I don't remember him as being a problem child, he was very nice,' one said.

After moving to Los Angeles, Ramirez was twice caught stealing cars, which meant that he had a local record and the police had his mugshot.

The night the police gave it to the newspapers, Ramirez was returning from Arizona after scoring some cocaine. He didn't know that he had been identified. He travelled back by Greyhound bus, dressed as usual in his favourite black T-shirt and pants.

He got back at 8.15am on 31 August and caught a local bus to Monterey Park, in East LA's barrio. He went into a convenience store and saw his own picture staring out at him from the newspapers on the counter. People were whispering and pointing.

THE CAPTURE

Ramirez ran out of the store and kept running for two miles. He started pulling a woman out of her car, to steal it. When passers-by ran to help, he jumped over a fence and tried to drive off in a Mustang, on which the owner was working. They grappled and he ran off.

He tried to grab another car, but the driver's husband attacked him with a steel rod. An angry crowd joined in until a police car arrived, and prevented a lynching. One of his assailants said: 'He said something Spanish about "I'm lucky the cops are coming" or something, because he knew that we were going to . . . everybody was going to finish him.'

Journalists and camera crews were swiftly on the scene and one of his captors described what had happened: 'Well, my sister was going to go to the store

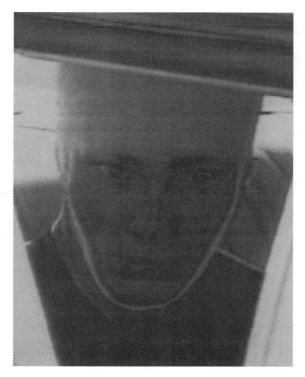

Richard Ramirez, his head bandaged from the beating he had received during his capture, being transferred to county jail. An escort of 50 police officers was needed as protection

he was brought from prison to be questioned by the police. He confessed to the investigators: 'I love to kill people, I love to watch them die. I love all that blood.'

The gaunt, black-clad figure claimed to have committed 20 murders. He was eventually charged with 14 counts of murder; five of attempted murder; two of kidnapping; seven of rape; 19 of burglary; six of robbery; and 15 charges of sexual assault.

His arrest was a personal triumph for Detective Sergeant Salerno, who had brought together the task force and led the hunt for the Night Stalker. A piece of evidence that eluded the searchers was the handgun Ramirez had thrown away during the chase. Despite a $5,000 reward, it was never turned in.

Police spokesman Joe Garza explained its importance: 'For lack of this weapon we may not be able to make a good case on some of these murders that we're investigating.'

But this was not allowed to delay Ramirez's first public appearance at his arraignment. Hiding behind his attorneys he gave an ambiguous reply when asked to plead.

Los Angeles Mayor Bradley almost jeopardised the case when honouring those who had cornered Ramirez. He said that whatever happened in court, he knew Ramirez was guilty – a statement that could have prejudiced the whole trial and which the defence lawyers jumped on with indignation.

CONFESSION AND RETRACTION

With so many crimes to consider, it took two years to bring Ramirez to the preliminary hearing on 6 March 1987. Then a number legal delays spun the process out by another two years. In that time, from his cell at St Quentin, he made a full confession, then retracted it, and constantly changed his mind about who he wanted to represent him.

Ramirez's first lawyer was a public defender, Alan Adashek, but his family in El Paso appointed a local attorney they knew to defend him. Then Ricky got the idea of getting the famous and flamboyant Melvin Belli, who visited him in prison, and then turned him down.

and she was going to open the car door, and suddenly the guy came and he tried to take away the car from her, but she started fighting him. And then, I don't know, someone called my brother-in-law, and he came and he started chasing him with a metal stick. And he got him over there and he hit him in the head.'

The arresting officer reported that when he got Ramirez into the police car, the Night Stalker began to weep. 'Shoot me,' he begged. 'Kill me. I don't deserve to live. Kill me now.' The crowd would have obliged, as it followed on foot to Hollenbeck police station.

Witnesses piled into a police car, and were driven away to record their statements. They were also staking their claim to a share of the rewards, which totalled $70,000.

MULTIPLE CHARGES

His head bandaged from the beating he had received, Ramirez was moved to the county jail, protected by 50 armed officers. On arrival in his holding cell, he seemed anxious to confess: 'I want the electric chair. They should have shot me in the street.'

Over the next few weeks there were numerous opportunities for the press to film the Night Stalker as

Throughout the preliminary hearings Ramirez persisted in flaunting Satanism, painting pentagrams on his hands and shouting 'Heil Satan'. He claimed to have no control over his actions as he was the child of Lucifer

The authorities were determined to ensure that Ramirez was given no opportunity to claim he had been denied an adequate defence. The arguments went on with District Attorney Ira Reiner trying to keep up the pressure: 'These are horrible crimes. Many investigators who went to the scene have described them as some of the most grotesque that they have seen in their experience.'

While the legal delays and arguments continued, the detectives of the task force had to sift through the 12,000 clues that had piled up over the months of investigations, and decide which were relevant to each of the 63 crimes for which Ramirez eventually be tried.

During the preliminary hearings, Ramirez changed his plea from guilty to not guilty, and his constant switching of attorneys infuriated the prosecution team. When he finally settled on two lawyers, both called Hernandez, they had so little time in which to prepare their case that for a while it seemed that the prosecution's worst nightmare might come true and that a mistrial might be called. However, a new judge ruled that the problems the defence lawyers faced were partly the fault of Ramirez's own intransigence and that the trial must go ahead as originally planned.

Richard Ramirez persisted in his flaunting of Satanism, and painted pentagrams on his hands which he frequently flashed to the press. The prosecution reckoned his interest in the occult was probably an attempt to build up an excuse for his blood lust. He had told detectives shortly after his arrest that he had no control over his actions as he was the child of Satan.

There were also widely varying interpretations of his favourite group's name, AC/DC. Some said it stood for 'Anti-Christ, Devil's Child'. The title of one of their songs was noted.

TRIAL AND CONVICTION

On 29 January 1989 the Night Stalker's trial began at last. His appearance had changed dramatically in the four years which had passed since his arrest: gone was the spiky hair and his rotting teeth had been replaced with a new set of false dentures. He wore a smart suit instead of his usual black T-shirt and trousers. Despite his new image, Ramirez refused to testify in his own defence and showed little interest in the proceedings.

For almost eight months the jury, selected from a pool of more than 1,500, was taken through the trail of murders, rapes and assaults which had terrorised Los Angeles almost four years before. The prosecution had built up a damning case to link Ramirez with most of the killings. This included identifications, shoe prints and other evidence left at the scenes of the crimes, the Toyota and the fingerprints. Ramirez's attorneys could do little to counter this except to claim that it was a case of mistaken identity.

The jury was unconvinced. On 20 September 1989 they found Richard Ramirez guilty of 13 murders and 30 other felonies and recommended that the death penalty be given.

In a melodramatic plea for mercy, his counsel claimed that Ramirez was a helpless victim, a man possessed by the devil. One of his lawyers concluded with the extraordinary words: 'Life imprisonment without parole means he'll never see Disneyland again.'

Ramirez himself seemed unimpressed as did the judge who gave him 13 death sentences. As he was led away, Ramirez sneered: 'Big deal. Death always goes with the territory. I'll see you in Disneyland.'

> **"I LOVE TO KILL PEOPLE, I LOVE TO WATCH THEM DIE. I LOVE ALL THAT BLOOD"**
>
> Richard Ramirez

During his trial, Richard Ramirez showed little interest in the proceedings. Even when the judge sentenced him to death, he merely sneered, 'Big deal'

To the police at the scene of a multiple killing, it seemed an open and shut case. A beautiful young model with a history of drug-taking, delusions and paranoia had killed her twin children, the parents who had adopted her and then herself. The father had managed to telephone his son as the girl had gone berserk, but the police arrived too late to avert the tragedy. But then a nephew and niece did their own investigating. Things were not quite as the police had assumed.

The Bamber Family Murders

I n the summer of 1985 the cities of London and Philadelphia both hosted Bob Geldof's Live Aid concerts to raise money for the starving. Less charitably, the French blew up the Greenpeace ship *Rainbow Warrior* in Auckland. On the murder front, Claus von Bulow was found not guilty of attempting to murder his wife, and a policeman was killed during the North London riots at Broadwater Farm.

In Essex, there is one small area which has seen no fewer than 18 murders in the last 40 years. The most widely publicised took place in White House Farm, near Tolleshunt D'Arcy, on 7 August 1985.

A young man, Jeremy Bamber, telephoned the local police station to say he had just had a call from the farm that had frightened him. It was his father, Nevill Bamber, who said: 'Your sister's gone crazy and she's got the gun.' Bamber's sister, Sheila, had a history of mental illness. There had been a shot and then silence.

When the police broke into the house, they found five bodies. Nevill Bamber had been shot and battered. Upstairs, they found the other four: in their blood-stained beds were Sheila's six-year-old twin boys, Daniel and Nicholas. They had both been shot several times. Daniel still had his thumb in his mouth. In the next room was 61-year-old June Bamber, outstretched on the floor, shot seven times. Sheila lay nearby, with two bullets in her head, apparently put there by herself.

The police found the weapon, an automatic rifle, on her chest and assumed that the girl, known to be mentally disturbed, had gone over the top, killing her parents, her children and herself.

The papers splashed the story of the 27-year-old model, nicknamed Bambi, who had murdered her wealthy parents and her children. The police washed the blood off the walls and burned the bedclothes.

At his parents' funeral, 24-year-old Jeremy, the one remaining member of the family, struck a tragic figure. He had specified cremation, and the service seemed a terrible ordeal for him. He appeared to burst into tears and staggered behind the coffins. He was supported by his girlfriend, Julie Mugford.

THE LIFE OF BAMBI

The villagers of Tolleshunt D'Arcy speculated how the strikingly attractive girl they had seen grow up could have reached the depths of killing her own twins and her parents. They recalled the rumours of the fast life she led as a model and whispered stories of drugs and paranoia.

The Bambers had adopted her at three months through the Church of England Children's Society. After she had been expelled from two schools, they sent her to Lucy Clayton's modelling agency. She learnt to exploit her good looks and long legs. But she was temperamental, too moody and unpredictable to be a top model.

She married a potter, Colin Caffell, though she was pregnant by another man. After a miscarriage and the birth of their twins, there was a break-up. She started having delusions – of being Joan of Arc, the Virgin Mary, and a white witch.

The police broke into her London flat and talked to people who knew her. They were told that Sheila had attempted suicide on a number of occasions. The tragedy at White House Farm seemed an almost predictable ending to her story. But not to everyone.

Julie Mugford helping to support boyfriend Jeremy Bamber at his parents' funeral. She later said that though he appeared to break down, there were no actual tears

Sheila Cafell, nicknamed Bambi, had a history of mental problems and seemed the perfect scapegoat for the murders

The Bambers' nephew, David Boutflour, didn't believe that the Sheila he had known was capable of murder, or could even handle a gun competently. His sister, Christine, was equally sceptical of the official murder and suicide theory. Together, they went back to the house and searched it again. Christine remembered that as children they had all sometimes climbed into a window that appeared to be locked when they didn't want the Bambers to know they had been out.

David found the silencer for the fatal rifle. It was in the gun cupboard and was said to have had blood and a hair inside it. They also tried the window, and found it could easily be opened and closed to look as if it were secured. So someone could have got in and out again, leaving an apparently locked-up house.

Sheila Caffell with her mother June Bamber (left) and her twin sons Nicholas and Daniel at the family home, White House Farm in Essex

JEREMY ACCUSED OF THEFT

A month after the killings, on 8 September, there was a new sensation when Jeremy Bamber was accused of theft. He was taken to Maldon Magistrates Court where he was charged with stealing £980 from the offices of a caravan site.

This had happened five months before the death of his father, who owned the site and had given his son a small financial interest in the company in return for some help there. Now Jeremy was accused of staging a phoney break-in of the offices. He was remanded and allowed out on bail, leaving the magistrates court with his sweater pulled up to hide him from photographers.

His solicitor revealed that, while in custody, his young client had also been questioned about the deaths at White House Farm. At a further hearing he was bailed again, and the police permitted him to go on a holiday abroad with a friend.

They flew to St Tropez in the South of France for a fortnight of sun, food, drink and fun. But he didn't take his supportive girlfriend, Julie Mugford, with whom he had had a row about another girl.

NOW A MURDER CHARGE

On her own and wrestling with her conscience, Julie Mugford decided to talk to the police. They jumped at the opportunity to question her without Jeremy Bamber nearby.

The police were waiting when Bamber's ferry docked at Dover on 30 September. The next day they charged Jeremy Bamber with murdering all five members of his family.

Jeremy, like Sheila, had been adopted at the age of three months through the Church of England Children's Society. Sent off to boarding school, he felt rejected. He took his resentment out on younger boys and was regarded as a bully. Perhaps resentment festered as he thought his parents loved Sheila, now engaged to Colin Caffell, more than him.

He worked on the farm, but at night he got up to whatever fun he could find locally. He was heard to complain about his parents and the wages he was

Arriving back home from his holiday in St Tropez, Jeremy Bamber found police waiting for him. He was arrested and remanded in custody for a year while they built up their case

paid, although they bought him a car, a house and land in the nearby village of Goldhanger.

Locally regarded as arrogant and vain, Bamber was said to accentuate his good looks with eye-liner, and he had a stream of local girls coming and going at his cottage. Among them was Julie Mugford, who said that she had heard Bamber hatch a plan to kill his parents and set fire to their house. But, she claimed, when Sheila became obsessed with religion and was hospitalised with a nervous breakdown, Jeremy had formed a new plan.

It was to lead him to the police court to be charged with five murders. He always maintained his innocence and never confessed.

THE SEARCH FOR CLUES

Outwardly confident, Jeremy remained smiling and convinced that his charm and looks would carry him through. And his sister certainly had been unhinged. Sheila had taken to shrieking at the neighbours and telling her analyst that her twin sons were trying to seduce her, then kill her. She was such an obvious

alternative suspect that the police asked for a series of remands while they searched for solid proof against Jeremy Bamber.

They tore his cottage apart in their pursuit of clinching evidence, and postponed his trial for over a year as they built up their case against Bamber. At White House Farm, they started again from scratch, going over every inch of the scene of the crimes. Ironically, they were hindered by the thorough cleaning up that the original investigators had given the farm months earlier.

The trial of Jeremy Bamber finally began at Chelmsford on 2 October 1986. A High Court judge, Mr Justice Drake, presided.

Bamber secured the services of one of the country's leading solicitors, Sir David Napley, who briefed Mr Geoffrey Rivlin QC as principal attorney for the defence. Leading for the Crown was another Queen's Counsel, Mr Anthony Arlidge, who set out the prosecution case: that this was a straightforward case of murder for money – specifically for an inheritance of property and shares worth £436,000.

THE CASE AGAINST BAMBER

At ten o'clock on 6 August, Jeremy Bamber was said to have telephoned his girlfriend Julie Mugford and told her 'tonight's the night'. Then he bicycled to the isolated farm from his cottage by back roads, so that he wouldn't be spotted. He arrived there between 1am and 2am, used a hacksaw blade to let himself in through the defective window, unlocked the gun cupboard, and took out a .22 Anschutz automatic rifle he had often used to shoot rabbits.

Nevill Bamber probably heard a noise and came downstairs to investigate, arriving just as Jeremy had put the silencer on. Bamber was said to have taken aim and shot in cold blood the man who had adopted him. As Nevill Bamber sank to his knees, Jeremy stepped up to him, and with shocking ferocity, battered him with the gun, swinging it like a club. The blows were so hard that the stock broke.

After pumping four further shots into the dying man, Jeremy went upstairs. June Bamber was reading the bible in bed. He sprayed her with bullets.

Now, said the prosecution, he moved to the next bedroom, where Sheila was sleeping. He placed the muzzle of the gun under her chin, where a suicide might shoot herself, and pulled the trigger. Along the corridor, his nephews were asleep. He crept in and emptied three shots into Nicholas, and five shots into his brother Daniel.

Mrs Bamber, not quite dead, had crawled into Sheila's room. Mr Arlidge said that Bamber finished her off with a shot between the eyes. He shot Sheila again, but without the silencer. Then he set up the fake suicide, leaving the gun on her chest.

He quit the house the way he had come in, and rode away on the bicycle he had come on. He had left a fingerprint on the gun that was overlooked, along with five dead bodies behind him.

At 3.26am he telephoned the police. But not by dialling 999: he wasted time looking up the local station. He told the police that when he had tried to call his father back the line was engaged. But the phone at the farm was left dangling and still connected so Bamber couldn't have got another dialling tone.

The prosecution claimed that another mistake overlooked at the time was that Bamber didn't take the natural action of rushing to the farm to see what

Sheila's six-year-old twins Nicholas and Daniel Caffell were shot several times whilst asleep. Jeremy Bamber claimed that Sheila was suicidal and wanted to take people with her

was wrong. The 40-strong police contingent, which took some time to assemble, overtook his car on the way to the house. Bamber arrived after they did, and told them: 'My sister is a nutter. She has gone doolally. She has gone mad before.'

It was not until 7.30am that the police broke through the kitchen door with a sledge-hammer and made their grue-some discoveries. They noticed how calm and collected Jeremy was, despite the appalling car-nage. When he was joined by Julie, the police later stated they had heard what sounded like a giggle as the couple whispered together.

> ## "MY SISTER IS A NUTTER. SHE HAS GONE DOOLALLY. SHE HAS GONE MAD BEFORE"
>
> Jeremy Bamber to police at the scene of the murders

However, to the scene-of-the-crime officer, Detective Inspector Ronald Cook, it seemed that a young mother, with a history of mental instability, had gone over the top. Cook assumed that what had happened was a pitiful domestic incident. In the wit-ness box, Cook admitted jumping to the wrong con-clusions, which led to his not wearing gloves when examining the gun, failing to look hard enough for the silencer, which was in the gun cupboard all the time, and losing the telltale hair on it when it was collected. Cook then testified that both Jeremy and Sheila's fin-gerprints were on the rifle.

VITAL EVIDENCE

David Boutflour, whose persistence had re-opened the case, gave evidence next. He told the court: 'We were just hunting for a needle in a haystack . . . We found it. We found it!'

He told the court how much Sheila loved her children and that he had never believed that she could possibly kill them. She knew nothing about guns and how they worked. Sheila couldn't have fired 25 shots with deadly accuracy. For one thing, her hand–eye co-ordination was hopeless. She couldn't even put baked beans on toast without missing the toast.

And how could the silencer have been in the cupboard if Sheila had shot herself with it on?

The murder gun was produced, along with the silencer that had had a hair – supposedly Sheila's – on it. With the silencer screwed on, the whole length was 36 inches, and her arms were simply not long enough to have reached the trigger with it on. A forensic scientist said she had tried holding the gun to her throat with the silencer on, but couldn't manage it. The jury left the courtroom under police escort to go to a nearby shoot-ing range where they heard the gun being fired, with and without the silencer on.

JULIE MUGFORD'S STORY

Then, on 9 October, Julie Mugford arrived to take the stand. Now the world heard her story of how Jeremy had spent months planning to kill his parents.

Bamber had abandoned his first plan, which was to drug them and burn the house down, because the insurance was too low. He had switched to shooting them, and implicating the sister everyone knew was a bit mad. Julie told of how he had phoned her at 3am to boast 'everything is going well'.

Later, Julie Mugford repeated to a reporter what she had said about Jeremy in court: 'It was the Christmas of 1984 when he first started talking about it. And he had this intention of burning down the house. And I just disregarded what he was saying really because he just said things to shock people. And I just followed up with a comment like don't be so ridiculous, you can't burn down the house, it's far too big and people would see it anyhow, and that's how seriously I took it at that stage. I just dismissed it as idle chit-chat, really.'

Julie claimed that she hadn't realised that Jeremy had actually gone through with his plan until the police came to collect her: 'Then at six o'clock in the morning when the police came to pick me up, that was when I first realised that there was something seriously wrong. And my worst fear was that it was Jeremy who had done something.'

She was asked why, with the knowledge she had, she didn't go to the police immediately or tell somebody that she suspected it was Jeremy who was responsible. She replied: 'Basically, because the police had been round and they had spoken to Jeremy, saying that things were as they looked. And that it was all murders and a suicide, and I didn't think that at that stage anyone would believe me, because it was obvious I was terribly shaken up about the whole affair, and also Jeremy was so terribly confident that nobody could do anything about it, and he said there was nothing I could do anyway. There was nothing I could have done to stop it, and there was nothing I could do now.

'I was very upset at the funeral because I had this thought in my mind about Jeremy doing all this, and he was there breaking down, supposedly, while I was actually upset feeling his guilt for him. Although he lost his legs and sort of buckled under a bit there were no actual tears when he was supposed to be crying. And as soon as he got in the car he started joking again.

Julie Mugford, who had dismissed Bamber's plans to murder his family as 'idle chit-chat', gave damning evidence in court which helped lead to his conviction

'As I kept on saying to him, I had to say something. And I couldn't keep them from questioning him. He became frightened of me which was making me frightened of him. Because he obviously was getting quite nervous about the fact that I wasn't prepared to, if you like, cover him any more because my conscience wouldn't let me. I couldn't let Sheila go through any more.'

Another damning piece of evidence was Julie's statement that when she arrived at the farm he had whispered: 'I should have been an actor.'

But Bamber shed tears in court when a letter was read from his mother marked 'Not to be opened until my death'. It said: 'I write to thank you for all you have given me.'

BALLISTICS EXPERTISE

A Home Office pathologist, Dr Peter Vanezis, said that Nevill Bamber had been shot eight times, four times in his skull, after he had already been immobilised by a savage beating with the butt of the gun.

Under cross-examination, Dr Vanezis accepted that Sheila had no marks that indicated whether she had been attacker or victim. But he said her wounds showed that she would have been disabled by the first of the two shots, so she could not have shot herself the second time.

Ballistics specialist Malcolm Fletcher testified that there would have been residue of bullet lubricant left on her hands if she had really fired the 25 shots. There wasn't. He, too, testified that Sheila was not tall enough to have managed to shoot herself with the silencer screwed on.

Julie testified that Jeremy had told her he had paid a mercenary, Matthew Macdonald, £2,000 to commit the murders. Macdonald testified that he was a plumber, not a mercenary. A false rumour had got about. He had been at home that night.

THE DEFENCE CASE

Mr Geoffrey Rivlin's case for the defence denied that Jeremy had committed the murders. Sheila Caffell had been solely responsible.

He called a psychiatrist, Dr John Bradley, who said that Sheila had a delusion that she was possessed by the devil. He told how Sheila believed she had the power to create evil and her children had it as well. Bradley went on to quote other cases where women had killed their children and then attempted suicide. These women had had the idea that some catastrophe was about to befall their offspring and one particular woman had thought she was so inadequate a mother that it was unfair for her children to go on living. Sheila may have felt the same.

On 16 October 1986 Bamber gave evidence on his own behalf. He continually smiled at the jury, which included five women. He insisted that he had a loving relationship with his parents, and accused Julie of making up stories out of spite, because they had had a row and split up.

When prosecuting counsel said that it was he – Bamber – who was not telling the truth, Jeremy answered: 'That is what you have got to establish,' reminding the jury that he was entitled to the benefit of any doubt.

On the night of the murder, he stated that he was at home watching television. After he went to bed he was woken up by his father's phone call for help. Jeremy insisted that Sheila was the murderer, saying: 'She wanted to go to heaven. She wanted to take people with her and she wanted to save the world.'

In his final speech, Bamber's counsel asked if he would have dared call the police if he really had been the murderer. The prosecutor replied that Bamber's fatal mistake was the phone call: he wanted the police to come, to prove he wasn't at the farm.

Summing up, Mr Justice Drake asked the jury to consider three key questions: 1) Did they believe Bamber or Mugford? 2) Could Sheila be the killer? 3) Did Nevill Bamber ring Jeremy?

The jury reported a disagreement among themselves, and the judge said he would accept a majority

> ## "JEREMY WAS SO TERRIBLY CONFIDENT THAT NOBODY COULD DO ANYTHING ABOUT IT"
>
> Julie Mugford

verdict. By ten votes to two they found Bamber guilty of all five murders. The judge sentenced him to life five times over, to serve at least 25 years.

THE AFTERMATH

There was an inquiry into the conduct of the police, and the Home Secretary admitted they had made mistakes. Bamber's application for a full appeal hearing was turned down in 1989.

David Boutflour was asked how he felt: 'Very sad. Feelings of relief, and a lot of sadness.' 'Why sadness?' 'Because no one wins. You can't bring them back.'

And Julie Mugford? Did she still feel any affection for the man she had loved? 'I feel something for him. But I just think he's a very sad man.'

In December 1993 Jeremy Bamber was still insisting his innocence and was waiting to hear whether a new appeal based on fresh evidence would be allowed.

Jeremy Bamber on his way to jail after being found guilty of the murders of his parents, his sister and his two nephews. He had remained unruffled throughout the trial but finally broke down when he was sentenced to life imprisonment

THE MAFIA IS THE MOST FAMOUS GROUP OF ORGANISED CRIMINALS IN THE WORLD, CONTROLLING MANY AREAS OF LEGITIMATE AMERICAN BUSINESS AS WELL AS THE SHADY WORLDS OF PORNOGRAPHY, DRUGS AND PROSTITUTION. THE FREQUENT WARS BETWEEN VARIOUS LEADERS AND THE CONSTANT STRUGGLES TO AVOID THE UPHOLDERS OF LAW AND ORDER HAVE LED TO MANY KILLINGS, TRIALS AND INVESTIGATING COMMITTEES. IN NEW YORK THE STREET MURDER OF BIG PAUL CASTELLANO IN 1985 WAS ONE OF THE LATEST LANDMARKS IN THE CONTINUING STORY.

New York Mafia Wars

Mikhail Gorbachev came to power in 1985 and was soon meeting President Ronald Reagan in Geneva. The lives of Americans overseas were threatened, with 39 held hostage on a TWA airline at Beirut and one elderly New Yorker actually killed by terrorists on the seized cruise liner *Achille Lauro*.

A double killing on 46th Street in New York on 16 December caused less media attention but had great significance in the long-running story of New York's Mafia wars. For the two men gunned down were Big Paul Castellano, the Mafia's boss of bosses, and his bodyguard, Thomas Bilotti.

Castellano's murder had been arranged by younger rivals within his own Gambino family, with the tacit approval of the other top bosses. Castellano was being prosecuted along with the Godfathers of the other main New York families in what became known as the Commission Trial.

They were pleading not guilty to ordering four murders and extorting more than $1 million from the New York concrete industry. As Big Paul was shepherded into court, the knives were already out

NEW YORK MAFIA WARS

for him. The FBI had bugged his house for several months, and the tapes implicated too many tentacles of the Mafia octopus. US Attorney Rudolph Giuliani couldn't disguise his pleasure at the indictments: 'This is a great day for law enforcement but this is a bad day, probably the worst, for the Mafia.'

Castellano was the latest victim in the two wars constantly being waged by top Mafiosi – against each other and against the authorities. In Castellano's case, his rivals got to him before the law.

UNDERWORLD STRUGGLE FOR SUPREMACY

These wars dated back to the early years of the century. The gangs which came to dominate bootlegging and prostitution in New York in the 1920s developed among the Jewish, Irish and Italian immigrants who had flooded into the city.

From Sicily came the Mafia, bringing with it ruthless violence and demanding obsessive secrecy and loyalty from its followers. By the end of the 1920s, the Moustache Petes, the ageing first generation of Mafia leaders, were locked in a bloody struggle among themselves for supremacy – the so-called Castellamarese wars.

New York's streets witnessed frequent shootings as the gunmen of the thuggish Guissepe Masseria struggled to beat off the challenge of the more urbane but equally ruthless Salvatore Maranzano. Masseria was finally gunned down on 15 April 1931 while enjoying a game of cards after lunch at the Nuovo Villa Tamara Restaurant on Coney Island. He had been invited there by one of his most trusted young lieutenants, Charles 'Lucky' Luciano, who had conveniently gone to the men's room when four gunmen burst in and slaughtered Masseria, leaving an Ace of Spades in his dead fingers.

This left Maranzano apparently supreme. He moved swiftly, calling a meeting of the Mafia and announcing that he would rule the whole thing in New York. La Cosa Nostra, as he called it, would be divided into five families, led by capos (bosses) including 'Lucky' Luciano. But Luciano was already plotting with his friend Meyer Lansky and other

young Mafiosi like Vito Genovese and Frank Costello to dispose of Maranzano. Maranzano was gunned down at his office near New York's Grand Central Station on 10 September 1931.

LUCKY RULES

Within weeks of Maranzano's murder, Chicago's gang leader Al Capone was hosting a national crime convention which was designed to formalise arrangements across the country. The New York gangsters accepted Luciano as the leader of the syndicate of five

Thomas E. Dewey led the authorities in their attack on organised crime in 1930s America. He succeeded in ousting both 'Lucky' Luciano and Vito Genovese

213

A Mafia bodyguard, gunned down in a Newark restaurant. His boss, king of the New York numbers racket Dutch Schultz, had gone to the bathroom where he was fatally wounded by one of gunmen

bosses were appalled by this. Such an assassination would force the authorities to act decisively to try to break the Mafia.

They decided instead that Dutch Schultz himself should be eliminated. On 23 October 1935 gunmen burst into the Palace Chop House in Newark, New Jersey, shooting Schultz's bodyguards dead at the table. Schultz had gone to the men's room but was gunned down there. He lingered on for several days before dying.

Ironically, it was Dewey who had his one-time saviour, 'Lucky' Luciano, arrested on a dubious charge of compulsory prostitution the following year. Dewey succeeded in getting Luciano sentenced to 30–50 years. However, Luciano continued to dominate the Mafia while in jail, working through his longtime associate Meyer Lansky, who was emerging as the brains behind the Mob, although as a Jew he was never formally a member of the Mafia.

Faced with a murder charge in 1937, Luciano's ally Vito Genovese fled to Italy, and Luciano himself, still an Italian citizen, also found himself back in the old country when he was deported in 1945.

COSTELLO TAKES OVER

By the late 1940s Frank Costello had emerged as the most powerful Mafia figure in New York, and it was he who became a reluctant star.

Quizzed by the Kefauver Committee in 1951 he was asked: 'You must have in your mind some things that you've done that you can speak of to your credit as American citizens. If so, what are they?' Costello replied: 'Paid my tax.'

It was these televised hearings that first made New Yorkers aware of the real power of the Mafia. Costello himself preferred anonymity and bribery to violence, but on occasions he would use the services of Alberto Anastasia and Murder Inc. Among others grateful to these hired killers was Vito Genovese, back from Italy with all his murder witnesses neatly disposed of.

Genovese was determined to reassert his control over the empire built up by 'Lucky' Luciano, who had

families which Maranzano had established. Over the next few years, under the leadership of Luciano, the Mafia emerged as the most cohesive and effective criminal force in the United States.

However, it continued to face competition from non-Italians such as Dutch Schultz. By 1933 Schultz had become the largest operator of numbers rackets in New York. Temporarily, at least, the Mafia had to compromise with him.

Other threats came from the authorities, now led by United States Attorney Thomas Dewey. When Dewey started putting increasing pressure on Schultz, the Dutchman demanded that he be killed. The other tried and failed to get back into the United States. He began by moving against a colleague of Costello who had been unfortunately talkative at the Kefauver hearings. After an argument, the syndicate bosses agreed that Willy Moretti must die. He was gunned down at Joe's Elbow Room on 4 October 1951.

Over the next five years Genovese prepared his final move. Frank Costello was the target. On 2 May 1957 Genovese sent a gunman to Costello's apartment. But he only grazed Costello's head. However, Costello soon discreetly retired and lived until the age of 82. The hitman, Vincente Gigante, was later to rise to greater heights.

Next, Albert Anastasia went for a haircut in the barber shop of the Park Sheraton Hotel. A gunman named Crazy Joe Gallo burst into the shop and shot him. Genovese and Meyer Lansky, whom Anastasia had offended, were behind the hit. They thus enabled Anastasia's underboss, Carlo Gambino, to take over as boss of the family.

Genovese now called a conference to claim the prized role of boss of bosses. This get-together, held at Apalachin in upstate New York, turned out to be a disaster for him.

Intrigued by the unusual sight of so many limousines, the local police set up roadblocks. They then detained 58 of the leading Mafia bosses. Genovese was humiliated and discredited. Within six months he was indicted on a narcotics charge, set up by Lansky and Costello. He got 15 years.

Frank Costello in the witness chair during the televised Kefauver Committee investigation in 1951. He 'retired' after an assassination attempt in 1957 and was one of the few top Mafiosi to survive to old age

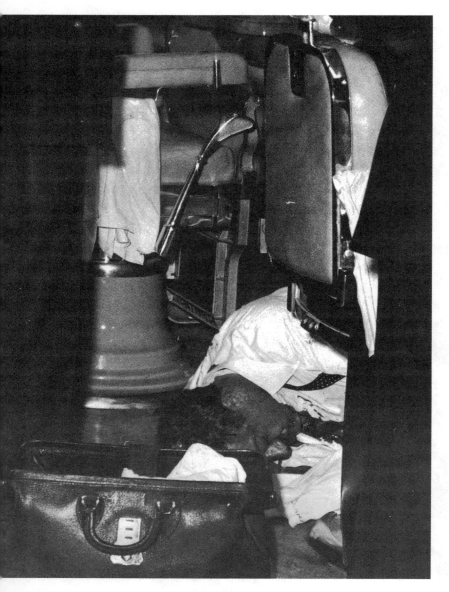

The body of Albert Anastasia, overlord and chief executioner of the hired assassin gang Murder Inc, gunned down in the barber shop of the Park Sheraton Hotel

the swearing-in ceremony, when he was 'made', and how he tossed a hot coal from hand to hand while repeating the following words: 'This is the way I burn if I expose this organisation.'

He took the senators through charts showing the organisation of the families, and showed his fear of what would happen to him: 'This is what I'm telling you, what I'm exposing, to you and the press, and everybody . . . This is my doom.'

Valachi's testimony was backed up by other witnesses such as Ralph Salerno of the New York Police Department. He expanded on the ruthlessness of the Mafia families and their love of euphemism to disguise the brutality of their activities: 'This is what a college boy might call his father: the old man. So in calling the boss of the gang the old man of the family – it has a nicer meaning. Another word that is kicked around quite a bit is respect. Everybody knows what that word means.'

INTERNECINE WARS

With Costello retired, Luciano in exile and Genovese in jail, another generation of men such as Anastasia's killer Crazy Joe Gallo and his brother Larry now waged open warfare against the last of Maranzano's original capos: men such as Joe Profaci and after he died in 1962, Joseph Magliocco. But Magliocco's plots against other families were betrayed by his underboss, Joe Colombo, who was installed in Magliocco's place. Joe Bonanno, the last surviving Maranzano capo, opened hostilities to become overall boss in 1967 but he was soon forced to retire.

During the 1960s the five families of the Mafia had undergone great changes. While Joe Gallo had been temporarily jailed, Colombo was the unchallenged head of the Genovese family. But in 1969, Vito Genovese died in prison and there was mutiny in the air against the high-profile Colombo. He was attracting too much attention as leader of the Italian-American Civil Rights League which he had founded.

So on 28 June 1971, Joe Gallo, now out of prison, had Joe Colombo gunned down during the second Italian-American Unity Day parade.

VALACHI TELLS ALL

There now appeared one of the most feared enemies of the Mob: Robert Kennedy, counsel to the Senate's McClennan Committee investigating racketeering, and later Attorney General.

It was to the McClennan Committee in 1962 that Joseph Valachi, gunman for Maranzano, Luciano and Genovese, broke his oath of silence and told all he knew about the Mafia. Genovese had put out a contract on him, and Valachi was determined to get his revenge. He described how Mafia members were told that they lived by the gun and by the night, and died by the gun and by the night. He demonstrated

Retribution was not long in coming. Within a year, Crazy Joe Gallo made the mistake of dining in Little Italy. In the finest traditions of gangland executions a lone gunman burst into the restaurant. Gallo took two slugs in his body, staggered into the street and died. His sister stood by his coffin and vowed: 'The streets are going to run with blood, Joey!' They did. At least 27 people, many of them innocent bystanders, died on the streets of New York in the next few weeks.

A portent of the future came after the kidnapping and murder in 1972 of the nephew of Carlo Gambino. One of the kidnappers, James McBratney, ended up dead on the floor of Snoope's Bar. The man who put him there was John Gotti. Despite previous convictions he pleaded self-defence and got only two years.

The grateful head of Gotti's family was Carlo Gambino, who was the most important of the new generation of bosses. A man of ruthless cunning, Gambino shunned publicity, and managed to survive both heart problems and a contract taken out on him in the 1960s. He died, like the fictional Godfather for whom he was a model, of a heart attack in October 1976 and was given a typically lavish funeral.

Shortly before his death, Carlo Gambino named his cousin Paul Castellano as head of the family, and

> ## "THE STREETS ARE GOING TO RUN WITH BLOOD!"
>
> Crazy Joe Gallo's sister vowing revenge at his funeral

'Lucky' Luciano, deported to Italy in 1945, collapsed and died of a heart attack at Capodichino Airport in Naples in January 1962. He had tried but failed to gain reentry to the United States

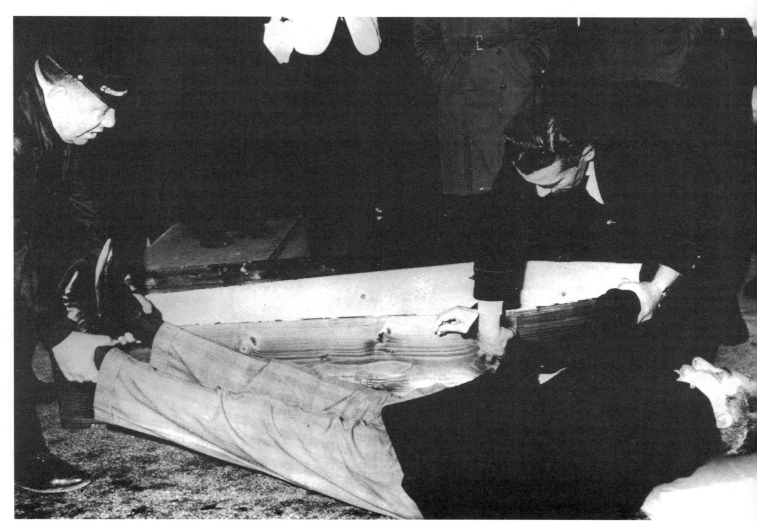

Big Paul was soon faced with the ambitious Carmine Galante, now head of the Bonanno family. This was neatly solved in the garden of a Brooklyn restaurant one July day in 1979. The 69-year-old Galante, who had only been paroled from a 20-year sentence in 1974, died with his cigar in his mouth.

THE PIZZA CONNECTION

The murdered man had been a partner of Gambino in setting up a string of pizza parlours as a front for the distribution of drugs and the laundering of the profits

Carmine Galante, shot dead with a cigar in his mouth at a Brooklyn restaurant on 12 July 1979. Four men in a car had opened fire with automatic weapons and shotguns

they made out of them. But, unknown to the Mob, the FBI was watching the Pizza Connection, as it came to be called. Secret meetings that decided the movement of heroin and cocaine were filmed on surveillance tapes.

The profits made from the Pizza Connection were staggering – $1.6 billion of heroin sold in grocery bags and shoe boxes across the counter and round the backs of the pizzerias.

The FBI took more than three years before it was satisfied that it had found enough evidence to

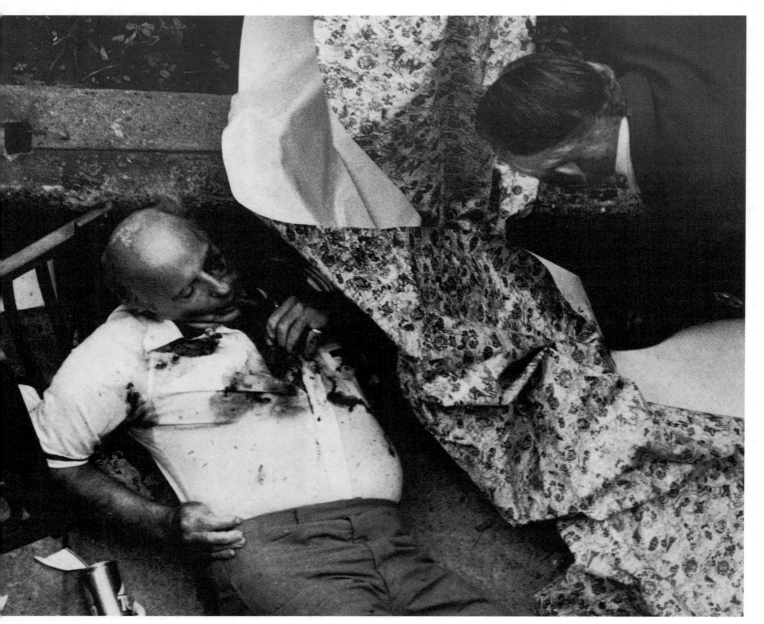

link the Mafia to the drugs. Then, in 1984, the police made their move and 38 key operatives were arrested in the sweep. It was estimated that they had made over $200 million profit during the previous twelve years, sending millions more to secret Swiss bank accounts.

Guns were an important part of the haul, proving that violence was an essential element of the operation. This was confirmed during the trial when one of the defendants was shot between sessions.

It eventually turned out to be the longest prosecution in federal history and a big feather in the cap of Chief Prosecutor Rudolph Giuliani: 'This case continues the offensive against organised crime drug dealing. Yesterday's arrest and charges reveal another heroin operation run by Sicilian immigrants using pizza parlours as a front for trafficking in large quantities of drugs.' Seventeen of the Pizza Mafiosi got sentences of up to 45 years.

> "THIS IS WHAT A COLLEGE BOY MIGHT CALL HIS FATHER: THE OLD MAN. SO IN CALLING THE BOSS OF THE GANG THE OLD MAN OF THE FAMILY — IT HAS A NICER MEANING. ANOTHER WORD THAT IS KICKED AROUND QUITE A BIT IS RESPECT. EVERYBODY KNOWS WHAT THAT WORD MEANS"
>
> Policeman Ralph Salerno describing the Mafia's love of euphemism to disguise the brutality of its activities

THE COMMISSION TRIAL

Now Giuliani turned his attention to the top dogs of the organisation, leading the prosecution in the 1985 Commission Trial, which had begun with the arrest on 25 February 1985 of the current leaders of the five Mafia families.

This ruling commission of the Mob pleaded not guilty to the charge that they authorised four murders, including Galante's, and extorted more than $1 million from the New York concrete industry.

Of the nine bosses finally indicted, the most important was Big Paul Castellano, the current capo di tutti capi (boss of bosses). He had allowed his defences to drop, and the FBI had been able to bug his house in Staten Island for four months.

They had planted a microphone in one of the lamps in the house and managed to record numerous incriminating meetings and telephone calls.

In the end, more than a hundred indictments stemmed from over 3,000 pages of transcripts of these recordings. A team of law enforcement officers was appointed to make the most of them.

Almost certain to be sent to jail in the Commission Trial, and already being criticised by younger Mafiosi for his conservative ways, Castellano now signed his death warrant, making two fatal errors which gave his younger rivals the excuse to strike him down: he failed to show respect when his underboss, Aniello Dellacroce, died, by ignoring the funeral; then Castellano appointed his driver Tommy Bilotti as Dellacroce's replacement, overlooking more senior gangsters who expected to be considered first for the underboss position.

On 16 December, Castellano and Tommy Bilotti emerged from Castellano's Lincoln Continental car to eat dinner at Sparks Steak House. Three men were waiting. They produced semi-automatics and loosed a barrage of bullets at close range. They finished Big Paul off with a coup de grâce to the head.

For the chief prosecutor, Rudolf Giuliani, the Commission Trial ended with one of the most complete victories the authorities had ever had in their long battle against the Mob. They had succeeded in getting more than eight sentences of 40–100 years handed down.

Giuliani and his team were cockahoop: 'Judge Alwyn gave the kind of sentence that you have to give to habitual criminals who at bottom are murderers. You put them in prison, hopefully for the rest of their lives. And that hopefully will also be the standard for the way the rest of them will be dealt with, as we go on and get more convictions of this type of organised criminal.'

Rudolf Giuliani suffered no illusions about the significance of this triumph. He knew that it was only a single victory in an ongoing war. A new generation of Mafia bosses immediately moved in to take over from the last of the men who had been foot-soldiers during the original Masseria-Maranzano struggle. Although they were outwardly more respectable than their predecessors, with wide interests in legitimate business, they could on occasions be just as ruthless.

> "TO BRING US BACK TO REALITY: THESE ARE HUMAN BEINGS WHO MAKE THEIR LIVING BY TAKING THE LIVES OF OTHER HUMAN BEINGS. THEY'RE DEDICATED TO DOING THAT"
>
> FBI Chief Prosecutor Rudolf Giuliani

GOTTI THE TEFLON DON

John Gotti took over Paul Castellano's family and he soon became known as the 'Teflon Don' because no charges could ever be made to stick. On the government's third attempt in January 1990 he was charged with having union leader John O'Connor shot and wounded, in revenge for O'Connor having one of the Gambino restaurants smashed up.

During the two-week trial the jury heard damning testimony. One of the gang who shot the offending union leader positively identified Gotti as the man who gave the orders. What the prosecution hoped would be the clinching evidence was a tape secretly recorded at the offices used by the Mafia leader and his cohorts.

Then, on 5 February 1990, came the moment of truth: 'How say you with respect to the defendant John Gotti, guilty or not guilty?' 'We find him not guilty,' was the verdict.

Yet again, John Gotti embraced his attorney Bruce Cutler and went free. After the trial was over, several members of the jury gave their reasons for finding him innocent: 'I did not find anything in those tapes that would lead me to believe Mr Gotti had a hand or caused this assault to take place.' 'In my mind there's no way that you could connect Mr Gotti up with what happened.'

Bruce Cutler admitted to being a little bit concerned when waiting for the jury's verdict: 'It's still up to twelve people, and so you get a little bit nervous. I do anyway. John doesn't, but we're all pleased with the result.'

So yet again the Teflon Don had managed to slip out of a sticky situation. He was well on the way to being hailed as the boss of bosses. But Gotti faced one challenger. That was the man who 30 years before had fired on Frank Costello: Vincente Giganti. Now head of the former Genovese family, he was ostensibly mentally ill, occasionally seen on the streets in pyjamas, and frequently in hospital.

But FBI agent Jules Bonavolonta was less than convinced: 'Crazy as a fox, he has played this game for many years.'

Colonel Clinton Pagano of the New Jersey state police was equally convinced that Gigante was keeping up a façade: 'A smart man would be smart enough to . . . to act a little crazy.'

Their suspicions seemed to be well-founded when surveillance film showed a normally dressed Gigante leaving his million-dollar town house off Park Avenue.

Bonavolonta said: 'He's been extremely smart, he's outwitted us for a long period of time. But I can tell you right now a commitment's gonna be made where it's gonna become extremely difficult for him to outwit us from here on out.'

Despite the FBI's confidence, all the signs were that another phase in the wars between rival Mafia gangs was building up in New York. The leaders of the two most powerful families were preparing to fight for supremacy.

John Gotti in court on
charges of planning
the murder of Big
Paul Castellano.
It had taken four
attempts before
the FBI was able to
make anything stick
to the 'Teflon Don'

Then fate intervened. John Gotti was arrested again, and yet again he looked dapper and unconcerned as he was taken into custody. This time the authorities had a new witness, Sammy 'The Bull' Gravano, who had been Gotti's closest lieutenant. Gravano testified that he had helped John Gotti plan the assassination of Big Paul Castellano. Then the pair of them had sat in a car and watched the shooting outside Sparks.

Gotti kept smiling even when he heard that his headquarters had been bugged. His lawyer Albert Krieger claimed that Sammy had lied in return for a lighter sentence: 'The description of the Castellano homicide as given by Gravano is a fiction.'

The jury found John Gotti guilty of murder. 'The tough line has gone, the Don is covered with velcro and every charge in the indictment stuck,' was the triumphant reaction of Prosecutor James Fox. Gotti was given a life sentence with no possibility of parole.

THE REALITY OF THE MAFIA

Despite these successes, the Mafia still dominates many areas outside its traditional pornography, prostitution and drugs. It has many legitimate interests and controls the waterfronts and airports through influence in the unions. The Mob infiltrates every level of the garment and food industries. It runs credit card scams, and music and video piracy operations.

Despite a façade of respectability, one must never forget the reality of the Mafia. As Prosecutor Rudolf Giuliani put it: 'To bring us back to reality, who we're dealing with and what we're dealing with: these are human beings who make their living by taking the lives of other human beings, they're destroying the lives of other human beings, they're dedicated to doing that. It's not an isolated act of passion maybe once in their life, it is something that they do over and over and over again, and if they don't take life they destroy life.

Index